Living in São Paulo
The L&T Guide

I dedicate this book to Youssef, Assaad and Mark who stood by me thru thick and thin. My thanks to Lynne and Maria Augusta who thought the idea brilliant and whose guidance was priceless throughout the process.
Leslie

For J.P., Zaba, Lilly & Pipo. I love you.
Tracy

Guia de São Paulo para estrangeiros

Living in São Paulo
The L&T Guide

Leslie Nicolas Nasr
Tracy Harrison Peixoto

Organização
Nanete Neves

LAROUSSE

Direção editorial	Soraia Luana Reis
Editora	Camila Werner
Coordenação editorial	Nanete Neves
Edição	Alexandre Bandeira
Produção editorial	Maíra Voltolini
Assistente de produção	Carolina Kuk de Freitas
Revisão	Beatriz de Freitas Moreira, Karen Clarke
Projeto gráfico e direção de arte	Artur Voltolini
Diagramação	Giovanna Angerami, Martha Tadaiéski e Silvana Martins
Ilustrações	Adriana Alves
Mapas	Abiuro
Gerente de produção	Fernando Borsetti

Dados Internacionais de Catalogação na Publicação (CIP)
(Câmara Brasileira do Livro, SP, Brasil)

Nasr, Leslie Nicolas
    Living in São Paulo : the L&T guide / Leslie Nicolas Nasr, Tracy
Harrison Peixoto ; organização Nanete Neves ; [ilustrações Adriana
Alves ; mapas Abiuro]. -- São Paulo : Larousse do Brasil, 2007.

    ISBN 978-85-7635-194-8

1. São Paulo (SP) - Descrição - Guias I. Peixoto, Tracy Harrison.
II. Neves, Nanete. III. Alves, Adriana. IV. Abiuro. V. Título.

07-0770   Cdd-918.1611

Índices para catálogo sistemático:
1. Guias : São Paulo : Cidade : Descrição 918.1611
2. São Paulo : Cidade : Descrição : Guias 918.1611

1ª edição 2007
Direitos da edição adquiridos por
Larousse do Brasil Participações Ltda.
Rua Afonso Brás, 473, 16º andar – São Paulo/SP – CEP 04511-011
Tel. (11) 3044-1515 – Fax (11) 3044-3437
E-mail: info@larousse.com.br – Site: www.larousse.com.br

Table of Contents

Introduction

Leslie's Introduction

People say that there are three things in life which are very upsetting; the first one is death, the second is the loss of a child, and the third is moving. Moving, most of the time, is a very rewarding experience. However as all experiences go, it does have its "ups and downs" and does not come without obstacles, especially when one has to face an unknown language, a different culture and unfamiliar customs. I have been very blessed, as over the years I have had a tremendous amount of help every time I moved - whether it was physical, emotional or financial. This is not the case for everyone and sometimes the most insignificant hurdle takes on gigantic proportions. I have therefore decided to use my own personal experiences and put down in writing what I hope will facilitate and render a practically "frustration free" move!

I think it is important for my readers to know why I specifically chose to do a guide on São Paulo. This is a cosmopolitan city that receives numerous tourists, as well as some of the most important financial institutions in the world. In fact after living in São Paulo for almost three years, I seriously think this city plays a major role in South America and coming from New York, I consider it to be the New York of South America! (No offence to people coming from other major cities.) Consequently, one would think the adaptation is not that difficult and would require the same amount of effort or time as moving to any other non-English speaking city. Well, not quite. The challenges one faces here seem at the beginning quite difficult to conquer – sometimes even impossible. The language is not the easiest to learn, despite its similarity to Spanish and

French. The way of life here is quite different from other places most of us have lived and on the whole this tends to leave one quite helpless and frustrated, with a feeling of incompetence which is a challenge in itself! I went through all of these feelings. It was not easy, it was not pretty.

However, I can now safely say that São Paulo has a lot to offer. It is a city so rich in so many different ways, that the experience leaves you a stronger, more educated individual, ready to tackle any challenge. Even more important, it leaves you eager to discover more. Once you reach that level, you will realize that you have indeed adapted well – and what a feeling that is! Think of it as learning something totally new for the very first time, almost forgetting how you used to do it and what you are used to. Apply baby steps to São Paulo, in order to fully appreciate and learn how this city and its people are different from others. Of course, it would be so much easier to move with a totally open mind, thinking: "I won't be comparing, this is not New York, London, etc."

The reality is that Brazil is in a different continent with its own rules, its own strengths and weaknesses, but is an unbelievable place to be. Once you discover São Paulo, you realize the numerous new experiences that you might not have in other cities in the world. People are helpful, welcoming, ready to socialize with newcomers, but they do it all in a "Brazilian way." Some behavior, which might appear rude elsewhere, is totally acceptable here. You will encounter different personalities; some you will like, some you won't. The beauty though is that you will always be faced with choices, and it is these choices that make São Paulo the city that it is.

ABOUT THE AUTHOR

Of Lebanese origin, Leslie Nasr has lived in ten different cities and six countries. She is a graduate of Wellesley College in Economics. Leslie has always been interested in different cultures, civilizations and languages. Leslie enjoys tremendously dealing with people and getting to know what is beneath the surface. Fluent in Arabic, French, English and now Portuguese, Leslie currently lives with her husband Youssef in New York. Their two sons also live in the United States.

Tracy's Introduction

I moved to São Paulo from New York City with a five-month-old baby and three months worth of intensive Portuguese lessons. I thought it would be easy to find an apartment and settle right in (Hah!). Even with the help of a relocation company, I spent weeks looking for apartments and then another month doing minor renovations to it (which is not uncommon in São Paulo). Lucky for me, I have an amazing Brazilian mother-in-law who had ALL of the "right" phone numbers and addresses! Over the past five years, I have added to and subtracted from this original list and so when Leslie came up with the idea to write a guide for foreigners living in or visiting São Paulo, I thought it would be the right time to share my secrets! **Bem-vindo!**

ABOUT THE AUTHOR

Tracy Harrison Peixoto was born in New York City. She grew up in San Francisco, Dallas & Washington, D.C. She graduated from Smith College and has a Master's degree in Architecture from U.C.L.A. She lives in São Paulo with her husband, Jorge, and their three children.

Our Objective

We wrote this guide for ex-patriates, executive spouses and foreign visitors here for business or pleasure. This guide is meant to aid its readers in the transition of moving to a huge metropolis where an unfamiliar language is spoken. We aimed to give readers an idea of what is available in São Paulo to make your stay more enjoyable and most of all, to help you understand the different customs so that you get familiar as quickly as possible with the "Brazilian way" of doing things. Make your own additions to the guide; you will no doubt find further information through other sources such as magazines, word of mouth, new acquaintances (**Paulistanos** love to help) and we are confident that in no time São Paulo will be "your home away from home!"

Brazilianism

Brazil is, in our view, a very "informal" country and the attitude of Brazilians reflects this. There is a certain "laisser aller" and a "laisser faire" which is widely acceptable. Punctuality is seldom respected unless you strongly stress it by adding on the invitation "English Time." It is common to wait awhile despite having made an appointment.

Party etiquette

Dinners at home tend to be served around 10 pm or even later. A good idea would be to snack before hand! Keeping the above in mind, it is practically unheard of to receive a "thank you" note from your guests. Sometimes, guests will call after the event to thank the hostess, but again, this is rare. Please never think that this is a reflection on the dinner you have just given. This is just another cultural difference.

Big parties are common in Brazil, especially when it is a wedding. You will generally receive the invitation only a few weeks before the actual event. Don't be alarmed if you see no "R.S.V.P.," as the guest count is rather "loose." You might be invited to a party verbally, but may still have to wait for the invitation to arrive by mail. The latter, believe it or not, might only arrive a day or so after the event. We would suggest checking with your hostess for confirmation, should that occur, and please don't be shy about it – it is perfectly ok!

A warm community

Brazilians love to greet with kisses and a strong handshake. This is a reflection of their warmth and hospitality. Depending on the city, the number of kisses varies, in São Paulo you get one or three, in Rio, two! This applies to both women and men, although men rarely kiss, but do a sort of hug/pat on the back greeting instead. Consequently, don't be taken aback when this happens upon meeting someone you have never seen before in your life – it is so natural, and is part of the Brazilian culture.

Brazilians are optimistic by nature and you will never hear someone not reply **Tudo bem (Everything's well)**. People tend to believe that if something is wrong, it won't be too long before the problem is solved, no matter the severity of it. In general, Brazilians don't like unpleasantness and it is against their nature to be burdened by it. This might be a little difficult to understand or accept at the beginning, but you will soon adapt and learn not to discuss certain things in public.

On New Year's Eve, Brazilians dress in white from top to bottom. (But don't forget to wear red panties for passion in the new year, never mind if they show thru!) And how Brazilians love new things! New shops, new restaurants, new apartments – renovations are extremely popular and are frequently undergone whether it is necessary or not!

Generally, it is not a Brazilian forte to be precise. Everything is, as we say in French, "à-peu-près." To give you an example, if asking how long it will take to get from point A to B, always allow extra time, as it will never be what you are told. Also, you will never get the same answer when asking different people the same question. Even the temperature and time indicators on the streets show different readings… Again, this is the charm of Brazil!

Expressions

In São Paulo, people have a special and informal way of greeting each other. *Oi…* (pronounced O-yyyyy) *Tudo bem? Tudo bom?* (Hello… All is well, All is good?). Please do not forget your salutations every time you speak to someone (even if you have already spoken to this person several times that day), because Brazilians take them very seriously and might feel slightly offended if they are not expressed! Inevitably at the end of a conversation the person says *um beijo* (stress the bei) = a kiss. Again, this is very natural and it is irrelevant whether you know this person or not!

You would frequently hear the word **magina**! (the first *i* is usually dropped) upon thanking someone. This is the Brazilian's response of "Oh please! Don't mention it," except

translated it means "imagine!" We would suggest you pay
close attention to the way this word is expressed, as depending
on the service rendered, the intonation varies a great deal.

People of **Sampa** (who were born in São Paulo) are
referred to as *Paulistanos*, the natives of Rio are called
Cariocas (men and women).

Incidentally if you like your coffee weak you should ask,
when in São Paulo, for a "*carioca!*" We still to this date don't
know if the two are related! And if you want ice with your
Coca Light (Diet Coke) ask for J-Lo (*gelo*)!

Faiths and superstition

Brazilians are quite religious. A beautiful expression used
when saying goodbye is: *Vai com Deus*. Literally translated
it means: Go with God (May God be with you). Another
expression commonly used to express disbelief is *Nossa*!
referring to "Nossa Senhora," Our Virgin Lady! Generally,
superstition is taken seriously in Brazil. Upon departing the
home of friends, the owner of the house has to open the
door for you, otherwise, if you do, it would signify that
you won't be coming back to visit.

It is considered bad luck to place your purse on the
floor. Servers in restaurants before doing anything else
will rush and place it on a chair next to you. The same in
shops, doctors offices, etc. Soon, you will get into the habit
of doing it and it will feel strange doing otherwise,
whether you are superstitious or not!

Learning the language

You will encounter numerous Anglo-Saxon names, but
they do not reflect the language spoken! Want to learn
Portuguese in the comfort of your home without spending a
dime? Watch the **novela das oito** (the nightly soap opera that
airs Monday to Saturday on TV Globo around 9 pm - even
though *das oito* means 8 pm – and lasts about 8-9 months).
You will also become quite familiar with colloquial
expressions used daily.

Be careful with your newly acquired Portuguese, every
word seems to have two meanings and one of them seems to
always have a sexual connotation! By the same token never
ever say *estou excitada* as this immediately implies you are

ready for... you know what! Instead you should say *eu estou tão animada!* (I am very animated, looking forward to…). Sometimes the same word in different cities has different meanings. In Rio, *bombeiros* mean plumber whereas in São Paulo it means fireman!

Speaking Portuguese

Pay particular attention when first learning the language, as stressing the wrong syllables will imply a different meaning. Certain words **might sound similar** but you will discover quickly that this is not the case. It is **crucial** to use the correct nasal sound otherwise the meaning is totally different. A good example is *massa* = pasta or *maçã* (massaaaan) = apple. This is no easy task and after three years I still pronounce those two words wrong, so be patient!

There are (unfortunately) many exceptions in Portuguese grammar. Do not let this deflate your enthusiasm! Brazilians LOVE to use contractions when speaking. We personally found that this created a lot of confusion at the beginning as no dictionary had the **né** for *não é?* = right? or **tá** for *está* = it is / yes / ok / it's fine (verb *estar*, to be, conjugated at the third person singular) or even **tou** for *estou* = I am (verb *estar*, to be, conjugated at the first person singular)!

There are certain daily expressions you will hear upon landing. They are used numerous times in a sentence and will deroute you completely if you are not familiar with them. Here are some examples:

> *Aí* and *então* depending on the sentence means therefore, so.

> *A gente* which mean we, the people. It is conjugated at the third person singular.

> *Linda* means beautiful. This is used to describe anything (people or objects). I will never forget that I was often referred to as "*Linda*" by my Brazilian cousin instead of Leslie and was heartbroken as I thought he could not remember my name!

> *Tá jóia* means cool, ok, right. *Tá legal*! means super, groovy!

> *Querida / Querido* (women / men) means darling, again very "loosely" used.

> *Mais ou menos* means "more or less." I don't recall using it that often in another language!

> *Zinho, zinha, ninha, ninho* are added to words in order to express "little," however it is more a way of talking and making something sound cute. It is used for everything: clothing, people...
> *Já* is constantly used to express it is done, I have done it, yes.
> *Filho, filha,* son, daughter. It is very strange, but parents often call their children this way instead of addressing them by their first names. Again, this shows affection – it is a term of endearment.
> The equivalent of "have a nice weekend" is *bom fim de semana.*

Getting out

The verb *viajar* is also used frequently. People seem to be travelling all the time here! *Paulistanos* loooove to get out of the city for the *fim de semana* (weekend). In general, if they don't own a house on the beach, they rent one. You will hear that they are travelling even though the distance could be as little as one hour away. Remember that Brazil is located in the southern hemisphere, therefore the summers start in December, when the schools have the equivalent of summer holidays in Europe and in the U.S. In Brazil the year really starts at the beginning of March, i.e. after **Carnaval**! It is crucial to keep this in mind when placing furniture orders (time of delivery will vary between 40-60 days,) planning renovations, or needing something repaired or fixed, as production factories and manufacturers tend to close during that period.

It is common for Brazilians to *emendar*, "take off" a few extra days when a public holiday falls either at the beginning of the week (Tuesday) or towards the end of the week (Thursday). Also beware if it is a "World Cup Year," they basically take off the month! There are a few "perks" to this abandonment of work – such as much lighter traffic, and less crowded shopping malls and restaurants!

Shopping

Sales people in general have a tendency to continue speaking to you in Portuguese, despite the fact that you made it clear you don't speak the language. It is important not to get frustrated. They are only trying to help and they don't know how else to do it. Just put that beautiful smile on, nod your head and take a deep breath. Before you know it, you will master the art of shopping in São Paulo!

Don't get upset if your beloved doesn't come home with that beautiful present that you so well deserve on February 14th . Here Valentine's Day is celebrated on June 12th . The date came from a commercial campaign created by a marketing agency in 1949 and was adopted by all Brazil very quickly. It is also St. Anthony's Day, the patron saint for anyone hoping for marriage.

Late dinners

Want to hear a funny contradiction? Brazilians don't usually eat dinner before 10 pm, but restaurants in São Paulo don't take reservations past 8:30 pm. It is extremely rare to get invited to dinner before 9 pm.

In restaurants, servers are as quick as lightening to take your drink orders. They will interrupt your conversation. Don't get annoyed. It is a fact. However, that is not the case with the menus. You should ask for them. Some restaurants include the "couvert" in the bill (bread, butter, patê, etc.) others don't, and you have to pay for it. A few restaurants have an English menu. If not, don't be shy in making the waiter or maître repeat what he is saying several times. Remember, YOU are the guest and you are trying your best to fit in. Upon taking away dishes, the equivalent of "how was everything" is "are you satisfied?", *satisfeita*?

As a last note, you should know that despite the fact that one might feel overwhelmed with the new culture, and despite the fact that it might seem to take a long time to adapt or to get to meet your new friends, Brazilians always welcome foreigners and are more than happy to open their doors to them. When moving to a new city, one always tends to think "oh I will do that later, oh I haven't got the time…" This is so cliché! Remember, time goes by very quickly and our best advice to you is try and enjoy your new life as soon as possible, as Brazil is a country that has tons to offer. Its diversity, size, and striking cultural differences from North to South makes it an intriguing and fabulous experience. When reflecting upon my three years here, I will always smile fondly and say I truly made the best out of it!

São Paulo

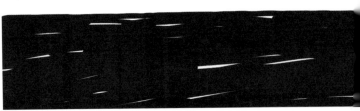

São Paulo was founded by Jesuits on January 25th, 1554.
Since then, it has experienced continuous and accelerated
growth; first being the departure city of the **Bandeiras**
expeditions to enlarge Brazil's frontiers, later becoming the
destination of many immigrants who came to work in the
fields, and afterwards in the developing industries. Italians,
Japanese, Germans, Lebanese and many others settled
in the city and brought their traditions, determining
São Paulo's cosmopolitan tendency. From 1870 to 1930,
the 15,000 inhabitant-city became a 2 million one. The
20th century brought an enormous growth in a short period
of time, attracting thousands of workers from all over Brazil,
mostly from the Northeast region. São Paulo was soon
to become the wealthiest and most important city in the
country; a business center connected to the whole world.

city facts and info

> **Population**
  20,5 million (Grande São Paulo, source: IBGE, Censo 2005)

> **Area**
  8,051 km²

> **Language**
  Portuguese

> **Currency**
  Real

> **Time Zone**
  GMT-3 hours

> **Country Code**
  55

> **City Code**
  11

> **Weather**
  Located in the southern hemisphere, Brazil's weather
  is known to be tropical. Consequently, São Paulo enjoys

longer summers with occasional heavy rain and much shorter, damp winters, with temperatures ranging between 10-19ºC. Summer starts around December until March with temperatures reaching up to 35º Celsius. Most of the time, the weather is still quite warm and pleasant up until June.

> Electricity / Voltage
Brazil has dual voltage: 110V. and 220V. Most homes have both currents. It is important to verify this fact before moving into an apartment, in order to label outlets accordingly.

> Measure
Brazil uses the metric system (meter, liter, kilogram) and Celsius for temperature. A quick conversion to simplify matters is to multiply the Celsius number x 2, then add 32 = Farenheit.

events

Business Expositions and Fairs
São Paulo has many business expositions and fairs during the year. Listed below are some sites for further information.

Anhembi (Pavilhão de Exposições do Anhembi)
Inaugurated in 1972 when it launched the first automotive fair (*Salão do Automóvel*). Considered to be one of the biggest enclosed event spaces in Latin America. Can hold up to four different events at one time, from businees fairs to artistic presentations.

🏠 Av. Olavo Fontoura, 1209, Santana

☎ 6226-0400

🌐 Check website for updated calendar of events
    www.anhembi.com.br

Expo Center Norte
Another important venue for business fairs, Center Norte's facilities include a shopping mall.

🏠 Rua José Bernardo Pinto, 333, Vila Guilherme

☎ 6224-5959

🌐 Check website for updated calendar of events
    www.centernorte.com.br/expo/

Pavilhão da Bienal no Ibirapuera

Calendar of events includes business fairs, art and architecture international exhibitions and biannual events and fashion shows.

🌐 Check the *calendário de eventos* section for updated information: www.cidadedesaopaulo.com

Some highlights

> **January**
  Couromoda, leather and shoes fair

> **January /July**
  São Paulo Fashion Week, fashion show

> **March**
  Bienal do Livro, international book fair, even years only

> **April**
  UD Brasil, household utilities

> **May**
  Casa Cor São Paulo, decoration show

> **June**
  Fenasoft, technology fair; **Fenit**, fabric industry fair

> **October**
  Salão do Automóvel, international car fair, even years only

festivities

Carnaval

Even though the *Carnaval* official day is the Tuesday of Carnival week, the celebrations start on Friday night and go up to Wednesday noon. Some *Escolas de Samba* (samba schools) have a day during the year where you can watch them hold tryouts for *Carnaval*. You can find out about each *escola* through the website. If you have the opportunity to attend the fantastically organized Rio *Carnaval*, don't miss it, as it is truly an unbelievable and unforgettable experience. The *Escolas de Samba* of São Paulo parade at its *Sambódromo*. The architect Oscar Niemeyer was behind the conception of the *Pólo Cultural e Esportivo Grande Otelo*, one of the biggest open spaces in the city, used for numerous events.

🌐 www.academiadosamba.com.br/escolassampa.htm

São Vito, Achiropita, and San Genaro

Traditional popular celebrations held by Italian immigrants. Italian food is served in tents on the streets, attracting thousands of people every year on the weekends. São Vito takes place at Pari district in July, Nossa Senhora da Achiropita at Bexiga district in August and San Genaro at Mooca district in September.

historical monuments and buildings

Arquivo Histórico Municipal

The Historical Municipal Archive holds a large number of blueprints, maps related to the city and layouts of buildings.

🏠 Praça Coronel Fernando Prestes, 152, Bom Retiro
☎ 3326-1010
🕐 Monday to Saturday office hours 9 am to 5 pm.

Capela do Morumbi

The chapel was restored and opened to public visits in 1980. The ruins were assumed to be of the Morumbi chapel, from when this district was a farm, around 1825. Today, it hosts art exhibitions and installations.

🏠 Av. Morumbi, 5387, Morumbi
☎ 3772-4301
🕐 Tuesday to Sunday, from 9 am to 5 pm.

Casa das Rosas

Inspired by French architecture, The House of the Roses was buit in 1935 by Ramos de Azevedo, and remodelled to receive the collection of work by the poet Haroldo de Campos. Today, it is a literature and poetry center.

🏠 Av. Paulista, 37, Paraíso
☎ 3285-6986
🕐 Tuesday to Sunday, from 10 am to 6 pm.
🌐 www.casadasrosas.sp.gov.br

Casa do Sítio da Ressaca

Inscriptions on the door and roof tiles of *Casa da Ressaca*
date it to at least 1719. In 1991, the place was used
for the *Acervo da Memória e do Viver Afro-Brasileiro*
(an event which celebrated African-Brazilian influences)
and holds exhibitions throughout the year. Advisable
to call before hand.

⌂ Centro Cultural Jabaquara
   Rua Arsênio Tavolieri, 45, Jabaquara
☎ 5011-2421
🕐 Tuesdays to Sundays, from 9 am to 5 pm.

Catedral da Sé

Inaugurated in 1954 to celebrate the 400th anniversary
of the city. The Sé Cathedral was built in the gothic style,
and the organ made by the Italian company Balbiani &
Bossi. The biggest church in São Paulo and a beautiful
venue for weddings.

⌂ Praça da Sé, Centro
☎ 3107-6832 / 3106-2709
🕐 Opened Monday to Friday 8 am to 7 pm, Saturday
   8 am to 5 pm, Sundays 8 am to 1 pm and 3 pm to 6 pm.
   Sundays mass 9 am, 11 am and 5 pm. There are daily
   (conducted) tours for a fee; reservations must be made
   in advance.

Catedral Ortodoxa

Inaugurated in January 1954 for the 400th anniversary
of the city, the Greek Orthodox Cathedral was blessed by
the Patriarch Elias IV in 1958. The original plan was based
on the Church of Santa Sofia in Constantinople, however
that did not materialize because of the nearby Paraíso
metro station.

⌂ Rua Vergueiro, 1515, Paraíso
☎ 5579-3835
🕐 Opened Monday to Friday 9 am to 1 pm and 3 pm
   to 6 pm, Saturday 10 am to 1 pm. Sundays the office
   is closed – mass at 10:30 am.
🌐 www.catedralortodoxa.com.br

Edificio Martinelli

The first skyscraper in São Paulo and by the 1920s it
was designated as the tallest building in South America.
In 1992, it was classified as a *Patrimônio Histórico*.

⌂ Rua Líbero Badaró, 505, Centro
☎ 3104-2477
◷ Monday, Wednesday and Friday 9 am to 10 am
   and 2:30 pm to 3:30 pm. Essential to schedule visits
   on weekends.
⊕ www.prediomartinelli.com.br

Estação da Luz

It was the first railway in São Paulo. Inaugurated in 1867, it was built by British investors and counted Barão de Mauá as its biggest shareholder. In view of the increase in population and the development of the economy, the station was remodelled, expanded and re-inaugurated in 1901. Sadly, the building caught fire in 1946, at the end of the British concession and had to be rebuilt. In 2004, the architecture was restored and the platform adapted for today's working trains. In 2006, the Museu da Língua Portuguesa (SEE MUSEUMS AT PAGE 94) was inaugurated on the premises.

⌂ Praça da Luz, Centro

Estação Júlio Prestes and Sala São Paulo

The old train station of Sorocaba has been divided into two parts, with one half still functioning as a working station and the other now transformed into the Sala São Paulo. The latter is the most modern and biggest concert hall in South America, with outstanding acoustics and the ability to accomodate the best Symphony orchestras in the world.

⌂ Praça Júlio Prestes, Centro
☎ 3367-9500
⊕ www.salasaopaulo.com.br

Fundação Bienal de São Paulo

The idea was conceived in the 1940s, and only materialized in1962. It was considered part of the cultural process of modernization, and enabled the city of São Paulo to integrate into the international art market in the 20th century.

⌂ Parque do Ibirapuera, Gate 3, Ibirapuera
☎ 5576-7600
◷ The time schedule and the entrance fee depends
   on the ongoing event.
⊕ www.bienalsaopaulo.org.br

Marco Zero

In the center of the *Praça da Sé* is the Marco Zero, inaugurated in 1934. It points the directions to the states that border São Paulo state, and it is the spot from where all the distances in the city are measured.

⌂ Praça da Sé, Centro

Mercado Municipal

The cast-iron structure of the old Beaux Arts palace supports a huge, two-story high area filled with stalls where fruit, spices, dried beef, fresh meat and fish, cheese and olives are sold from five in the morning until four in the afternoon. Open air restaurants are located on the mezzanine/balcony level where one can enjoy a snack or a meal and have a perfect view of the enormous and beautiful stained glass windows on the opposite wall. Popular with residents and tourists alike, the mercado is very crowded at weekends; although the restaurants are closed on Monday, stalls do businnes as usual.

⌂ Rua da Cantareira, 306, Centro

☎ 3228-0673

⊙ Opened Mondays to Saturdays, 6 am to 6 pm, and Sundays and Holidays, 6 am to 4 pm

⊕ www.mercadomunicipalamedacom.br

Monumento à Independência

Inaugurated in 1922, celebrating the 100th anniversary of the Independence of Brazil. The artist Ettore Ximenez created 131 sculptures in bronze. Inside the monument is the Imperial Chapel, where, in a crypt, D. Pedro I and Princess Leopoldina's remains rest.

⌂ Parque da Independência, Ipiranga

Monumento às Bandeiras

This monument, by Victor Brecheret, represents the memory of the Portuguese *Bandeirantes*, the native Brazilian guides and the African slaves who participated in the *Bandeiras* – expeditions to enlarge Brazil's frontiers. It was inaugurated in 1953.

⌂ Praça Armando Salles de Oliveira, in front of Parque do Ibirapuera

Mosteiro de São Bento

One of the major historical sites in the country, this
Monastery was founded in 1598 by Frei Mauro Teixeira of
the Benedictine Order. In 1646 Fernão Dias Paes Leme
financed a new church, built on condition that his family
could be buried there. Dom Miguel Kruse was assigned to
run the establishment in 1900; he ordered the church rebuilt
and, in 1903, the Colégio São Bento was incorporated and is
where Dom Miguel opened the first school of philosophy in
Brazil. Today, the Benedictine complex includes the Basílica
Nossa Senhora da Assunção, the Monastery and the College.
Known for its magnificent organ that boasts 6,000 pipes and
its Gregorian chants sung by two dozen monks, the
Benedictines also make delicious breads, cakes and jams that
are offered for sale in the church shop.

- Rua São Bento, Centro
- 3328-8799
- Church office is opened Mondays to Fridays 6 am to
  6:30 pm, Thursdays 6 am to 8 am and 2 pm to 6:30 pm,
  Saturdays and Sundays 6 am to noon and 4 pm to 6 pm.
  Mass with Gregorian chant, Mondays to Fridays at 7 am,
  Saturdays at 6 am, Sundays at 10 am.
- www.mosteiro.org.br

Obelisco Mausoléu aos Heróis de 32

Four big Italian mosaic panels compose this monument,
erected in memory of the heroes who died in the
Constitutionalist Rebellion of 1932, when the estate
of São Paulo lost the battle for a constitutionalist regime
against the federal government of Getúlio Vargas.

- Parque do Ibirapuera

Pátio do Colégio

Pátio do Colégio could be considered the historical
beginning of São Paulo, where priest Manuel de Paiva,
Manuel da Nóbrega and José de Anchieta celebrated the first
mass and founded the village *São Paulo de Piratininga* in
January 25th, 1554. Father José de Anchieta decided that the
place was a good location to build a house for the Jesuits
to live in and to provide a catechism school for the native
Indians. Both the house and the school were built by the
Indian Tribal Chief Tibiriçá and were inaugurated on

November 1st, 1556. Throughout the years, Pátio do Colégio has been transformed many times for different institutions and has been used as a Governor House, a home for the clergy, and even the site of metal smelting, for the production of money. In 1882, one of the original wings was torn down. In 1954 new construction took place in order to restore the original building. The project was undertaken by the Companhia de Jesus (who represented the Brazilian Education Society) who had acquired the land. Today, the Museum Padre Anchieta, the Church Beat José de Anchieta, and the House of Anchieta, reflect this fabulous history.

You will also see the monument Glória Imortal aos Fundadores de São Paulo, inaugurated in 1925. The woman on top of the monument represents the city, and carries laurels – for glory, a sickle – for work and a torch – for religion and culture.

⌂ Praça Pátio do Colégio, 84, Centro

☎ 3105-6899

◷ Church opened Sundays to Sundays 9 am to 5 pm, mass Mondays to Fridays at noon, Saturdays no mass, Sundays at 10 am. Museum opened Tuesdays to Sundays from 9 am to 5 pm. Entrance fee applies.

⊕ www.pateocollegio.com.br

Solar da Marquesa de Santos

The origins of this building are not known, however the architectural characteristics lead us to believe that it was built in the middle of the 18th century. It has been used for various purposes and transformed several times. In 1975, it became the home of the Municipal Secretary of Culture. In 1984, access to the building was prohibited due to physical deterioration. It was only in 1991, when the solar was restored, that visits were allowed again. Antique furniture and permanent and temporary exhibitions are on display, as well as eight thousand photo negatives of the city.

⌂ Rua Roberto Simonsen, 136, Centro

☎ 3241-4238

◷ Opened Thursdays to Sundays, from 9 am to 5 pm.

Teatro Municipal de São Paulo e Museu

During the last decade of the 19th century, industry was growing and coffee was becoming the most important commodity in the Brazilian economy. São Paulo, with its so-called "coffee barons," wanted to be on a level with the great cultural centers of the world at that time. The only theater able to stage big events, Teatro São Paulo, in the city center, had been lost in a fire in 1898. Therefore, it was a must to build a space to receive the great international companies.

In 1903, the architect Ramos de Azevedo started building the theatre, a task that lasted eight years. The architecture of the Theater was influenced by the Paris Opera House and externally has baroque and Renaissance features reminiscent of the 17th century. Its interior is full of art pieces, a delight to the spectator's eyes. The opening staged an opera – *Hamlet* – with an audience of 20,000 people. This is how São Paulo became part of the international cultural route. Names such as Maria Callas, Caruso, Toscanini, Rubinstein, Ana Pawlova, Nijinsky, Isadora Duncan, Nureyev, Margot Fonteyn, Baryshnikov, Duke Ellington, Ella Fitzgerald, Vivien Leigh have performed here.

The Theater is also famous for having been the host of the Modern Art Week of 1922, a landmark event in Brazilian art.

Through the years it has undergone two major renovations. The first, in 1951 installed the G. Tamburini organ. The second, from 1986 to 1991, was done by the City Hall (Departamento de Patrimônio Histórico, Secretaria Municipal de Cultura), restoring the building and implementing more modern structures and equipment.

Today, the Municipal Theater coordinates music and dance schools: the Muncipal Symphonic Orchestra, the Experimental Orchestra of Repertoire, the City Ballet, the String Quartet, the Lyric Chorus, and the Paulistano Chorus. Its calendar includes national and international events.

Almost a century old, with its art, history, and dream settings, the Municipal Theater wants to receive everyone with open doors and wishes to continue to have the same meaning and importance to the people of São Paulo as it had on September 12th, 1911.

Praça Ramos de Azevedo, Centro (the museum is at the lower Viaduto do Chá, beneath the theater)

3222-8698 (ticket office) / 3241-3815 (museum)

www.prefeitura.sp.gov.br/theatromunicipal

Teatro São Pedro

Inaugurated on January 17th, 1917, Teatro São Pedro has always hosted various events such as films, plays, operettas, and music concerts. In 1984, it was designated

as a *Patrimônio Histórico*, even though the original
architecture had been modified and fallen into disrepair.
The restored theater opened in 1998, with modern
equipment for illumination, acoustics and air
conditioning. It was important to preserve the memory of
the artistic community of the early 20th century. There are
800 seats and 350 parking spaces available in a nearby
parking garage. Open Wednesdays to Sundays, 2 pm to
7 pm or until the show starts – for concerts during the
day, the ticket office opens at 10 am.

⌂ Rua Barra Funda, 171, Campos Eliseos

☎ 3667-0499

⊕ www.teatrosaopedro.sp.gov.br

Terraço do Edifício Itália

With a beautiful panoramic view of the city, it was
inaugurated in 1967. One of the highest points in São Paulo,
it offers a restaurant and a Piano Bar, where you can have a
caipirinha (SEE GLOSSARY AT PAGE 212) while watching the sunset.

⌂ Av. Ipiranga, 344, Centro

☎ 2189-2929

⊕ www.terracoitalia.com.br

Scheduling visits beforehand by telephone is advisable.

holidays

Fixed Public and Religious Holidays

> **JAN 1** New Year's Day

> **JAN 25** São Paulo Founder's day

> **ABR 21** Tiradentes

> **MAY 1** Labor Day

> **JUL 9** Soldado Constitucionalista (only São Paulo)

> **SEPT 7** Independence Day

> **OCT 12** Patron Saint of Brazil, Nossa Senhora Aparecida

> **NOV 2** All Souls' Day

> **NOV 15** Proclamation of the Republic

> **NOV 20** Dia da Consciência Negra (some cities only, including São Paulo)

> **DEC 25** Christmas – *Natal*

Fluctuating Public Religious Holidays

Year / Holiday	2006	2007	2008	2009	2010
Tuesday of Carnival	Feb 28	Feb 20	Feb 5	Feb 24	Feb 16
Good Friday	Apr 14	Apr 6	Apr 21	Apr 10	Apr 2
Easter	Apr 16	Apr 8	Apr 23	Apr 12	Apr 4
Corpus Christi	Jun 15	Jun 7	May 22	Jun 11	Jun 3

Commercial Holidays

> **Children's Day** October 12

> **Father's Day** Second Sunday of August

> **Mother's Day** Second Sunday of May

> **Valentine's Day** June 12

serra da cantareira · cantareira

Neighborhood Map

lapa

parque vila-lobos

jaguaré

vila madalena · r. heitor penteado

marginal do pinheiros

jd. paulista

pinheiros

av. rebouças

cidade univesitária

ZONASUDOESTE

av. 9 de julho

av. prof. francisco morato

av. brig. faria lima

joquey clube

vila olímpia

est. do morumbi

soc. hípica paulista

itaim

parque alfredo volpi

av. 9 de julho

av. morumbi

morumbi

palácio do governo

ZONASUL

neighborhoods

Alto da Boa Vista

A very popular area among ex-pats, this neighborhood offers mainly houses. You will find good commercial infrastructure at two great international schools, Chapel (American) and Escola Suíço-Brasileira (Swiss). **Chácara Flora** is a gated community in this neighborhood which has the feel of an American suburb. Great location for those working in Brooklin and on Avenida das Nações Unidas.

Bexiga

Pronounced "bee-shee-ga" and officially called Bela Vista, this district was occupied by Italian artisans and ex-slaves. Its name refers to the ulcers on the skin caused by smallpox. Today it has many traditional Italian restaurants, theaters, an antique fair on Sundays (SEE ANTIQUES AT PAGE 74) and is home to the *Vai-Vai samba school*, one of the biggest in the city.

Bom Retiro

The Jewish community settled this area and has opened many fabric and clothing manufacturers and retail stores over the last century. Today, the Korean community has taken over a large share of this district's markets. Bolivians, Orthodox Jews and Koreans have found a melting pot in this neighborhood. It is full of restaurants with typical ethnic cuisine, supermarkets and inexpensive clothing stores. Here you will find *Parque da Luz*, one of the older parks in the city, just outside the *Pinacoteca do Estado* and in front of the *Museu da Língua Portuguesa*. (SEE MUSEUMS AT PAGE 94).

Brás, Mooca, Pari

A mostly industrial district at the edge of the east side of São Paulo. Populated by Italians, Spanish and Portuguese immigrants, it is still a great place for Italian food. Brás is known for its inexpensive clothing and linen stores – some of excellent quality.

Brooklin / Campo Belo

Since the 1990s what was once a mostly residential neighborhood has now developed into a large and modern office area. Also home to the Hípica Paulista, for those who enjoy riding horses.

Centro

The old section of town combines old world charm with mayhem.The classic architectural buildings mainly house government and financial offices. In the evening, Centro offers some of the best venues for classical music. During the day, however, walk around *Rua 25 de Março* to shop for all your arts and crafts needs, party supplies and costumes (especially for Halloween and **Carnaval**). There are all sorts of kitchen supplies, fabrics, bedding, and shoes for sale, at considerably less cost than what you will find in the malls. The best time to go is in the morning or early afternoon. Try to avoid Fridays and Saturdays. Pedestrians only so the best way to get there is by taxi or metro (São Bento station).

Cidade Jardim

Once you leave Itaim and on your way to Morumbi be careful not blink or you may miss this well esconsced neighborhood with only very upscale homes. The Jockey Club, located in Cidade Jardim, is a great place to spend an afternoon (SEE MORE INFO UNDER RESTAURANTS, PAGE 114).

Itaim / Vila Olímpia

Full of commercial buildings, bars, restaurants and nightclubs these neighborhoods are rapidly becoming another financial center in São Paulo (in addition to Avenida Paulista). Itaim is full of residential buildings (and construction sites!) and grows more and more popular everyday.

Higienópolis / Pacaembu

If you are looking for charming historical apartments with high ceilings and ample space, then Higienópolis may be for you. Here you will find a good mix of churches, synagogues and shopping centers and it is also very well located for those who will work around Avenida Paulista. Pacaembu is adjacent to Higienópolis and is better suited for those looking for homes instead of apartments.

Jardins

The name Jardins refers to a number of neighborhoods including **Jardim Europa**, **Jardim Paulista**, **Jardim América**, which are mainly residential, and **Cerqueira César**, which is a mix of apartment buildings & shops.

Cerqueira César is home to some of the best hotels, restaurants and the most famous shopping street in São Paulo, Rua Oscar Freire. This area also has some of the most beautiful homes, and apartments in the city. Look carefully and you will locate great finds, from homes in tucked away **vilas** to boutiques with the most up to date fashions. It is also home to Casa Santa Luzia a supermarket that carries the very best of everything! In our opinion there is a certain "je ne sais quoi" that makes the Jardins special!

Liberdade

Traditionally a Japanese neighborhood, Liberdade now has small Chinese and Korean communities as well. This rich mix of cultures offers amazing restaurants, ethnic food stores, linen shops and household equipment, and is where you can find the best sushis in town.

Moema

A middle-class neighborhood close to Parque do Ibirapuera, Moema offers a good mix of green areas and commercial spaces. Be aware of the noise pollution from airplanes during the day and the many bars and restaurants at night.

Morumbi

A sprawling neighborhood which offers large apartments, many with playgrounds and pools, and large homes. It is home to one of the best hospitals in São Paulo, Albert Einstein, and the Governors residence, which contrast sharply with the many slums that pepper the neighborhood. Very well located for those whose children will attend the American School, Graded. However, be ready for heavy traffic.

Pinheiros

Between the Pinheiros River and Vila Madalena, this residential neighborhood is home to CEASA and has as its most defining landmark the Praça Panamericana. It is located across the river from the largest university in Brasil, The University of São Paulo (USP).

Santana / Tucuruvi

In the northern part of the city, this neighborhood is a mix of lower income commerce and residences. Check out the Serra da Cantareira and the Pavilhão do Anhembi.

Vila Madalena

The bohemian section of São Paulo, this neighborhood has tons of charm. Small boutiques, little cafes and restaurants line quaint narrow streets. A great residential area as well.

Vila Nova Conceição

A charming neighborhood located next to Moema and in front of Parque do Ibirapuera. It is full of upsacale apartment buildings with wide, well paved sidewalks and very little in the way of commerce. It is the most expensive area per square meter in the city!

safety: some personal advice...

The following information was not easy to write, because the intentions were certainly not to scare any visitor, whether coming for business or pleasure, nor any newcomer who already has enough on their minds and does not need a whole list of "do's and don'ts."

However, Brazil is notorious for being unsafe. In fact, it is one of the first things that we are told when planning a trip here! Keeping that in mind, anyone who comes to São Paulo should be aware of the basic precautions, which should be undertaken and are essential in order to avoid any unfortunate incident.

Like any other big city, São Paulo has its share of problems, made worse, due to the huge discrepancy between rich and poor. Thefts are common and thieves vary in age from small children to adults, men or women.

The weapons used to conduct robberies are various, ranging from guns to pieces of glass. It is therefore highly advisable to NEVER RESIST AN ASSAULT, as the perpetrators tend to vanish once they get what they want.

Ten basic recommended steps to follow:

> Always carry some change with you. It is recommended to carry R$ 50,00, at least.

> Avoid wearing jewellery, nice watches, or anything glittery that might attract attention.

> Keep important papers at home, or in the safe at the hotel (RNE, CPF, driving license). Either carry copies or, better yet, write the corresponding numbers on a piece of paper that you will have with you at all times, as you do not have to provide the actual card, but only the corresponding number. Of course, if you are driving, you will need a copy of your driving license.

> When withdrawing money at an ATM, even inside the bank or in a shopping mall, look around – as quite frequently the robber is watching you. Do not be fooled by their physical appearance as many of them are dressed quite respectably.

> If asked for directions, whether by a male or a female, do not stop to answer – this is a trick used quite often.

> In cars, we strongly suggest keeping your doors locked and windows closed… rolled up.

> Always enquire whether the area you would like to visit is safe, as some are notoriously known not to be!

> If you live in a house (as opposed to an apartment), upon entering your garage or your parking area, please take the time to look around before exiting your car.

> We would recommend refraining from buying anything (chewing gum, flowers, etc.) when stopped at either a red light or in a traffic jam. Some robberies are conducted in broad daylight and in good areas.

> Last, but not least – at home, keep your valuables in more than one safe place, but be prepared to let the contents of one safe go, should (God Forbid), your building come under siege.

Most buildings have cameras and security guards who will identify your visitors at length and doormen will call you before allowing them entry. In addition to that, identify your visitor through the door viewer, keep the chain on until you are ready to open the door and please get into the habit of locking your doors at all times.

telephones

City codes

CAPITALS IN BRAZIL

capital	state	code
Aracaju	SE – Sergipe	79
Belém	PA – Pará	91
Belo Horizonte	MG – Minas Gerais	31
Boa Vista	RR – Roraima	95
Brasília	DF – Distrito Federal	61
Campo Grande	MS – Mato Grosso do Sul	67
Cuiabá	MT – Mato Grosso	65
Curitiba	PR – Paraná	41
Florianópolis	SC – Santa Catarina	48
Fortaleza	CE – Ceará	85
Goiânia	GO – Goiás	62
João Pessoa	PB – Paraíba	83
Macapá	AP – Amapá	96
Maceió	AL – Alagoas	82
Manaus	AM – Amazonas	92
Natal	RN – Rio Grande do Norte	84
Palmas	TO – Tocantins	63
Porto Alegre	RS – Rio Grande do Sul	51
Porto Velho	RO – Rondônia	69
Recife	PE – Pernambuco	81
Rio Branco	AC – Acre	68
Rio de Janeiro	RJ – Rio de Janeiro	21
Salvador	BA – Bahia	71
São Luís	MA – Maranhão	98
São Paulo	SP – São Paulo	11
Vitória	ES – Espírito Santo	27
Teresina	PI – Piauí	86

CITIES IN THE STATE OF SÃO PAULO

city	code
Águas de Lindóia	19
Americana	19
Araçatuba	18
Atibaia	11
Barretos	17
Barueri	11
Bauru	14
Bebedouro	17
Bertioga	13
Campinas	19
Campos do Jordão	12
Franca	16
Guaratinguetá	12
Guarujá	13
Ilhabela	12
Itu	11
Marília	14
Ourinhos	14
Piracicaba	19
Presidente Prudente	18
Rio Claro	19
Ribeirão Preto	16
Santa Bárbara do Oeste	19
Santos	13
São José do Rio Preto	17
São José dos Campos	12
São Sebastião	12
Sorocaba	15
Taquaritinga	16
Taubaté	12

City Services Telephones

Alarm clock
☎ 134

Correct Time
☎ 130

Crematorium
⌂ Av. Francisco Falconi, 437, Vila Alpina
☎ 6347-3549 / 6345-5937
⊕ http://portal.prefeitura.sp.gov.br/empresas_autarquias/
servico_funerario

Eletricity Company
AES Eletropaulo. Emergency in the electric
distribution system.
☎ 0800 72 72 196 to transfer the name on the bill
0800 72 72 120 to establish electrical connections

Fedex
For addresses and information:
☎ 0800 703 3339
⊕ www.fedex.com.br

Funeral Service
The Mayor's Office (Prefeitura) in the city of São Paulo is
the only office permitted to carry out the necessary
arrangements, should a death occur.
☎ 3247-7000
⊕ http://portal.prefeitura.sp.gov.br/empresas_autarquias/
servico_funerario

Should you need to send the body overseas, the
department known as *fiscalização* will be able to
help you.

Gas Company
Comgás
☎ 0800 11 01 97

Phone Telegrams
☎ 0800 550 135

Post Office Services

Called *Correios*. All post offices provide telegram and express mail service, and the Zip Code (CEP) of the different city zones.

☎ 0800 57 00 100

🌐 www.correios.com.br

Procon

Proteção ao Consumidor, in other words consumer protection agency. Believe it or not, this agency does a good job! It might take a little longer than it would elsewhere, but if you persevere, follow up with phone calls and appear in court when the time comes, you will be rewarded. Don't be intimidated and do ask the help of your Portuguese teacher should you feel you need it. I did! The agency also provides a list of companies that have been problematic to clients.

☎ 151

🌐 www.procon.sp.gov.br

Telephone Information

For new listings, local telephone information.

☎ 102. Information for new listings in other cities:
15 (or 21) + 21 (Rio's code) + number 102

Traffic Department

Detran, for information about taxes or fines related to your vehicle.

☎ 154

Water Departament

Sabesp

☎ 195

Emergency Phone Numbers

HEALTH

SEE MORE HOSPITALS AND THEIR ADDRESSES UNDER HEALTH, PAGE 148.

Ambulance

In case of a car accident, if someone does not feel well in a public place, or at home.

☎ 192

Hospital Oswaldo Cruz
☎ 6163-1119

Hospital Albert Einstein
☎ 3747-0200

Hospital Sírio Libanês
☎ 3155-0200

Hospital Sociedade Beneficência Portuguesa
☎ 3505-5190

Instituto Butantan
In case of an accident involving scorpions, snakes or spiders. Hospital Vital Brasil inside the "Instituto Butantan" 24-hour service.
⌂ Av. Vital Brasil, 1500, Butantã
☎ 3726-7962
⊕ www.butantan.gov.br

Pasteur Institute
In case of dog, cat and bat bites (prophylaxis to human hydrophobia).
⌂ Av. Paulista, 393, Cerqueira César
☎ 3288-0088
⊕ www.pasteur.saude.sp.gov.br

Poison Control Center
Centro de Controle de Intoxicação, medication and chemical products.
⌂ Hospital Municipal Sabóia
  Rua Francisco de Paula Quintanilha Ribeiro, 860, Jabaquara
☎ 5012-5311

CRIME / FIRE SERVICES

Child abuse
SOS Criança.
☎ 3207-9422

Denouncement
Make annonymous denunciations at *Disque Denúncia*.
☎ 181

Fire Department
☎ 193

Lost / Stolen documents
If your personal papers (ID, check) have either been stolen or lost, you must first call the police (or report the incident through the Internet), in order to get a file number (or B.O., *Boletim de Ocorrência*). You then call the number below to report the incident. This way, you are protected from any spending carried out by the person who has your documents.
☎ 0800 11 15 22

Police
In case of robbery, threatening situations, or whenever you need police intervention. In case of car theft without assault, loss of papers, stolen ID and missing persons, the report can be filed through the Internet, or in person at the police station. Should an assault occur, the report can only be filed at the police station, or by phone.
☎ 190
⊕ www.ssp.sp.gov.br

Police for Tourist Assistance
Deatur
☎ 3120-6782
🕐 Monday to Friday 8 am to 8 pm, Weekends 1 pm to 6 pm.

TRAFFIC

CET
For traffic information and help about anything related to traffic, as traffic interruption during public events.
☎ 156

Traffic accidents
☎ 156 or 190

Traffic accidents – legal advice
Call them if you need help solving a dispute about a traffic accident. They will be there immediately.
☎ 0800 644 2020

Tow Trucks

Usually, if a breakdown occurs in the city, you should call your own insurance company.

ROADSIDE ASSISTANCE

In case of car problems or accidents on the following highways, please call the numbers below (or your insurance company). They represent various companies (eg. AutoBan, for the Bandeirantes highway) which have contracts with the respective highways. You will be assisted quickly and a tow truck will be sent to you and will take you to the nearest garage, at no charge.

AutoBan
Rodovias Anhangüera and Bandeirantes
☎ 0800 055 5550
🌐 www.autoban.com.br

Dersa
Rodovias D. Pedro I, Ayrton Senna and Carvalho Pinto
☎ 0800 055 5510
🌐 www.dersa.sp.gov.br

Centrovias
Rodovia Washington Luiz
☎ 0800 17 8998
🌐 www.centrovias.com.br

Ecovias
Rodovias Anchieta and Imigrantes
☎ 0800 19 78 78
🌐 www.ecovias.com.br

Nova Dutra
Rodovia Presidente Dutra
☎ 0800 017 3536
🌐 www.novadutra.com.br

Viaoeste
Rodovias Castelo Branco and Raposo Tavares
☎ 0800 701 5555
🌐 www.viaoeste.com.br

Making Phone Calls

Anatel
Government Agency that coordinates all communication companies in Brazil.
☎ 0800 33 20 01

COLLECT CALLS

From São Paulo city to São Paulo city:
☎ 9090 + number

From São Paulo to other city in Brazil:
☎ 90 + operator's code + city code + number

TELEPHONE COMPANIES
In São Paulo, there are two major telephone companies:

Embratel
Operators who speak English are available.
☎ 0800 70 32 100

Telefônica
Only Portuguese spoken.
☎ 0800 777 1515

REPORTING PROBLEMS
Both companies provide billing information, time zones and country and city codes.

Embratel
☎ 103-21

Telefônica
☎ 103-15

CELL PHONES
There are four cell phone companies in São Paulo. They have stores scattered all over the city, and usually have a kiosk or a store in shopping centers as well.

Claro
☎ 1052
🌐 www.claro.com.br

Oi
☎ 1057
🌐 www.oi.com.br

Tim
☎ 0800 741 4141
🌐 www.tim.com.br

Vivo
☎ 1058
🌐 www.vivo.com.br

LONG DISTANCE CALLS
Operator's codes for long distance calling, both national
and international.

Embratel
☎ code 21
🌐 www.embratel.com.br

Intelig
☎ code 23
🌐 www.intelig.com.br

Telefônica
☎ code 15
🌐 www.telefonica.com.br

Each operator offers different prices and discounts.

DDD National Direct Dialing, long distance calls within Brazil
For long distance calls within Brazil (DDD), you dial:
☎ 0 + operator's code + city code + the number

DDI International Direct Dialing
For international, overseas calls (DDI), you dial:
☎ 00 + operator's code + country code + city code +
the number

Transportation Map

traffic and transportation

Buses

IN THE CITY
For information on bus lines, or for complaints, call SPTrans.
☎ 156
🌐 www.sptrans.com.br and choose *itinerário*

LEAVING THE CITY
All bus stations have access to a metro station.

Estação Barra Funda
From here, buses go to the south of São Paulo, as well as the states of Paraná, Goiás, Mato Grosso do Sul and Rondônia.
📍 Rua Mário de Andrade, 664, Barra Funda
☎ 3392-2110

Estação Jabaquara
Santos and the Litoral South of São Paulo State.
📍 Av. dos Jequitibás, Jabaquara

Estação Tietê
One of the biggest stations in South America, serves almost all of Brazil, in addition to four countries: Argentina, Chile, Paraguay and Uruguay.
📍 Av. Cruzeiro do Sul, 1800

Socicam
Company whitch administrates all São Paulo's buses terminals. Check the site to find information about all terminals, routes and destinations.
☎ 3235-0322
🌐 www.socicam.com.br

Bus ticket delivery

Passagem Expressa em Domicílio
📍 Rua Eng. Andrade Jr, 227, Belém
☎ 6618-2044
🕗 Monday to Friday, from 8:30 am to 5:30 pm.
🌐 www.passagem-em-domicilio.com.br

Driving in São Paulo

ZONA AZUL
This is designated by posted signs and reflects the areas in the city where you are allowed to park for a limited time (one to two hours), with a permission paper which you can buy either at newsstands, in authorized locations or even from the Zona Azul inspector who supervises the area. There are people in the street who sell the permit as well, but it is not advisable to purchase from them.

RODÍZIO
With the intention of reducing pollution and traffic in the streets, the expanded central areas of the city are inaccessible for some cars during the week between the hours of 7 am to 10 am, and 5 pm to 8 pm. The last number on the license plate determines which day of the week a car cannot be driven during those times, as shown in the box below.

Mondays	Tuesdays	Wednesday	Thursday	Friday
1 and 2	3 and 4	5 and 6	7 and 8	9 and 0

For more information about the prohibited areas, go to www.cetsp.com.br and click on **rodízio**.

Subway
Clean and very organized, this is São Paulo's best form of public transport. Nowadays there are four different lines: blue, red, green, and purple (SEE MAP AT PAGE 46)
☎ 3371-7274
🕐 Everyday, from 5 am to midnight.
🌐 www.metro.sp.gov.br

Taxi
There are three kinds of taxis in São Paulo, the common, the special, and the radio taxi.

COMMON

Ponto de Táxi or taxi stands are quite widespread in the city. These taxis are a safe way to move around but, unfortunately, most do not work overnight. You will often find the taxi stands at the foot of residential buildings. We suggest, at least at the beginning and until you familiarize yourself well with the city and the language, to always carry with you the name and cellular number of a person who speaks Portuguese, as well as your home address. Another helpful hint is to have the security guard of the condominium in which you live call a taxi for you and explain where you are going. If your needs for a taxi are quite frequent, it isn't a bad idea to get to know a specific driver whose services you can trust.

SPECIAL AND RADIO TAXIS

You can also call for a taxi – it usually takes from 15 minutes to half an hour to arrive. They work 24 hours.

Central Rádio Táxi

☏ 5069-0404

⊕ www.centralradiotaxi.com.br

Ligue Táxi

With enough notice, they will provide a bilingual driver.

☏ 3866-3030

⊕ www.ligue-taxi.com.br

Rádio Táxi Vermelho e Branco

☏ 3146-4000

⊕ www.radiotaxivermelhoebranco.com.br

> When taking down an address, take your time, have the name of the street spelled for you (the number in the address always comes after the name of the street) and ask what **bairro** (region) it is located in, as this will cut down tremendously on the time it takes to get to your destination. All taxis are required to have meters. Taxis at airports are safe.

Táxi Aéreo

Small airplanes are available for rent. They normally charge by distance (number of kilometers). Also available for rent are helicopters, whose fees are based on the number of hours. The bill is calculated on travel time, and not on the number of people. If the aircraft is available, the destination (any city or country, including the U.S.A. and Europe) does not pose a problem.

> It is advisable to schedule trips in advance, in order to receive an estimate of cost.

Using helicopters is quite common, as business people enjoy this mode of transportation due to the security and time saved. It is easy to find buildings with heliports on their roofs!

Aero Express
☎ 5031-8684

Aero Flyer
☎ 5096-3303 / cel. 9917-0310

Global
☎ 5070-6000
🌐 www.globaltaxiaereo.com.br

Líder
☎ 0800 970 2020
🌐 www.lideraviacao.com.br

Luma Táxi Aéreo
☎ 5535-1736
🌐 www.lumataxiaereo.com.br

Tam Jatos Executivos
☎ 4002-7000
🌐 www.tamjatos.com.br

Trains

CPTM
City trains information.
☎ 0800 055 0121
🌐 www.cptm.sp.gov.br

City Sections

airlines

Aerolineas Argentinas
☎ 0800 707 3313
🌐 www.aerolineasargentinas.com

Aero Mexico
☎ 3253-3888
🌐 www.aeromexico.com

Air France
☎ 4003-9955
🌐 www.airfrance.com.br

Air Canada
☎ 3254-6630
🌐 www.aircanada.com.br

Alitalia
☎ 2171-7610
🌐 www.alitalia.com.br

American Airlines
☎ 4502-4000
🌐 www.aa.com.br

BRA Transportes Aéreos
Take advantage of their promotions.
☎ 6445-4310
🌐 www.voebra.com.br

British Airways
☎ 3145-9700
🌐 www.ba.com

Continental Airlines
☎ 2122-7500
🌐 www.continental.com

Copa Airlines
☎ 3549-2672
🌐 www.copaair.com

Gol Linhas Aéreas
☎ 0800 280 0465
🌐 www.voegol.com.br

Iberia Airlines
☎ 3218-7130
🌐 www.iberia.com.br

Jal Japan Airlines
☎ 3175-2270
🌐 www.jal.com.br

KLM Airlines
☎ 3049-0900
🌐 www.klm.com.br

Lloyd Aereo Boliviano
☎ 3258-8111
🌐 www.labairlines.com.br

Lufthansa
☎ 3048-5800
🌐 www.lufthansa.com

Pantanal
☎ 0800 602 5888
🌐 www.voepantanal.com.br

Pluna
☎ 5091-7000
🌐 www.pluna.aero

South African Airways
☎ 3065-5115
🌐 www.flysaa.com

Swiss
☎ 3049-2720
🌐 www.swiss.com

Tam
☎ 4002-5700
🌐 www.tam.com.br

Tap
☎ 2131-1200
🌐 www.flytap.com.br

United Airlines
☎ 3145-4200
🌐 www.united.com.br

Varig
☎ 4003-7000
🌐 www.varig.com.br

Airport Shuttle Bus

Airport Bus Service
There are special bus lines connecting São Paulo International Airport (Guarulhos) to Congonhas Airport, Praça da República (downtown), Tietê Interstate Bus Terminal, Barra Funda Interstate Bus Terminal, Itaim and the Circle Line of the metro and Hotels Circuit (Paulista and Augusta).
☎ 6221-0244
🕐 24-hour service
🌐 www.airportbusservice.com.br

Airports
This is a useful web link in English, French, and Spanish. It explains the transport of animals, travel of minors, refunds and endorsements of tickets, overbooking, bad service, loss of baggage, flight cancellation, hand baggage, flight delays and ID card presentation.

To get information about flights arriving and departing from both airports, use the "on-line flights" link shown on the first page.

For services available at the airports, click on "airports", choose "Sudeste" region, on "São Paulo" then on "Guarulhos Airport" or on "Congonhas Airport" and you will find a list of available services (post office, pharmacies, banks) that are open 24 hours a day. Other services, such as dining areas, masseuses and libraries are available at the airports as well.
🌐 www.infraero.gov.br

Keep in mind while packing that porters are non-existent at both airports, but you will find plenty of available trolleys at no charge!

Congonhas International Airport
Mostly domestic flights.
📍 Av. Washington Luiz, Campo Belo
☎ 5090-9000

São Paulo International Airport / Guarulhos (Cumbica)
International and domestic flights.
📍 Rodovia Helio Schmidt, Guarulhos
☎ 6445-2945

banks

Private banks

ABN AMRO Real
🌐 www.bancoreal.com.br

BMG
🌐 www.bancobmg.com.br

Bradesco
🌐 www.bradesco.com.br

Citibank
🌐 www.citibank.com.br

HSBC
🌐 www.hsbc.com.br

Itaú
🌐 www.itau.com.br

Rural
🌐 www.rural.com.br

Safra
🌐 www.safranet.com.br

Santander
🌐 www.santander.com.br

Sudameris
🌐 www.sudameris.com.br

Unibanco
🌐 www.unibanco.com.br

Governments banks
Federal and State banks

Banco do Brasil
🌐 www.bancodobrasil.com.br

Nossa Caixa
🌐 www.nossacaixa.com.br

Caixa Econômica Federal
🌐 www.caixaeconomicafederal.
com.br

charities

If you are interested in making donations or helping in any way, you are sure to find somewhere that will be very gratefull for your help

AACC – Associação de Apoio à Criança com Câncer
For children with cancer.
☎ 5084-5434
🌐 www.aacc.org.br

Ação Criança
For children living in dangerous or inadequate conditions.
☎ 3289-7400
🌐 www.acaocrianca.org.br

Ação da Cidadania
☎ 3362-8266
🌐 www.acaodacidadania.org.br

APAE – Associação de Pais e Amigos dos Excepcionais
☎ 5080-7000
🌐 www.apaesp.org.br

Associação Cruz Verde
☎ 5579-7335
🌐 www.cruzverde org.br

Casas André Luiz
☎ 6457-7733
🌐 www.andreluiz.org.br

CDI – Comitê para Democratização da Informática
Accepts computer parts, printers,

or anything related to computers.
☎ 3666-0911
🌐 www.cdi.org.br

Exército de Salvação
☎ 5562-2285
🌐 www.exercitodesalvacao.org.br

Fraternidade Irmã Clara
Accepts clothes, furniture and other items. You can donate by telephone. They will collect your donations the next day.
🏠 Av. Pacaembu, 40, Barra Funda
☎ 3666-2727
🌐 www.ficfeliz.org.br

Fundação Dorina Nowill
Has helped blind people since 1946. Also prints books in Braille.
🏠 Rua Dr. Diogo de Faria, 558, Vila Mariana
☎ 5087-0999
🌐 www.fundacaodorina.org.br

Lar da Tia Edna
Accepts clothes and small items, that are then sold in their bazaar.
🏠 Rua Luís Góes, 262, Saúde
☎ 2577-2043

Lar da Tia Maria
🏠 Praça Rafael Mendes de Carvalho, 65, Alto do Mandaqui
☎ 6283-6568

Lar Escola São Francisco
Accepts clothes, furniture and other items, that are then sold in their bazaar.
☎ 5908-7899
🌐 www.lesf.org.br

Projeto Arrastão
☎ 5841-3366
🌐 www.arrastao.org.br

Rede Voluntária de Combate ao Câncer Carmem Prudente
🏠 Rua Antônio Prudente, 211, second basement, Liberdade
☎ 2189-5000
🌐 www.hcanc.org.br

consulates

Argentina
🏠 Av. Paulista, 2313, mezzanine, Cerqueira César
☎ 3897-9522
🌐 www.brasil.embajada-argentina.gov.ar

Armenia
🏠 Av. São Luís, 192, room 1301, Centro
☎ 3255-7707
🌐 www.consulados.com.br/consulados/armenia.html

Australia
🏠 Alameda Min. Rocha Azevedo, 456, second floor, Jardins
☎ 2112-6200
🌐 www.australian-consulate.org.br

Austria
🏠 Av. Dr. Cardoso de Melo, 1340, room 71, Building Network Empresarial, Vila Olímpia
☎ 3842-7500
🌐 www.austria.org.br

Bangladesh Consulate Honorary

📍 Rua Princesa Isabel, 1740, Brooklin

☎ 5533-2838

🌐 www.consulados.com.br/consulados/bangladesh.html

Belgium

📍 Av. Paulista, 2073, Conjunto Nacional Horsa I Building, rooms 1303/1310, Cerqueira César

☎ 3171-1596 / 3171-1599 / 3171-1603 / 3171-1606

🌐 www.diplomatie.be/saopaulo

Bolivia

📍 Av. Paulista, 1439, ninth floor, room 92, Cerqueira César

☎ 3289-0443

🌐 www.consulados.com.br/consulados/bolivia.html

Canada

📍 Av. das Nações Unidas, 12901, North Tower, sixteenth floor, Brooklin

☎ 5509-4321 / 5509-4343

🌐 www.canada.org.br

Cape Verde Islands Consulate Honorary

📍 Av. Prof. Alfonso Bovero, 1057, ninth floor, room 97/99, Sumaré

☎ 3871-0017 / 3863-2071 / 3868-2934

🌐 www.consulados.com.br/consulados/caboverde.html

Chile

📍 Av. Paulista, 1009, tenth floor, Cerqueira César

☎ 3284-2044

🌐 www.congechilesaopaulo.org.br

China

📍 Rua Estados Unidos, 1071, Jardins

☎ 3082-9877 / 3082-9084

🌐 www.saopaulo.china-consulate.org

Colombia

📍 Rua Tenente Negrão, 140, ninth floor, room 92, Itaim

☎ 3078-0322

🌐 www.consulados.com.br/consulados/colombia.html

Costa Rica

📍 Rua Monte Alegre, 523, room 22, Perdizes

☎ 3875-3430 / 3875-2570

🌐 www.consulados.com.br/consulados/costarica.html

Croatia Consulate Honorary

📍 Av. Brig. Faria Lima, 2012, room 32, Itaim

☎ 3815-4375

🌐 www.consulados.com.br/consulados/croacia.html

Cuba

📍 Rua Cardoso de Almeida, 2115, Perdizes

☎ 3873-4537 / 3873-2800

🌐 www.embaixadacuba.org.br

Czech Republic

📍 Av. Morumbi, 635, Jardim Guedala

3031-1729 / 3031-8997
www.mfa.cz/saopaulo

Denmark
Rua Oscar Freire, 379,
room 31, Jardins
3061-3625
www.gksaopaulo.um.dk

Dominican Republic Consulate
Alameda Jaú, 1742,
room 91, Jardins
3898-1120 / 3086-3926
www.consulados.com.br/consulados/republicadominicana.html

Ecuador
Rua Diogo Moreira, 132,
room 1308, Pinheiros
3032-9909
www.consulecuadorsp.com.br

Estonia
Av. Morumbi, 6901,
sixth floor, Morumbi
4667-1529 / 3759-3800
www.consulados.com.br/consulados/estonia.html

Finland
Rua Machado Bittencourt, 190,
room 607, Vila Clementino
5087-9542
www.finlandia.org.br

France
Av. Paulista, 1842, North
Tower, fourteenth floor,
Cerqueira César
3371-5400
www.ambafrance.org.br

Gana Consulate Honorary
Rua Belini, 231,
Alto de Pinheiros
3021-1687
www.consulados.com.br/consulados/gana.html

Germany
Av. Brig. Faria Lima, 2092,
twelfth floor, Itaim
3097-6644
www.sao-paulo.diplo.de

Greece
Av. Paulista, 2073, Conjunto
Nacional Horsa II Building,
twenty-third floor, room
2303, Cerqueira César
3251-0675
www.emb-grecia.org.br

Guatemala
Rua Itapeva, 378, fourth floor,
room 44, Bela Vista
3285-0586
www.consulados.com.br/consulados/guatemala.html

Iceland Consulate Honorary
Rua Conde D'Eu, 618,
Santo Amaro
5547-0700
www.consulados.com.br/consulados/islandia.html

Jordan Consulate Honorary
Av. Paulista, 326, fifteenth
floor, room 158/159, Paraíso
3285-5521
consuladojordaniasp@yahoo.com.br

Korea (South)

⌂ Av. Paulista, 37, ninth floor, room 91, Paraíso
☎ 3141-1278
🌐 www.consulados.com.br/ consulados/coreiadosul.html

Latvia Consulate Honorary

⌂ Rua Jacques Felix, 586, room 12, Vila Nova Conceição
☎ 5182-8925 / 3842-0687
🌐 www.consulados.com.br/ consulados/letonia.html

Lebanon

⌂ Av. Paulista, 688, sixteenth floor, Bela Vista
☎ 3262-0604 / 3262-0534
🌐 www.consulados.com.br/ consulados/libano.html

Lithuania Consulate Honorary

⌂ Rua Manoel Pereira Guimarães, 87
☎ 5681-9658 / 5523-9184
🌐 www.consulados.com.br/ consulados/lituania.html

Malawi

⌂ Rua Américo Brasiliense, 1943, Chácara Santo Antônio
☎ 5181-5433
🌐 www.consulados.com.br/ consulados/malaui.html

Malta Consulate

⌂ Rua Xavier de Almeida, 227, Ipiranga
☎ 6914-4420
🌐 www.consulados.com.br/ consulados/malta.html

Mexico

⌂ Rua Holanda, 274, Jardim Europa
☎ 3081-4144 / 3081-4921
🌐 www.mexico.org.br

Morocco

⌂ Rua Formosa, 51, seventh floor, Centro
☎ 3256-2146
🌐 www.consulados.com.br/ consulados/marrocos.html

Mozambique Consulate Honorary

⌂ Rua Líbero Badaró, 425, twentieth floor, Centro
☎ 3107-3102
🌐 www.consulados.com.br/ consulados/mocambique.html

Netherlands

⌂ Av. Brig. Faria Lima, 1779, third floor, Itaim
☎ 3811-3300
🌐 www.embaixada- holanda.org.br

New Zealand

⌂ Alameda Campinas, 579, fifteenth floor, Jardins
☎ 3148-0616
🌐 www.novazelandia.org.br

Norway

⌂ Rua General Almerio de Moura, 780, Morumbi
☎ 3759-2379 / 5549-5031
🌐 www.noruega.org.br

Panama

⌂ Rua Augusta, 1642, room 6-A, Jardins

☎ 3266-2923 / 3222-8722
🌐 www.consulados.com.br/
consulados/panama.html

Paraguay
🏠 Rua Bandeira Paulista,
600, room 153, Itaim
☎ 3167-7793
🌐 www.paraguaysp.com.br

Peru
🏠 Rua Venezuela, 36,
Jardim Paulista
☎ 3063-5952 / 3063-5968
🌐 www.consuladoperusp.com.br

Philippines Consulate Honorary
🏠 Praça da República, 32,
first floor, Centro
☎ 3259-4966
🌐 www.consulados.com.br/
consulados/filipinas.html

Poland
🏠 Rua Monte Alegre,
1791, Perdizes
☎ 3672-3778 / 3672-5778
🌐 www.consuladopoloniasp.
org.br

Portugal
🏠 Rua Canadá, 324, Jardins
☎ 3084-1800
🌐 www.consuladoportugalsp.
org.br

Russia
🏠 Avenida Lineu de Paula
Machado, 1366,
Jardim Everest
☎ 3814-1246 / 3814-4100
🌐 www.sao-paulo.mid.ru

San Marino
🏠 Rua XV de Novembro,
228, Centro
☎ 3168-9725
🌐 www.geocities.com/
infosanmarino

Senegal Consulate Honorary
🏠 Av. Brig. Faria Lima,
201, eleventh floor,
Pinheiros
☎ 3034-1319
🌐 www.consuladosenegalsp.
org.br

South Africa
🏠 Av. Paulista, 1754,
twelfth floor, Cerqueira César
☎ 3265-0449
🌐 www.africadosul.org.br

Spain
🏠 Av. Bernardino de Campos,
98, first floor, Vila Mariana
☎ 3059-1800
🌐 www.consuladoespanhasp.
org.br

Suriname Consulate Honorary
🏠 Rua Said Aiach, 135, Paraíso
☎ 3884-7868
🌐 www.consulados.com.br/
consulados/suriname.html

Sweden Consulate Honorary
🏠 Rua Arandu, 205, room 1009,
Brooklin
☎ 5506-9994
🌐 www.consulados.com.br/
consulados/suecia.html

Switzerland Consulate

🏠 Av. Paulista, 1754,
fourth floor, Cerqueira César
☎ 3372-8200
🌐 www.consulados.com.br/
consulados/suica.html

Syria

🏠 Av. Paulista, 326,
sixth floor, Paraíso
☎ 3285-5578 / 3288-0060
🌐 www.consulados.com.br/
consulados/siria.html

Taiwan Representative Office

🏠 Av. Paulista, 1294,
twenty-first floor, room
21-A, Cerqueira César
☎ 3285-6988
🌐 www.consulados.com.br/
consulados/taiwan.html

Thailand

🏠 Alameda Dinamarca,
467, Alphaville I,
Barueri
☎ 4195-2820
🌐 www.thaiconsul.com

United Kingdom

🏠 Rua Ferreira de Araújo,
741, second floor,
Pinheiros
☎ 3094-2700
🌐 www.britishembassy.gov.uk

United States of America

🏠 Rua Henri Dunant, 500,
Chácara Santo Antônio
☎ 5186-7000 and 5181-8730 for

after hours calls
🌐 www.consuladoamericanosp.
org.br

Venezuela Consulate

🏠 Rua General Fonseca Teles,
564, Itaim
☎ 3887-2318 / 3887-4583
🌐 www.consulados.com.br/
consulados/venezuela.html

Upon landing in São Paulo you are asked to fill in an immigration form. It is important that you keep the stamped copy, as you have to give it back upon exiting. If you need to translate documents, SEE TRANSLATION AT PAGE 64

documentation

Forwarding Agents

Agência Despac

Only vehicle documents.
🏠 Rua Pascal, 911, Campo Belo
☎ 3213-7689 / 3213-7685 /
fax 5044-9723

Agência Flavio de Despachos

Vehicle documents.
🏠 Av. Brig. Luiz Antonio,
3785, Itaim
☎ fax 3887-0438

Augusto de Leoni Assessoria de Despacho

🏠 Rua Bráulio Gomes, 141,
fourth floor, Centro
☎ 3258-3388 / fax 3159-2386

Despachante Andorinha

Vehicle documents.

⊕ Rua Dr. Alceu de Campos
   Rodrigues, 566, room 6,
   Vila Nova Conceição

☎ fax 3845-6406

Marco Zero

Car documents and auto school.

⊕ Rua Oscar Freire, 2095,
   Jardins

☎ fax 3081-4930

Relemar Despachos

Vehicle documents.

⊕ Av. Nossa Senhora do Sabará,
   2190, second floor,
   Santo Amaro

☎ fax 5631-3403

⊕ www.relemar.com.br

Robi Assessoria

Car documents and auto school.

⊕ Rua Gomes de Carvalho,
   1176, Vila Olímpia

☎ fax 3849-5127

Notary Public's Office / Registry Office

Cartórios are a Brazilian phenomenon. You will inevitably be
required to have a document
notarized (*autenticada*). This
requires that you visit an official
cartório and register your signature. Bring all of your domestic
and international documents
with you. Visit the website to
locate the one nearest you.

⊕ www.mj.gov.br/cartorio/
   index.htm

Driving License

Detran is the official department
that issues driver's licenses.

⊕ Av. Pedro Álvares Cabral,
   Ibirapuera

☎ 2189-9724

⊕ www.detran.sp.gov.br

Our tips for visiting the
Detran website:

Click on *serviços*; then click on
habilitação; then *estrangeiros*;
this is going to open
Selecione a opção desejada –
Select the desired option:

1) *Estrangeiros dirigindo
no Brasil* – Foreigner driving
in Brazil;

2) *Estrangeiros renovando a
licença provisória* – Foreigner
renewing their temporary
license;

3) *Brasileiro habilitado em
outro país* – Brazilians driving
overseas.

RNE Registro Nacional de Estrangeiros

A national identity card for foreigners issued by the Federal
Police Office that regulates
foreigner's papers.

To facilitate matters upon
your arrival, ir is advisable
to enquire at the Brazilian con-
sulate in your country before
you move, to verify what documents you will need on arrival
to finalize your RNE.

☎ 3616-5000

⊕ www.dpf.gov.br

It is advisable to carry a copy of your RNE card (Brazilian Identification card which indicates your permanent residency) at all times, as very often you are asked to give the number.

(search) type: *estrangeiros* (foreigners). Add the information you need, eg: *estrangeiros* visa...(visa for foreigners). You will be informed about the laws which apply to foreigners.

CPF
(CPF = *Cadastro de Pessoa Física*)

The CPF card is essential, as it is a type of identification necessary for people who reside in Brazil. You will be asked for your CPF number when opening bank accounts, paying taxes, declaring income, etc.

☎ 0300 780 300
🌐 www.receita.fazenda.gov.br

The CPF card is also requested from people who do not live in the country, but who wish to buy property and/or do business.

VISA
Brazil issues various kinds of visa. The most sought-after are the tourist and business visas. Each is normally issued for a duration of ninety days. For further information about visas, visit the following link:

🌐 www.dpf.gov.br.

Each country has different visa requirements. Another useful link is www.planalto.gov.br. Click on *legislação* (legislation), then under the word *buscar*

Translation

Andrart Traduções
Official and personal translation in English, French, Spanish, Italian, German, Japanese and Portuguese.

⌂ Rua da Consolação, 331, first floor, room 102, Consolação
☎ 3259-7848
🌐 www.andrart.com

JUST – Traduções Joanita Haimerl
Official and personal translation in English, German, Spanish and Portuguese.

⌂ Rua Líbero Badaró, 488, seventh floor, Centro
☎ 3106-7383
🌐 www.just-traduz.com.br

libraries

Biblioteca do Centro Cultural São Paulo
⌂ Rua Vergueiro, 1000, Paraíso
☎ 3277-3611
🌐 www.centrocultural.sp.gov.br

Biblioteca do Memorial da América Latina
SEE MORE INFORMATION ABOUT

CULTURAL CENTERS AT PAGE **91**.

📍 Av. Auro Soares de Moura
   Andrade, 664, Barra Funda
☎ 3823-4732
🌐 www.memorial.sp.gov.br

Biblioteca Mário de Andrade

📍 Rua da Consolação, 94,
   Centro
☎ 3256-5270

Biblioteca Monteiro Lobato

📍 Rua General Jardim, 485,
   Vila Buarque
☎ 3256-4122

hotels

Blue Tree Towers Nações Unidas

📍 Rua Fernandes Moreira, 1371,
   Chácara Santo Antônio
☎ 5189-6555
   For more locations:
🌐 www.bluetree.com.br

Clarion Berrini

📍 Rua Alcides Lourenço
   da Rocha, 136, Brooklin
☎ 2137-4500

Clarion Jardim Europa

📍 Rua Jerônimo da Veiga,
   248, Itaim
☎ 3702-9000
🌐 www.atlantica-hotels.com

This website is also for Hotel
Quality Suites, Comfort,
Radisson and Park Suites.

Crowne Plaza Hotel

📍 Rua Frei Caneca, 1360,
   Cerqueira César
☎ 4501-8000
🌐 www.ichotelsgroup.com.br

Caesar Business

📍 Av. Paulista, 2181,
   Cerqueira César
☎ 3066-6666

Ceasar Park

📍 Rua das Olimpíadas, 205,
   Vila Olímpia
☎ 3049-6622
🌐 www.caesarpark.com.br

Emiliano

An elegant, boutique hotel and
a quiet place to enjoy lunch
or dinner, the location of the
Emiliano is perfect for those
of you who are ready to shop
'til they drop!

📍 Rua Oscar Freire, 384, Jardins
☎ 3068-4399
🌐 www.emiliano.com.br

Estanplaza

For bookings and addresses:
☎ 3059-3277
🌐 www.estanplaza.com.br

Fasano

Step into the world of luxury,
European intimacy and outstanding service. Need we
say more? Generally, visitors
in a new city prefer to experience fine dining in restaurants
outside hotels, however, a
must in São Paulo is to dine
at the Fasano. The elegant ambi-
ence and the exceptional quality

of the food make it a memorable night.

Do not forget to visit the kitchen – you are in for a surprise!

Before or after dining, relax to the sounds of the music in Baretto, the hotel bar.

On a last note, did you notice that the name of the street is the same as the hotel? How cool is that?!

🏠 Rua Vittorio Fasano, 88, Jardins
☎ 3896-4000
🌐 www.fasano.com.br

For a casual lunch, try Nono Rugero, located on the first floor. Serves a buffet and a la carte, as well as brunch on the weekend. Weather permitting, you can also sit outside.

Feller
☎ 3016-7594
🌐 www.fellersolution.com.br

Formule 1 / Accor Hotels
Very inexpensive and conveniently located.
🏠 Av. Nove de Julho, 3597, Jardins
☎ 3886-4600
🌐 www.accorhotels.com.br/formule1

Grand Hyatt
A relative newcomer on the scene, the Grand Hyatt is noted for its fabulous spa and restaurant "Eau," which often enjoys the talents of renowned acclaimed international chefs. Space available for rent, with choice of room space, depending on the size of the event.

🏠 Av. das Nações Unidas, 13301, Brooklin
☎ 6838-1234
🌐 www.saopaulo.hyatt.com

Hilton
🏠 Av. das Nações Unidas, 12901, Brooklin
☎ 6845-0000 / 0800 596 0000
🌐 www.hilton.com

Ibis / Accor Hotels
Bed and breakfast.
🏠 Av. Paulista, 2355, Jardins
☎ 3523-3000
🌐 www.accorhotels.com.br/ibis

Intercontinental
🏠 Alameda Santos, 1123, Jardins
☎ 3179-2600
🌐 www.intercontinental ameda.com

L'Hotel
🏠 Alameda Campinas, 266, Bela Vista
☎ 2183-0500 / 0800 130 080
🌐 www.lhotel.com.br

Maksoud Plaza Hotel
🏠 Alameda Campinas, 150, Jardins
☎ 3145-8000 / 0800 134 411 (Brazil) 1 888 55 11 333 (U.S.A.)
🌐 www.maksoud.com.br

Marriott
For bookings and addresses:
☎ 0800 703 1612
🌐 www.marriott.com.br

Meliá Comfort Paulista
🏠 Rua Haddock Lobo, 294, Cerqueira César
☎ 3123-6200
🌐 www.solmelia.com

Park Plaza

🏠 Alameda Lorena,
360, Jardins
☎ 3058-4055
🌐 www.parkplaza.com.br

Paulista Wall Street

🏠 Rua Itapeva, 636,
Bela Vista
☎ 3141-3000
🌐 www.paulistawallstreet.com.br

Pergamon Hotel

🏠 Rua Frei Caneca, 80,
Consolação
☎ 3123-2021
🌐 www.pergamon.com.br

Renaissance
São Paulo Hotel

One of the top hotels in São
Paulo, the Renaissance has
a fabulous gym with personal
trainers on site, ready to help.
Don't forget to check out the
theater room, which always has
a good schedule.

SEE THEATERS AT PAGE 100.

🏠 Alameda Santos, 2233, Jardins
☎ 3069-2233
🌐 www.marriottbrasil.com

Sofitel Hotel

For bookings and addresses:
☎ 2122-8000
🌐 www.accorhotels.com.br

Transamérica São Paulo

🏠 Av. das Nações Unidas,
18591, Santo Amaro
☎ 5693-4511 / 0800 012 6060
🌐 www.transamerica.com.br

L&T's best!

Unique Hotel

As the name indicates, the
architecture of the Unique
Hotel is truly unique, designed
by Ruy Othake. Built like a ship,
with windows in the shape of
portholes, this hotel is one of
a kind! We strongly recommend having a drink at the bar,
and going up to the top-floor
"Sky Restaurant" to savour
the different cuisines served.

As reservations are only
accepted for guests staying in
the hotel, an "earlier" dinner
is recommended.

For the younger crowd, the
adjoining bar is quite a scene,
especially during weekends.

🏠 Av. Brig. Luiz Antonio,
4700, Jardim Paulista
☎ 3055-4710
🌐 www.hotelunique.com.br

Extended stay
apartments

Flat Fortune

🏠 Rua Haddock Lobo,
804, Jardins
☎ 3085-9511
🌐 www.fortuneresidence.com.br

Residence George V

🏠 Rua Roquette Pinto, 9,
Alto de Pinheiros
☎ 3030-0700

For more addresses
and reservation:
☎ 0800 773 4663
🌐 www.george-v.com.br

The Palace

🏠 Alameda dos Anapurus,
1661, Moema
☎ 5095-2199
🌐 www.thepalace.com.br

Transamerica Flat Opera

⌂ Alameda Lorena,
   1748, Jardins
☎ 3062-2666
   For bookings and more
   addresses:
☎ 0800 12 44 00
🌐 www.transamericaflats.com.br

maps and guides

tourist information

CIT – Centrais de Informação Turística

The CITs are located in many spots in the city, and provide information on tourism, entertainment, leisure and public utilities. They offer maps and folders, and also organize city tours by appointment. English, French and Spanish spoken; maps are in Japanese, German, French, Italian, English and Spanish.

⌂ Av. Paulista, in front of Parque Trianon, across from MASP
☎ 6226-0400

🌐 www.cidadedesaopaulo.com
   www.visitesaopaulo.com

Address and route information

You can buy the "Guia Ruas São Paulo" at any newstand or in any bookshop, always useful to keep it in the car. It has complete and detailed lists and maps of all streets and avenues, including those in the outskirts of the city.

You can also check these websites for routes and maps:

🌐 www.apontador.com.br
   www.guiamais.com.br/ruas
   www.maplink.com.br

cultural guides

Magazines and newspapers provide weekly cultural guides. *Veja São Paulo* ("Vejinha") comes with *Veja* magazine on Saturdays, *Guia da Folha* comes in the *Folha de São Paulo* newspaper on Fridays and the *Guia Caderno 2* comes in *Estado de São Paulo* newspaper, also on Fridays.

🌐 http://vejinha.abril.com.br
   www.estado.com.br
   www1.folha.uol.com.br/guia

Mapa das Artes

Every other month this compact art map is released. It is great to carry around because of its clear format, which lists all the art institutions and galleries in the city. You will only be able to collect your copy by asking at the art galleries or museums, or check the website.

🌐 ww.mapadasartes.com.br

religions

All religious denominations have a home here. Catholic, Protestants and Greek Orthodox Churches, Jewish synagogues and Muslim Mosques co-exist side by side. Religious holidays are observed by the different factions.

Baptist Church

Igreja Batista de Vila Mariana
⌂ Rua Joaquim Távora, 598
☎ 5539-7633
   For more locations:
🌐 www.ibvm.org.br

Buddhism – Templo Zu Lai

Estrada Municipal Fernando Nobre, 1461, Cotia

11 4612-2895

www.templozulai.org.br

Calvary International Church

Sundays Services conducted in English: 8 am First morning Worship; 10:40 am Morning Worship; 15:00 pm Afternoon Prayer Meeting.

Rua Barão do Triunfo, 1670, Brooklin

5041-2541

Office hours open Mondays to Fridays, from 9 am to 5 pm.

www.calvary.org.br

Greek Orthodox – Catedral Ortodoxa

FOR MORE INFORMATION SEE HISTORICAL MONUMENTS AT PAGE 21.

Rua Vergueiro, 1515, Paraíso

5579-3835

www.catedralortodoxa.com.br

Kardecism – Federação Espírita do Estado de São Paulo

Rua Maria Paula, 140, Allan Kardec Building, Bela Vista

3115-5544

For more locations: www.feesp.com.br

Luteran Church

Rua Verbo Divino, 392, Granja Julieta
For more locations

www.luteranos.com.br

Mosques – Sociedade Beneficente Muçulmana

The first Islamic temple was inaugurated in São Paulo in 1955 in the Cambuci neighborhood. There are now about 40 temples in the city.

Av. do Estado, 5382, Cambuci

3208-6789

Our Lady Help of Christians Parish (Catholic)

Mass conducted in English: 7:15 am Monday and Wednesday; 8:15 am every Friday; 18:30 pm every Saturday; 10:30 am every Sunday; 10:30 am and 18:30 pm last Sunday of every month.

Rua Vigário João de Pontes, 537, Chácara Flora

5541-9183

www.chapelparish.org

Sampa Community Church

Services in English: 5:55 pm Sunday.

The Alumni Building
Av. Brasiliense, 65, Sto Amaro

www.sampacommunity.com

St. Paul's Anglican Episcopal Church

Services in English: 10:00 am Sunday

Rua Comendador Elias Zarzur, 1239, Alto da Boa Vista

5686-2180

www.catedral-anglicana.org.br

Synagogues – Federação Israelita do Estado de São Paulo

Ask by letter, fax or e-mail for the list of the city's synagogues.

3088-0111

www.fisesp.org.br
www.netjudaica.com.br
This site gives you more religious information.

Our Sections

In "Our Sections" we have tried to come up with as much useful information as possible and we have divided the items into what we hope will be easy to navigate sections.

- Home decoration, housing;
- Leisure and travel cultural, outings, bars & restaurants, templates for the weekend;
- Personal beauty, education, fitness, health;
- Shopping & Stores clothing, cars, discount and megastores, grocery stores and more;
- Social clubs, party help

We recommend keeping a copy of the guide in your purse!

Home

decoration and utilities

Antique shops

Anno Domini Antiguidades
⌂ Alameda Gabriel Monteiro da Silva, 65, Jardins
☎ 3064-2929
🌐 www.annodominiantigui-dades.com.br

Basile
⌂ Alameda Lorena, 2050, Jardins
☎ 3083-7553
⌂ Rua da Consolação, 3125, Jardins
☎ 3062-2799

L&T's best!
Herrero Móveis e Antiguidades
Eclectic shop run by an Argentine family. If they don't have what you're looking for, they'll go out of their way to find it!
⌂ Rua João Cachoeira, 159, Itaim
☎ 3168-4469

Ilustrata Gravuras Antigas
⌂ Rua João Cachoeira, 233, store 6, Itaim
☎ 3079-6086

Oswaldo Kathalian
⌂ Rua Haddock Lobo, 858, Jardins
☎ 3082-9002

Passado Composto
See Furniture section at page 79

Patrimônio Antiguidades
Specializes in Brazilian furniture and tribal art.
⌂ Alameda Min. Rocha Azevedo, 1068, Jardins
☎ 3064-1750 / 3081-8307

Tony Antiguidades
⌂ Rua Estados Unidos, 1470, Jardins
☎ 3062-8488 / 3085-5891
🕐 Mondays to Fridays, from 1 pm to 7 pm.

Antique Markets
Feira de Antiguidades e Design, MuBE, and outside the Museum of Modern Art (MASP) are a joy to visit, and you can still find bargains if you are ready to hang on and negotiate. English and French are often spoken (at the very least understood), so be careful when showing too much interest – you might weaken your bargaining power!

L&T's best!
Feira de Antiguidades e Design, MuBE
One of the best in the city. Great way to start your Christmas shopping ahead of time!
⌂ Av. Europa, 218, Jardim Europa
☎ 3081-8611
🕐 Sundays, from 10 am to 6 pm.
🌐 www.mube.art.br

Feira do Bexiga
Similar to Benedito Calixto, next to traditional Italian restaurants.

Big variety of door handles and other antiques.
- 🏠 Praça Dom Orione
- 🕐 Sundays, from 9 am to 7 pm.

MASP

Next to one of the most important art museums of São Paulo.
- 🏠 Av. Paulista, 1578
- ☎ 3081-8611
- 🕐 Sundays, from 9 am to 6 pm.

Praça Benedito Calixto

Has similar goodies at more affordable prices. Also crafts.
- 🏠 Pinheiros
- ☎ 3081-8611
- 🕐 Saturdays, from 9 am to 7 pm.

Antique repairs

FOR SILVER REPAIR SEE PAGE 82.

Bassoi Cristais e Presentes
- 🏠 Rua Belmiro Braga, 138, Pinheiros
- ☎ 3813-1772

Restauração Tabapuã

China, metal, crystal.
- 🏠 Rua Tabapuã, 398, Itaim
- ☎ 3167-1683 / 3167-7781
- 🌐 www.restauracaotabapua.com.br

Robles Prata de Lei
- 🏠 Rua Oscar Freire, 285, Jardins
- ☎ 3081-0222
- 🌐 www.robles.com.br

Artisanal Market

Embu das Artes

Small town just outside São Paulo known for its furniture, crafts and restaurants.
- 🏠 Rodovia Régis Bittencourt, km 282
- ☎ 11 4704-6565 (English speakers and guides)
- 🕐 Saturdays and Sundays, from 9:30 am to 7 pm.

Feira de Artes da Água Branca
- 🏠 Parque da Água Branca, Pavilhões 1, 2 e 3 Av. Francisco Matarazzo, 455, Água Branca
- ☎ 3675-7436
- 🕐 First or second Sunday of the month, from 8 am to 6 pm.
- 🌐 www.assamapab.org.br

Praça da Liberdade

Famous oriental neighborhood.
- 🏠 Liberdade
- 🕐 Sundays, from 9 am to 7 pm.

Shopping S.P. Market
- 🏠 Av. das Nações Unidas, 22540, Interlagos
- ☎ 5682-3666
- 🕐 Sundays.

Cable TV and Internet

Cable TV allows you access to many different channels, some in English. Package deals are available for subscription and can be paired up with an Internet provider. Many buildings have it already installed. Monthly fees apply. If the contract is in your name, make sure to cancel the service at least a few days before your moving date, for it will take some time. It is best to make an appointment to have the boxes removed.

NET
☎ 0800 726 0800
🌐 www.nettv.globo.com
    (for cable TV)
    www.virtua.com.br
    (Internet service)

Sky + Direct TV
Cable TV (not Internet).
☎ 4004-2808
🌐 www.skytv.com.br

Speedy
Only Internet service.
☎ 0800 12 15 20
🌐 www.speedy.com.br

TVA
☎ 3038-5500
🌐 www.tva.com.br (for cable TV)
    www.ajato.com.br
    (for Internet service)

Carpenters

12 polegadas
Furniture, frames and special projects. Leonardo Padilha is an up-scale carpenter with a college degree in Fine Arts. The furniture you need, with contemporary design.
📍 Rua Assis, 132, Barra Funda
☎ 3392-1323
🌐 www.12polegadas.com.br

Atelier Thierry Marcenaria Francesa
Furniture.
📍 Rua Alba, 1431,
    Vila Santa Catarina
☎ cel. 8222-0445
📍 Showroom: Shopping Campo Belo, Rua Antonio de Macedo Soares, 1102, loja 20

Depósito das Artes
Frames and mirrors.
📍 Rua Bela Cintra, 1543, Jardins
☎ 3061-0640

Fastframe
Only frames.
📍 Alameda Gabriel Monteiro da Silva, 2121, Jardim Paulistano
☎ 3060-8335
🌐 www.fastframe.com.br

Iran Molduras
Frames and mirrors.
📍 Rua José Maria Lisboa, 1260, Jardins
    3081-9107

For repairs

Click Molduras
Principally framers but also are knowledgeable and trustworthy when it comes to repairs and restorations. Sells some.
📍 Rua João Cachoeira, 289, Itaim
☎ 3079-0203 / 3079-6775

Furniture Ramiro do Carmo
Ramiro will come to your home

and estimate what has to be repaired. He will then decide whether he will do the repair on the premises or take it away. Very professional and pleasant.
☎ 3768-4270 / cel. 8374-5748

Molduraria Freitas
Restoration of doors, furniture and frames.
⌂ Rua José Maria Lisboa, 1135, Jardins
☎ 3085-6260
⊕ www.moldurariafreitas.com.br

Curtain makers / Fabrics

Aladim Decorações
Fabric for decoration, curtains.
⌂ Praça Ragueb Chofi, 392/410, Centro (around Rua 25 de Março)
☎ 3229-5111
⊕ www.aladimdecor.com.br

ARTecidos
⌂ Rua Dr. Melo Alves, 258, Jardins
☎ 3896-1622
⊕ www.artecidos.com.br

Casa do Tapeceiro
Fabric for decoration, mattresses.
⌂ Rua Jairo Góis, 94, Brás
☎ 3227-6385 / 3229-0640
⊕ www.casadotapeceiro.com.br

Donatelli São Gabriel
⌂ Av. São Gabriel, 102, Jardim Paulista
☎ 3885-6988
⊕ www.donatelli.com.br

Emporio Beraldin
Silk, fur, fabric for decoration.
⌂ Rua Mateus Grou, 604, Pinheiros
☎ 3030-3956
⊕ www.emporioberaldin.com.br

Cinerama
Huge selection of fabrics at great prices.
⌂ Rua João Cachoeira, 432, Itaim
☎ 3168-5455
For other locations:
⊕ www.cinerama.com.br

Formatex
⌂ Rua das Fiandeiras, 326, Vila Olímpia
☎ 4082-8000
⊕ www.formatex.com.br

LARMOD
Fabrics and accessories.
⌂ Alameda Gabriel Monteiro da Silva, 413, Jardim América
☎ 3065-1944
⊕ www.larmod.com.br

Lily Cortinas
Need curtains? Created by an expat, so you will not have any problems with language! Go see all of the fabrics they have available, or supply your own and they will do the rest!
⌂ Rua Cônego Eugênio Leite, 233, Jardins
☎ 3082-3687

LJ
Sofamaker and repairer.
⌂ Rua André Saraiva, 180, Vila Sônia
☎ 3749-9926

Prints

They carry a collection of their own designs; will dye to match any color you like.

🔌 Rua Dr. Melo Alves, 661, Jardins
☎ 3083-7587

Cleaners (sofa, carpets and rugs)

FOR DRYCLEANERS SEE PAGE 164.

Lavanderia Elite

🔌 Rua Maestro Carlos Cruz, 22, Butantã
☎ 3726-1699

Designer, Architect and Renovation

Ana Lúcia Salama

Architect.

🔌 Av. Macuco, 726, room 1702, Moema
☎ 5054-6972

L&T's best!

Candida Tabet

A fantastic eye for detail, innovative ideas, great precision, skill and professionalism. No praise should be considered too much for describing Candida Tabet's work. She's an architect with a wide experience in commercial and residential construction, locally and overseas!

🔌 Rua Fidalga, 505, Pinheiros
☎ 3034-0046
🌐 www.candidatabet.com

Cristina Allegri

Interior designer.

🔌 Rua Gumercindo Saraiva, 10, house 1, Jardim Europa
☎ 3083-4340

Estúdio Campana

The internationally-awarded Brazilian designers, brothers Fernando e Humberto Campana.

🔌 Rua Barão de Tatuí, 219, Santa Cecília
☎ 3825-3408
🌐 www.campanas.com.br

Etel Interiores

Interior Design Studio.

🔌 Alameda Gabriel Monteiro da Silva, 1834, Jardim América
☎ 3064-1266
🌐 www.etelinteriores.com.br

Flavio Miranda

Designer.

🔌 Rua Haddock Lobo, 1398, Jardins
☎ 3085-6746 / 3082-6715
🌐 www.flaviomiranda.com

Lacaz Broggin

They will do everything, from designing a new house, to organizing and acting as general contractor on your project.

🔌 Av. São Gabriel, 201, room 303, Itaim
☎ 3704-7334
🌐 www.lacazbroggin.com.br

Marcos Lisboa

Designer.

🔌 Rua São Carlos do Pinhal, 345, room 604, Bela Vista
3283-1382

Norea de Vitto and Beto Galvez

Architecture and decoration.

🏠 Rua Cônego Eugênio Leite, 513, room 22, Pinheiros

☎ 3062-1913 / 3085-5035

Petro Engenharia

🏠 Rua Campevas, 115, room 2, Perdizes

☎ 3877-1100

🌐 www.petroengenharia.com.br

Electrical & Electronics Repair

Boutique do Telefone

Repairs cell phones, cordless, regular, answering machines, faxes.

🏠 Shopping Iguatemi
Av. Brig. Faria Lima, 2232, third floor, Jardim Paulista

☎ 3819-8866

🌐 www.boutiquedotelefone.com.br

Computer Eletrônica

🏠 Rua Oscar Freire, 975, Jardins

☎ 3088-7221

Jardins Service Assistência Técnica

🏠 Alameda Franca, 181, Jardins

☎ 3288-2823

Oficinas Poppy

Shoe repair, key cutting, electrician, repairs of refrigerators and dishwashers.

🏠 Alameda Min. Rocha Azevedo, 1195, Jardins

☎ 3082-3087

Synchron

🏠 Alameda Santos, 1203, Jardins

☎ 3251-0097 / 3289-7088

Fire place – barbecue shops

Artesania Espanhola

Crystal chandeliers, fireplace equipment, torches.

🏠 Rua da Consolação, 2927, Jardins

☎ 3082-9158

Gegê

Pre-moulded fireplaces, barbecues and accessories for both.

🏠 Av. dos Bandeirantes, 3460, Campo Belo

☎ 5533-7041

🌐 www.gegelar.com.br

Furniture

Several of the following shops also carry accessories and soft furnishings.

> Take a walk up and down Alameda Gabriel Monteiro da Silva (Jardins) and Rua Teodoro Sampaio (Pinheiros). You'll find plenty of furniture, lighting and kitchen showrooms.

Artefacto

🏠 Rua Haddock Lobo, 1405, Jardins

☎ 3087-7000

🌐 www.artefacto.com.br

Bettoni

Box springs, sofas, armchairs,
pillows, sofa beds.

🏠 Rua Augusta, 2917, Jardins

☎ 3085-3826 / 3083-4057

🌐 www.sofa-cama.com.br

Depósito São Martinho

🏠 Av. Europa, 615, Jardim Europa

☎ 3083-1433

🌐 www.depositosaomartinho.
com.br

Embu das Artes

SEE ARTISANAL MARKET FOR DETAILS
AT PAGE 75.

Empório Jorge Elias

🏠 Rua Dr. Melo Alves, 549, Jardins

☎ 3085-6785

🌐 www.jorgeelias.com.br

Empório Raízes

🏠 Alameda Tietê, 496, Jardins

☎ 3083-4694

Entreposto

A great source for furniture,
fabric & home furnishings.

🏠 Av. Cidade Jardim, 187,
Jardim Europa

☎ 3061-9797

🌐 www.entreposto.com.br

Etna

Modern design in furniture
for adults, babies and kids.
Also kitchen utensils and
home decoration.

🏠 Av. Luís Carlos Berrini, 2001,
Brooklin

☎ 2161-7600

🌐 www.etna.com.br

House Garden

🏠 Alameda Gabriel Monteiro
da Silva, 1218, Jardim Paulista

☎ 3081-7999 / 3087-7777

🌐 www.housegarden.com.br

Jacaré do Brasil

🏠 Rua Dr. Melo Alves, 555, Jardins

☎ 3081-6109

🌐 www.jacaredobrasil.com.br

Lar Center

A shopping mall for furniture,
lighting and kitchen equipment.

🏠 Av. Otto Baumgartt, 500,
Vila Guilherme

☎ 6224-5959

🌐 www.larcenter.com.br

Leroy Merlin

🏠 Rua Magalhães de Castro,
12000, Morumbi

☎ 3759-5800

🌐 www.leroymerlin.com

L'oeil

Decoration, furniture, rugs, items
for both indoors and outdoors.

🏠 Rua Bela Cintra, 2009, Jardins

☎ 3085-3211

🌐 www.loeil.com.br

Micasa

A very modern, hip shop
without the "craziness" of
some of today's designs. You
will find very appealing, innovative furniture which is
extremely comfortable. The
lines are clean, which makes
the pieces easy to work with,
mixing them with either
modern or antique pieces.

Rua Estados Unidos, 2109,
Jardins
3088-1238
www.micasa.com.br

Passado Composto
Modern furniture and antiques.
Alameda Lorena, 1996, Jardins
3088-9128
www.passadocomposto.com.br

Recanto do Artesanato Junco Rattan e Vime
Your source for baskets!
Av. Morumbi, 7849, Brooklin
5533-6841
www.recantodoartesanato.
com.br

Tok & Stok
Brazilian equivalent of Ikea. A
full line of baby, teen and adult
furniture. Also kitchen utensils
and houseware.
Av. Eusébio Matoso, 1231,
Pinheiros
3813-2800
For more locations:
www.tokstok.com.br

Shopping D&D
SEE SHOPS & STORES AT PAGE 154.

Vitória's Decorações
Calçada das Orquídeas, 119,
Centro Comercial, Barueri
11 4191-6113 / 4193-6360
www.vitoriadecor.com.br

Wood's
Garden and home furniture.
Rua Dr. Virgílio de Carvalho
Pinto, 69, Pinheiros

3085-5289 / 3062-1454
www.woods.com.br

Furniture Rental

John Richard
Rua Sion, 66, Veleiros
0800 771 5352
www.johnrichard.com.br

Home Appliance Stores

Casas Bahia
One of the largest chains in Brazil,
with a big selection of appliances,
electronics & inexpensive furniture.
0800 888 8008
For all locations:
www.casasbahia.com.br

Fast Shop
Also sales by telephone.
3232-3100
For all locations:
www.fastshop.com.br

Ponto Frio
Also sales by telephone.
0800 286 1855
For all locations:
www.pontofrio.com.br

Kitchen Utensils / Houseware Stores
Some restaurants have a "kitchen
section" with items for sale. Please
do keep in mind that "imported
items", however insignificant,
are more expensive…

Artmix
⌂ Rua Armando Penteado, 56, Higienópolis
☎ 3661-1769
🌐 www.artmix.com.br

Barra Doce
⌂ Av. dos Eucaliptos, 301, Moema
☎ 5543-6652 / 5533-3560
🌐 www.barradoce.com.br

M. Dragonetti
The best place I have found in São Paulo for pots & pans and all of your baking needs! A must (as they say in *Sampa*)!
⌂ Av. Santo Amaro, 898, Vila Nova Conceição
☎ 3846-8782
🌐 www.dragonetti.com.br

S Brasil Cabides
All kind of hangers.
⌂ Rua Iguatemi, 22, Itaim
☎ 3168-8206

Spicy
Staff are knowledgeable. Returns for exchanges are accepted at all stores.
⌂ Rua Haddock Lobo, 746, Jardins
☎ 3062-8377
   0800 16 83 88 (client service)
🌐 For more locations:
   www.spicy.com.br

Utilplast
Utilplast carries a wide selection of local and imported articles for kitchen, bath, camping, including small electrical appliances and gadgets. Staff is knowledgeable and ready to get the item if it is not available in the store.
⌂ Alameda Lorena, 1931, Jardins
☎ 3088-0862
   0800 16 83 88 (client service)
🌐 www.utilplast.com.br

Silver repair

Robles Prata de Lei (main shop)
⌂ Rua Oscar Freire, 285, Jardins
☎ 3081-0222
🌐 For other locations:
   www.robles.com.br

Linen Stores

Blue Gardenia Bed & Bath
⌂ Alameda Lorena, 1986, Jardins
☎ 3063-4343
🌐 www.bluegardenia.com.br

Cecilia Dale
Furniture, gifts, glass, silverware, great holiday stuff (Christmas, Eastern), imported and sophisticated linens.
⌂ Rua Dr. Melo Alves, 513, Jardins
☎ 3064-2644
🌐 For more locations:
   www.ceciliadale.com.br

Fernanda Salles Show Room
⌂ Rua Domingos Oswaldo Batalha, 185, Indianópolis
☎ 5581-5726 / 5589-8458
🌐 www.fernandaenxovais.com.br

Girassol
🏠 Rua Dr. Melo Alves, 428, Jardins
☎ 3085-6929

M. Martan
🏠 Av. Sumaré, 1177, Sumaré
☎ 3873-8114 / 0800 723 7222
🌐 For more locations:
www.mmartan.com.br

Mundo do Enxoval
🏠 Av. Lavandisca, 223, Moema
☎ 5051-3732
🌐 For more locations:
www.mundodoenxoval.com.br

Sabie Enxovais Corporativos
🏠 Rua dos Patriotas, 897, 16-A,
Ipiranga
☎ 0800 772 2911
🌐 www.sabie.com.br

Trousseau
🏠 Rua Escobar Ortiz, 482,
Vila Nova Conceição
☎ 3044-3582
🌐 For more locations:
www.trousseau.com.br

Victoria Mill
🏠 Rua Augusta, 2803, Jardins
☎ 3085-8513

Rugs

Beto Altílio
🏠 Rua Conselheiro Zacarias, 379,
Jardim Paulista
☎ 3052-2970

Cor e Forma
🏠 Alameda Min. Rocha
Azevedo, 983, Jardins
☎ 3088-7439
🌐 www.coreforma.com.br

Fenícia
🏠 Alameda dos Maracatins, 63,
Moema
☎ 5051-4228
🌐 www.feniciatapetes.com.br

Hariz Tapetes Orientais
🏠 Av. Sabiá, 668, Moema
☎ 5051-6370
🌐 www.hariz.com.br

Santa Monica Tapetes e Carpetes
🏠 Alameda Gabriel Monteiro
da Silva, 660, Jardim América
☎ 3085-1866 / 0800 16 02 55
🌐 For more locations:
www.smonica.com.br

Rug repairs

FOR RUG CLEANERS SEE PAGE 78

Restauradora de Tapetes Porteleki
Concerned about your antique carpets? Don't be, as the professionals of Porteleki take great care in cleaning and restoring them for you. Someone will come to your home for an estimate, pick up your rug and deliver upon completion.
At the shop, you will also find some beautiful carpets for sale.
🏠 Rua Dr. Afonso Baccari, 61,
Vila Clementino
☎ 5579-0223 / 5579-2903
🌐 www.porteleki.com.br

housing

Construction Shops

Casa & Construção
Similar to Home Depot in the U.S.A., Casa & Construção is a mega store for all your construction needs.
- Av. Brasil, 1860, Jardim Paulista
- 3891-1157
- For more locations: www.cec.com.br

Should you wish to do your shopping from the comfort of your own home, dial the Service Center: 4001-0100!

Construri
- Rua Padre João Manoel, 891, Jardins
- 3082-9866

Jardim América Materiais de Construção
- Alameda Lorena, 1371, Jardins
- 3083-0219 / 3083-2509

Telha Norte
Showroom.
- Av. Brasil, 2200, Jardim América
- 3082-8544

Doors & Windows

GG Esquadrias & Vidraçaria
- Av. Senador Teotônio Vilela, 7243, Jardim São Rafael
- 5925-2611 / cel. 9416-4826
- www.ggesquadrias.com.br

Domestic Help
Let's face it. This is one of the highlights of living in Brazil! Most foreigners will hire at least one housekeeper while they're here. You may find employees by word of mouth – ask your doorman, your friends' housekeepers – but there are also some very reputable agencies to assist in the search (they charge a fee, but most have a satisfaction guaranteed policy – check on this beforehand). Also important is to have all the facts about terms of agreement and contracts. Get everything written (hiring, firing, etc.), to avoid problems later on with maids, nannies, gardeners, butlers, drivers, or cooks.

Jobber
Any type of domestic help.
- Av. Santo Amaro, 499, Vila Nova Conceição
- 3045-0032

Lisboa Recrutamentos
- Rua Maceió, 87, first floor, Consolação
- 3257-2506
- www.empregadosdomesticos. com.br

Nursery School
Baby-sitting and maid services.
- Av. Brig. Luiz Antonio, 4444, Jardim Paulista
- 3052-1609
- www.escoladebaba.com.br

Prendas Domésticas

Any domestic help can be provided.

🏠 Rua Borges Lagoa, 26, Vila Mariana

☎ 5572-6878

🌐 www.prendasdomesticas.com.br

Tramit Brasil

Provides all type of domestic help.

🏠 Rua França Pinto, 76, Vila Mariana

☎ 5084-7118

🌐 For more locations: www.tramitbrasil.com.br

Uniforms

Home staff in São Paulo usually wear a uniform. It is the norm rather than the exception. No offense is taken.

Eli Confecção

🏠 Rua Jerônimo da Veiga, 149, Itaim

☎ 3079-4764 / 3167-4092

Il Settantuno Work Fashion

🏠 Rua José Maria Lisboa, 1260, Jardins

☎ 3088-1156

🌐 www.settantuno.com.br

RPI

🏠 Alameda Itu, 1068, Jardins

☎ 3062-0979 / 3088-1686

🌐 www.uniformesitu.com.br

Hardware Store

YOU MAY ALSO FIND ANTIQUE AND DESIGNED HANDLES AT THE FEIRA DO BEXIGA (SEE ANTIQUE MARKETS AT PAGE 75).

Artesania Espanhola

Crystal chandeliers, equipment for fireplaces and torches.

🏠 Rua da Consolação, 2927, Jardins

☎ 3082-9158

Bovex

Also items for bathrooms.

🏠 Rua Itapura, 1284, Tatuapé

☎ 2296-6661

🌐 www.bovex.com.br

Ferragens Floresta

🏠 Rua Paes Leme, 238/244, Pinheiros

☎ 3034-6122

🌐 www.ferragensfloresta.com.br

Keyato

🏠 Alameda dos Maracatins, 787, Moema

☎ 5055-9533

🌐 www.keyato.com.br

Multicoisas

🏠 Alameda Tietê, 207, Jardins

☎ 3082-1919

🌐 For more locations: www.multicoisas.com.br

Open Puxadores e Complementos

🏠 Alameda Gabriel Monteiro da Silva, 1319, Jardim Paulista

☎ 3898-1809

For more locations:

🌐 www.openpuxadores.com.br

Illumination

Benaide
Shades and lamps to order.
⌂ Rua Tangará, 182,
Vila Mariana
☎ 5084-5374

La Lampe
⌂ Alameda Gabriel Monteiro da
Silva, 1258, Jardim Paulistano
☎ 3069-3949
🌐 www.lalampe.com.br

Lustreco
⌂ Av. Pres. Juscelino Kubitschek,
1139/1151, Itaim
☎ 3845-5463 / 3845-8077
🌐 www.lustreco.com.br

Locksmith
24-hour service

Chaveiro Caconde
Offers 24-hour service.
Locksmith for cars and homes,
also repairs mechanical and elec-
trical automobile problems.
⌂ Rua Caconde, 27,
Jardins
☎ 3885-9114

Chaveiro e Copiadora
Laminating and photocopying.
⌂ Av. Brig. Luiz Antonio, 2013,
store 12, Supermercado Extra
parking lot, Bela Vista
☎ 3284-5192 / cel. 9225-3341

Chaveiro Presidente
24-hour service locksmith.
Mobile operation – can reach

you anywhere in the city
in 20 minutes.
⌂ Rua Bom Pastor, 1592,
Ipiranga
☎ 6161-4030 / 0800 16 40 23

Chaveiro Silva
24-hour service. Also key
copying.
⌂ Rua Pintassilgo, 576, Moema
☎ 5542-4030 / 5533-6367

Moving Companies

A Lusitana
☎ 3601-1921
🌐 www.lusitana.com.br

Fink
☎ 3835-3399
🌐 www.fink.com.br

Granero
☎ 3760-9000
🌐 www.granero.com.br

L&T's best!

Millenium
A smaller company compared
to Granero and Fink, though
the service does not suffer as a
result. Individual attention,
excellent packers (especially
when it comes to fine, antique
objects), constant communication between the client and the
firm. The representative speaks
fluent English and is ready to
help with all of the paperwork.
☎ 3619-1900
🌐 www.milleniumtransportes.
com.br

Paint

Multicolor Decorações
⌂ Alameda Lorena, 814,
  Jardins
☎ 3081-2679

Tintas Depósito
⌂ Rua Joaquim Floriano,
  827, Itaim
☎ 3078-8680 / 3078-3212

Painter

Alimac Pinturas
⌂ Rua Antonio de Sousa
  Bastos, 355,
  Jardim Ipanema
☎ 5660-7759

Real Estate Agencies

São Paulo offers apartments
and houses for all budgets and
tastes. It is interesting to know
that there are a number of apartments that are rented almost
exclusively to ex-pats. These
apartments are generally "move
in ready," but it is
also possible to find a great
apartment or house for rent that
needs minor (sometimes major)
renovations. It is crucial that the
cost of these renovations, or simple repairs, be negotiated with
the owner beforehand in the
rental agreement. Normally
the owner will discount some
or all of the work.

Perhaps the easiest thing for
you to do is to hire an architect
who will serve as a general
contractor and organize the
various subcontractors. You can
save some money if you buy
your own material, or you can
let them handle everything.

Coelho da Fonseca
☎ 3882-4000
⊕ www.coelhodafonseca.com.br

Lopes
One of the most traditional real
estate agencies in São Paulo,
Lopes will assist you in your
search for apartments or houses
for rental throughout the city.
☎ 3067-0500
⊕ www.lopes.com.br

Marcos E. Monteiro
Specializes in the Jardim Europa,
Jardim Paulista, Jardim Guedala
and Itaim neighborhoods.
⌂ Rua Dr. Melo Alves,
  550, Jardins
☎ 3085-8675 / 3062-8426 /
  cel.8199 8889

Mendes de Castro
Specializes in the Jardins
neighborhood.
⌂ Rua Groenlândia, 1925,
  Jardim Europa
☎ 3061-5322
⊕ www.mendesdecastro.com.br

Seaport
Beach rentals along the Litoral
Norte of São Paulo.
⌂ Rua Prof. Carlos de Carvalho,
  164, tenth floor, Itaim
☎ 3167-5665
⊕ www.seaport.com.br

Leisure & Travel

cultural

Brazilians have a good "joie de vivre", love to relax and have a good time. This once more is illustrated in venues that lead to entertainment and fun!

Tickets

For tickets and information:
- 🌐 www.bilheteria.com
- 🌐 www.ingresso.com.br
- 🌐 www.ticketmaster.com.br

(FOR CULTURAL GUIDES SEE PAGE **68**)

Art Galleries

A favorite "passe temps" for us, the art galleries in São Paulo, are quite diverse and most interesting. An excellent place to start your "initiation and integration" to Latin American culture! Most of the staff will converse in either English or French and will offer extensive explanations on what is displayed. Quite a few participate in international art fairs (Miami, Basel, Spain...) held throughout the year in various countries. Some even hold their own auctions.

Most galleries open Tuesday to Friday, from 10 am to 8 pm, Saturday from 10 am to 1 pm, and/or by appointments.

Arte Aplicada
- 🏠 Rua Haddock Lobo, 1406, Jardins
- ☎ 3062-5128 / 3064-4725
- 🌐 www.arteaplicada.com.br

Dan Galeria
Contemporary and modern art with an emphasis on Brazilian artists and contemporary Latin American artists such as Soto, Cruz Diaz, Marco Magge. English and French spoken.
- 🏠 Rua Estados Unidos, 1638, Jardins
- ☎ 3083-4600
- 🌐 www.dangaleria.com.br

Galeria de Arte Horizonte
Contemporary art.
- 🏠 Rua João Lourenço, 79, Vila Nova Conceição
- ☎ 3044-1057

Galeria Fortes Vilaça
Contemporary art.
English spoken.
- 🏠 Rua Fradique Coutinho, 1500, Vila Madalena
- ☎ 3032-7066
- 🌐 www.fortesvilaca.com.br

Galeria Luisa Strina
Contemporary art. Luisa has an excellent reputation and knows the local and international markets inside and out. English and French spoken.
- 🏠 Rua Oscar Freire, 502, Jardins
- ☎ 3088-2471
- 🌐 www.galerialuisastrina.com.br

Galeria Nara Rosler
Contemporary and modern art. English spoken.
- 🏠 Av. Europa, 655, Jardim Paulistano
- ☎ 3063-2344
- 🌐 www.nararoesler.com.br

Galeria Thomas Cohn

Contemporary art, with emphasis on paintings. English spoken.
- Av. Europa, 641, Jardim Paulistano
- 3083-3355
- www.thomascohn.com.br

Galeria Vermelho

Cutting-edge contemporary Brazilian art, this gallery occupies an entire *vila*, with a view of the Pacaembu neighborhood and a nice restaurant on the premises. They often present performances and live acts. English spoken.
- Rua Minas Gerais, 350, Higienópolis
- 3257-2033
- www.galeriavermelho.com.br

Marília Razuk Galeria de Arte

Contemporary and modern art. Young and up-coming artists are shown here among already established artists. Provides very good explanations and guidance. English and French spoken.
- Av. Nove de Julho, 5719, store 2, Itaim
- 3079-0853
- www.galeriamariliarazuk.com.br

Millan Antonio

Contemporary and modern art, another young, dynamic excellent art gallery not to be missed! French and English spoken.
- Rua Fradique Coutinho, 1360, Pinheiros
- 3031-6007
- www.millanantonio.com.br

Valoart Galerias de Arte
- Rua Bela Cintra, 2006, Jardins
- 3081-8489 / 3081-8764

Classical Music Rooms

Concerts are extremely enjoyable as they do not require any translation and are held in some of the best acoustic halls.

Auditório da Pinacoteca
SEE INFO AT PAGE 99.

Memorial da América Latina
SEE INFO AT PAGE 92.

Sala São Paulo
SEE INFO AT PAGE 23.

Teatro Municipal
SEE INFO AT PAGE 27.

Cultural Association

Mozarteum
Society which sponsors and produces classical music events.
- 3815-6377
- www.mozarteum.org.br

Cultural Centers

Centro da Cultura Judaica
- Rua Oscar Freire, 2500, Jardins
- 3065-4333
- www.culturajudaica.org.br

Centro Cultural Banco do Brasil

Movie theater and fine arts. For guided visits in English, call 3113-3649.

🏠 Rua Alvares Penteado, 112, Centro

☎ 3113-3651

🌐 www.bb.com.br/cultura

Centro Cultural Fiesp

🏠 Av. Paulista, 1313, Cerqueira César

☎ 3146-7405

🌐 www.sesisp.org.br

Centro Cultural do Liceu de Artes e Ofícios

Inaugurated in 1980, this Cultural Center holds a permanent exhibition known as "Arte e Humanismo" (Art and Humanism). On display are life-size models of classical history. Thanks to advanced technology and clever use of lighting equipment, displayed sculptures from Ancient Greece to the Renaissance seem to come to life!

🏠 Rua da Cantareira, 1351, Luz

☎ 2155-3300

🌐 www.liceuescola.com.br

A guided tour must be scheduled in advance. Tours at 9 am, 10:30 am, 2 pm and 4 pm Mondays to Fridays. Entrance fee applies.

Centro Cultural São Paulo

🏠 Rua Vergueiro, 1000, Paraíso

☎ 3277-3611

🌐 www.centroculturalamedasp. gov.br

Cultura Inglesa – Centro Brasileiro Britânico

🏠 Rua Ferreira de Araújo, 741, Pinheiros

☎ 3039-0500

🌐 http://agenda.culturainglesa sp.com.br

Instituto Goethe

🏠 Rua Lisboa, 974, Pinheiros

☎ 3088-4288

🌐 www.goethe.de/saopaulo

Instituto Itaú Cultural

🏠 Av. Paulista, 149, Paraíso

☎ 2168-1700

🌐 www.itauculturalamedaorg.br

Instituto Moreira Salles

🏠 Rua Piauí, 844, first floor, Higienópolis

☎ 3825-2560

🌐 www.ims.com.br

Instituto Tomie Ohtake

🏠 Av. Brig. Faria Lima, 201 (entrance by Rua Coropés, 88), Pinheiros

🌐 www.institutotomieohtake. org.br

Memorial da América Latina

Internationally renowned architect Oscar Niemeyer planned the complex in order to unite the different cultures of Latin American countries. As well as the headquarters of the Latin

American Parliament, permanent and temporary exhibitions about crafts and artesanal work of the continent are constantly on display.
Books and films in the library help to increase knowledge about this part of the world. One of the biggest auditoriums in São Paulo state is located there.

⊕ Av. Auro Soares de Moura Andrade, 664, Barra Funda
☎ 3823-4600
🌐 www.memorialamedasp.gov.br

Paço das Artes
This gallery was created to exhibit various types of visual art.

⊕ Av. da Universidade, 1, Cidade Universitária
☎ 3814-4832
🌐 www.pacodasartes.sp.gov.br

SESC SP
Founded in 1946, the Social Service of Commerce promotes social well-being and cultural development in venues scattered all over the country. Activities include sports, music, theatre, dance, exhibitions, workshops and events. Many important national and international shows, lectures and events take place in some of their venues, including the Antunes Filho's theatre group, and the Videobrasil International Video Festival, among others.

☎ 0800 11 8220
🌐 For more locations:
www.sescsp.com.br

Movie Theaters
Many of the movie theaters are located in shopping malls (SEE SHOPPING CENTERS AT PAGE 195). For the most part they are extremely comfortable, clean and very modern. As for the movies, some of the major releases happen almost simultaneously with the U.S. (although this is rare). You can check for movies in the daily newspapers. The two most common are **Folha de S.Paulo** and **O Estado de S. Paulo.** www.ingresso.com. Here are some of the better and cult movie theaters outside shopping malls:

Cinemateca Brasileira
Has the biggest collection of films in Latin America. The collection includes about 30,000 titles made since 1895. Fiction, documentary, news, publicity films, family features, both national and international. The television footage goes back to what was produced by the very first Brazilian T.V. company, "TV Tupi". Has a library, a closed and open projection room and a small café.

⊕ Largo Senador Raul Cardoso, 207, Vila Clementino
☎ 5084-2177 / 5084-3366
🌐 www.cinemateca.com.br

Library hours: 9 am to 1 pm. The office is open 9 am to 6 pm. The projection room depends on availability. Entrance fee applies only for film viewing.

Cinesesc

Here you can choose to watch the movie from the large window in the coffee shop.

⌂ Rua Augusta, 2075,
   Cerqueira César

☎ 3082-0213

🌐 www.sescsp.com.br/sesc/
   unidades/cinesesc.htm

Cinusp

⌂ Rua do Anfiteatro, 181,
   Colméia Building,
   Cidade Universitária

☎ 3091-3540

🌐 www.usp.br/cinusp

Espaço Unibanco

⌂ Rua Augusta, 1470,
   Cerqueira César

☎ 3288-6780

HSBC Belas Artes

⌂ Rua da Consolação, 2423,
   Consolação

☎ 3258-4092

🌐 www.hsbcbelasartes.com.br

Museums

Estação Pinacoteca

Inaugurated in 1914, it was designed as a warehouse. In 2002, a remodelling project by Haron Cohen created a space for temporary and permanent exhibitions. Contains a library, an auditorium, and a coffee shop.

⌂ Largo General Osório, 66, Luz

☎ 3337-0185

🌐 www.cultura.sp.gov.br
   (click on link "museus")

Fundação Maria Luisa e Oscar Americano

Maria Luisa and Oscar Americano Foundation was created by the patron of the arts, Oscar Americano, in March of 1974. It consists of a park that covers an area of 75,000 m^2 as well as the couple's home where they lived for many years with their children. On the tour, you can visit the two bedrooms, left intact, as well as other rooms showing the family art collection (engraving, sculpture, painting) and some of the treasures that belonged to the Brazilian imperial family in the 19th century. The Foundation offers concerts and other cultural events, classes in music, philosophy, art and history, to name a few. Space available to rent for events.

⌂ Av. Morumbi, 4077, Morumbi

☎ 3742-0077

🕐 Tuesdays to Fridays
   from 11 am to 5 pm,
   Saturdays and Sundays
   from 10 am to 5 pm.
   Park and tea room:
   Tuesdays to Sundays
   from 11:30 am to 6 pm.
   Free entrance.

🌐 www.fundacaooscaramerica
   no.org.br

MAB (Museu de Arte Brasileira) – FAAP (Fundação Armando Alvares Penteado)

FAAP is an institution which integrates a college with a museum. The museum is the best place to showcase the work done by the students. It is quite unique, as a certain space is "given" to the students to exhibit their work in industrial design, fashion, etc. Consequently, the museum has more temporary exhibitions than permanent ones. The museum's own artefacts are only exhibited a few times a year. Important international exhibitions are featured as well. Tour guides should be scheduled in advance, with a minimum of 10 people required.

⌂ Rua Alagoas, 903, Pacaembu

☏ 3662-7198

⊙ Tuesdays to Fridays
   from 10 am to 8 pm,
   Saturdays and Sundays
   from 1 pm to 5 pm.
   Free entrance.

⊕ www.faap.br/museu/museu

MAC – Museu de Arte Contemporânea da Universidade de São Paulo

The University of São Paulo Museum of Contemporary Art was founded in 1963. It represents the very first specialized collection of 20th century art work in Latin America. There are around 8,000 works of contemporary art, from paintings, drawings, photographs to engravings and sculptures. The museum holds permanent and temporary exhibitions, as well as classes and seminars about the arts.

⌂ Rua da Reitoria, 109-A,
   Cidade Universitária

☏ 3091-3538 / 3091-3039

⊕ www.macvirtualamedausp.br

Anita Malfatti, Di Cavalcanti, Brecheret, Tarsila, Portinari, Rego Monteiro, De Chirico, Modigliani, Boccioni and Picasso, are some of the famous artists whose work has been displayed here.

MAM – Museu de Arte Moderna

The Museum of Modern Art was founded in 1948 by art patron Francisco Matarazzo and is one of the first modern art museums of South America. Italian-born architect Lina Bo Bardi designed the building, which is located inside Ibirapuera Park, facing a Sculpture Garden designed by landscape architect Roberto Burle Marx. MAM has two exhibition halls, an auditorium, a studio and a restaurant, with a collection of about 4,000 pieces of art, including paintings, prints, drawings, photographs and sculptures. You will find important works of art by Brazilian artists such as Portinari, Di Cavalcanti, Tarsila do Amaral and Brecheret, plus a significant collection of Brazilian contemporay art. The MAM holds permanent and temporary exhibitions, classes, has a library and a gift shop. It is possible to rent a space for events. Guided tours (minimum 10 people) should be scheduled in advance. Entrance fee applies.

⌂ Ibirapuera Park, Gate 3,
   Ibirapuera

☏ 5085-1300

⊙ Tuesdays to Sundays and
   holidays, from 10 am to 6 pm.

⊕ www.mam.org.br

MASP – Museu de Arte de São Paulo

Founded on October 2nd, 1947, by art patron and media mogul Assis Chateaubriand, and Italian- born journalist and art dealer Pietro Maria Bardi, at Rua 7 de Abril. In November 1968, the second new building was inaugurated at Avenida Paulista in the presence of Queen Elizabeth II of England. The architecture of the building is quite unusual; the design concept having been created by Lina Bo Bardi, Pietro Maria's wife.

The Art Museum of São Paulo is considered to be one of the most important European cultural heritage museums in Latin America, and perhaps the most important Brazilian museum. Works of artists such as Rafael, Andrea Mantegna, Botticceli, Bellini, Rembrandt, Frans Hals, Cranach, Memling, Velázquéz, Goya, Nattier, Delacroix, Renoir, Manet, Monet, Cézanne, Degas, Van Gogh, Toulouse-Lautrec, have been displayed here.

The museum holds permanent and temporary exhibitions, and is used to host many different events throughout the year. It also has a restaurant, a library and an auditorium. Tour groups have to be scheduled in advance.

🏠 Av. Paulista, 1578, Cerqueira César

☎ 3251-5644

🕐 Tuesdays to Sundays, from 11 am to 6 pm. Entrance fee applies.

🌐 www.masp.art.br

Memorial do Imigrante

The construction of the Memorial started in 1886 and took two years to finish. In 1888, the building was ready to receive all the immigrants who arrived in São Paulo, with permission from the government, to work in agriculture. In 1986, it became what it is today, a museum to commemorate the memories of immigrants. It is composed of a garden, an auditorium, an old lodging-house, as well as an old train station with a functional steam engine, and a department which encompasses a collection of documents showing the history and relating the memories of the families who arrived in Brazil. This is done through lists of names, photos and papers gathered from the government and collected from the ships that anchored in Brazil. All of these documents can be viewed by the public. A very interesting way of discovering one's ancestors and roots! Holds permanent and temporary exhibitions also. Guided visits for groups can be scheduled in advance.

🏠 Rua Visconde de Parnaíba, 1316, Mooca

☎ 6692-7804

🕐 Tuesdays to Sundays, from 10 am to 5 pm. Entrance fee applies.

🌐 www.memorialdoimigrante. sp.gov.br

The steam engine has tours only on Sundays and holidays.

97

MIS – Museu da Imagem e do Som

The Museum of Image and Sound was created on May 29th, 1970, with the purpose of preserving the past memory and present evidence of the great contributions that music, cinema, photos, and graphic arts bring to the art world. The MIS holds more than 200,000 images, 1,600 VHS tapes and 12,750 titles in Super 8 and 16mm films. It is best to get up-dated monthly scheduled information on films, shows, exhibitions, cultural exchange, national and international events. A tour guide can be provided for a minimum of 15 people, if booked in advance.

- Av. Europa, 158, Jardim Europa
- 3088-0896 / 3062-9197 / 3081-4417
- Tuesdays to Sundays from 10 am to 8 pm, sometimes later (depending on the program). Entrance fee applies for some events.
- www.mis.sp.gov.br

L&T's best!

MuBE – Museu Brasileiro da Escultura

Created after the dream of Brazilian artist Marilisa Rathsam, the museum was inaugurated in 1995. This was quite a challenge as it came during an economic period known not to be one of the best in São Paulo! A variety of activities is offered for adults and adolescents, such as classes in sculpture, painting and design. It has an auditorium, a gift shop and restaurant facilities. Also, on Sundays, it hosts the best antique fair in the city.

SEE ANTIQUES AT PAGE 74

- Av. Europa, 218, Jardim Europa
- 3081-8611
- Tuesdays to Sundays, from 10 am to 7 pm. Free entrance.
- www.mube.art.br

Museu Afro-Brasileiro

The museum focuses on African cultural history in Brazil. It holds around 5,000 pieces of art done by national and international artists, all related to the Afro theme.

- Ibirapuera Park, Gate 10, Ibirapuera
- 5579-0593
- Tuesdays to Mondays, from 10 am to 5 pm. Free entrance.
- www.museuafrobrasil. prodam.sp.gov.br

Museu da Casa Brasileira

The compound known as Solar Fábio Prado was built in the 1940s in an area covering 15,000 square meters. The museum was inaugurated in 1972 with a permanent exhibition of furniture, objects, and equipment, called "Habitat in Brazil." It also has a library with plenty of information on design, a very nice restaurant

(SEE RESTAURANTS AT PAGE 114), and
a beautiful garden. The space
is available for events; however,
only companies can do so.
If required, when you visit
the museum a guide can
be provided. Big groups to be
scheduled in advance.

🏠 Av. Brig. Faria Lima, 2705,
    Jardim Paulistano
☎ 3032-3727 / 3032-2564
🕐 Tuesdays to Sundays,
    from 10 am to 6 pm.
    Entrance fee applies.
🌐 www.mcb.sp.gov.br

Museu da Língua Portuguesa

This museum informs the
public about the language,
history, and literature of
Brazilian Portuguese. This is
explained through images and
video presentations. Entrance
fee applies. Half price available.

🏠 Estação da Luz
    Praça da Luz
☎ 3326-0775
🕐 Tuesdays to Sundays,
    from 10 am to 5 pm.
🌐 www.museudalinguaportu-
    guesa.org.br

Museu de Arte Sacra

The Museum of Sacred Art was
founded by Frei Antonio Galvão in
1774, and it was acknowledged as
an important heritage site in 1943.
The complex is also home to nuns
who dedicate their lives to prayer.

The museum holds about
4,000 important pieces
of Brazilian sacred art.

Permanent and temporary
exhibitions are held.
Guided tours should
be scheduled in advance.

🏠 Av. Tiradentes, 676, Luz
☎ 3326-1373
🕐 Tuesdays to Sundays,
    from 11 am to 6 pm.
    Entrance fee applies.
🌐 www.artesacra.sp.gov.br

Museu de Zoologia da USP

Holds displays of stuffed,
classified animals from tropical
rainforest habitats. The museum
holds cultural and scientific
activities, temporary and
permanent exhibitions as well.
The library stocks 73,850
editions, amongst them maps,
books and manuscripts. Group
tours are to be scheduled
in advance. The gift shop
has interesting souvenirs.

🏠 Av. Nazaré, 481, Ipiranga
☎ 6165-8100
🕐 Tuesdays to Sundays,
    from 10 am to 5 pm.
    Entrance fee applies.
🌐 www.mz.usp.br

Museu Lasar Segall

A compound with a museum and
cinema was inaugurated in 1987,
in the house where the artist
Lasar Segall (painter and
sculptor) lived until his death.
He was born in 1891 in a Russian
city named Vilna, today
Lithuania's capitol, and he came
to Brazil in 1911. Art classes
are conducted in the museum.

🏠 Rua Berta, 111, Vila Mariana
☎ 5574-7322
🕐 Tuesdays to Saturdays
from 2 pm to 7 pm,
Sundays from 2 pm to 6 pm.
Free entrance (for the cinema,
entrance fee applies).
🌐 www.museusegall.org.br

Museu Paulista – Ipiranga

The first monument built to
commemorate the Independence
of Brazil, it was inaugurated
on September 7th (Independence
Day), 1895, with the intention
of turning it into a scientific
museum. However, it is known
today to be a historical museum,
holding approximately 100,000
pieces of Brazilian history in
a heritage library of books and
manuscripts. Guided tours
to be scheduled in advance.
🏠 Parque da Independência,
Ipiranga
☎ 6165-8000
🕐 Tuesdays to Sundays,
from 9 am to 17 pm.
Entrance fee applies.
🌐 www.mp.usp.br

Palácio dos Bandeirantes

Bandeirantes Palace is the head-
quarter for the State of São
Paulo Government.
Construction on the building
started in 1955. The intention
was for it to be the site of the
foundation of art patron, Count
Francisco Matarazzo. Since then
it was the home of two more
foundations, the Getúlio Vargas
Foundation and the Foundation
of São Paulo. In April 1964,
the State government moved
from Campos Elísios
neighborhood to the Morumbi
neighborhood, into the Palácio
dos Bandeirantes. The palace
holds an impressive colletion
with 1,680 works of art.
Works of Almeida Jr., Oscar
Pereira da Silva and Pedro
Américo, amongst many other
artists, are displayed. Tour
guides should be scheduled
in advance.
🏠 Av. Morumbi, 4500, Morumbi
☎ 2193-8282 / 2193-8094
🕐 Saturdays and Sundays,
from 1 pm to 5 pm.
Free entrance.
🌐 www.acervo.sp.gov.br

Pinacoteca do Estado

The building follows a Neo-
Renaissance Italian style.
The project was completed
by architect Ramos de Azevedo, in
1897. Originally, it was built to be a
school of arts and crafts, with the
intention of providing São Paulo
with artisans and technicians.
Since then it has been transformed many times to serve
different institutions. During
the 1990s, the museum underwent a big restoration by Paulo
Mendes da Rocha, and for that
reason was able to receive
the Rodin sculptures in 1998. It
holds temporary and also
permanent exhibitions
(around 4,000 works of art).
There is always something
happening in the auditorium

and one can host events in a designated space there, available for rent. Some of the Brazilian artists featured are: Almeida Junior, Pedro Alexandrino, Oscar Pereira, Cândido Portinari, Anita Malfati, Victor Brecheret, Tarsila do Amaral, Di Cavalcanti. Guides can be scheduled in advance.

- Praça da Luz, 2, Luz
- 3229-9844
- Thursdays to Sundays, from 10 am to 5:30 pm. Entrance fee applies.
- www.cultura.sp.gov.br (click on link "museus")

Shows and Concert Houses

Auditório Ibirapuera

Inaugurated in 2005, by architect Oscar Niemeyer, this building completes the original project built by the architect in Ibirapuera Park. It has a great concert hall and includes a music school for children and teenagers.

The 20- meter wall behind the stage can be opened, allowing some concerts to be open to the park.

- Ibirapuera Park, Ibirapuera
- 5908-4299
- www.auditorioibirapuera. com.br

Citibank Hall

- Av. Jamaris, 213, Moema
- 6846-6040
- www.citibankhall.com.br

Credicard Hall

- Av. das Nações Unidas, 17955, Vila Almeida
- 6846-6010
- www.credicardhall.com.br

Tom Brasil Nações Unidas

- Rua Bragança Paulista, 1281, Chácara Santo Antônio
- 2163-2100
- www.tombr.com.br

Via Funchal

- Rua Funchal, 65, Vila Olímpia
- 3897-4456 / 3089-6999
- www.viafunchalamedacom.br

Theaters

Auditório Cultura Inglesa Higienópolis

- Av. Higienópolis, 449, Higienópolis
- 3826-4322
- www.culturainglesasp.com.br

TBC – Teatro Brasileiro de Comédia

- Rua Major Diogo, 315, Bela Vista
- 3104-5523

Teatro Abril

- Av. Brig. Luiz Antonio, 411, Bela Vista
- 6846-6060
- www.teatroabril.com.br

Teatro Alfa

- Rua Bento Branco de Andrade Filho, 722, Santo Amaro

☎ 5693-4000
🌐 www.teatroalfa.com.br

Teatro Aliança Francesa
🏠 Rua General Jardim, 182,
Vila Buarque
☎ 3129-5730

Teatro de Arena Eugênio Kusnet
🏠 Rua Teodoro Baima, 94, Centro
☎ 3662-5177
🌐 www.funarte.gov.br

Teatro Artur Azevedo
🏠 Av. Paes de Barros, 955, Mooca
☎ 6605-8007

Teatro Augusta
🏠 Rua Augusta, 943, Consolação
☎ 3151-2464 / 3151-4141
🌐 www.teatroaugusta.com.br

Teatro Bibi Ferreira
🏠 Av. Brig. Luiz Antonio, 931,
Bela Vista
☎ 3105-3129
🌐 www.teatrobibiferreira.com.br

Teatro Brigadeiro
🏠 Av. Brig. Luiz Antonio, 884,
Bela Vista
☎ 3107-5774 / 3115-2637

Teatro do Centro da Terra
🏠 Rua Piracuama, 19, Sumaré
☎ 3675-1595
🌐 www.centrodaterra.com.br

Teatro Crowne Plaza
🏠 Rua Frei Caneca, 1360,
Cerqueira César
☎ 3289-0985

Teatro Cultura Artística
🏠 Rua Nestor Pestana, 196,
Centro
☎ 3258-3344
🌐 www.culturaartistica.com.br

Teatro Cultura Inglesa Pinheiros
🏠 Rua Dep. Lacerda Franco,
333, Pinheiros
☎ 3814-0100
🌐 www.culturainglesasp.com.br

Teatro FAAP
🏠 Rua Alagoas, 903,
Higienópolis
☎ 3662-7233
🌐 www.faap.br/teatro

Teatro Fábrica São Paulo
🏠 Rua da Consolação, 1623,
Consolação
☎ 3255-5922
🌐 www.fabricasaopaulo.com.br

Teatro Fecomercio
🏠 Rua Dr. Plínio Barreto, 285,
Bela Vista
☎ 3188-4141
🌐 www.fecomercioeventos.
com.br

Teatro Folha
🏠 Shopping Pátio Higienópolis
Av. Higienópolis, 618,
Higienópolis
☎ 3823-2323
🌐 www.teatrofolha.com.br

Teatro Galpão dos Folias
🏠 Rua Ana Cintra, 213,
Santa Cecília
☎ 3361-2223

Teatro Humboldt
Av. Eng. Alberto Kuhlmann, 525, Interlagos
5686-4055
www.teatrohumboldt.com.br

Teatro Imprensa
Rua Jaceguai, 400, Bela Vista
3241-4203

Teatro João Caetano
Rua Borges Lagoa, 650, Vila Clementino
5573-3774

Teatro Maria Della Costa
Rua Paim, 72, Bela Vista
3256-9115
www.apetesp.org.br/mariadellacosta

Teatro Martins Pena
Largo do Rosário, 20, Centro
2293-6630

Teatro da Memória – Instituto Cultural Capobianco
Rua Álvaro de Carvalho, 97, Centro
3237-1187
www.institutocapobianco.org.br

Teatro Municipal
(See page 27)

Teatro Oficina
Stage to one of Brazilian's finest theater companies today.
Rua Jaceguai, 520, Bela Vista
3106-5300 / 3101-2938
www.teatroficina.com.br

Teatro Paulo Eiró
Av. Adolfo Pinheiro, 765, Santo Amaro
5546-0449

Teatro Popular do Sesi
Free tickets, limited audience.
Av. Paulista, 1313, Cerqueira César
3146-7405
www.sesisp.org.br

Teatro Procópio Ferreira
Rua Augusta, 2823, Cerqueira César
3083-4475
www.teatroprocopioferreira.com.br

Teatro Renaissance
Alameda Santos, 2233, Cerqueira César
3188-4151

Teatro Ruth Escobar
Rua dos Ingleses, 209, Bela Vista
3289-2358
www.ruthescobar.apetesp.org.br

Teatro São Pedro
Rua Barra Funda, 171, Barra Funda
3667-0499
www.teatrosaopedro.sp.gov.br

Teatro Sérgio Cardoso
Rua Rui Barbosa, 153, Bela Vista
3288-0136
www.teatrosergiocardoso.sp.gov.br

Teatro Shopping Frei Caneca

⌂ Shopping Frei Caneca
Rua Frei Caneca, 569,
sixth floor, Bela Vista
☎ 3472-2229
⊕ www.teatroshoppingfreicaneca.com.br

Teatro Tuca

⌂ Rua Monte Alegre, 1024,
Perdizes
☎ 3188-4156
⊕ www.teatrotuca.com.br

Teatro Vivo

⌂ Av. Dr. Chucri Zaidan, 860,
Brooklin
☎ 5105-1520

TUSP – Teatro Universidade de São Paulo – CEUMA

⌂ Rua Maria Antônia, 294,
Higienópolis
☎ 3259-8342
⊕ www.usp.br/tusp

outings

Cycling

Bike shops
Bike Tech

You can buy the "the whole kit and caboodle" for a great bike ride (bikes, helmets, pads, clothing). Repairs bikes as well.
⌂ Rua da Consolação, 3344,
Jardins
☎ 3088-1922 / 3891-2290
⊕ www.biketechjardins.com.br

Cycling in the city
Faria Lima

⌂ Av. Brig. Faria Lima,
Pinheiros, 1,3 km long

Roberto Marinho

⌂ Av. Jorn. Roberto Marinho,
Brooklin, 0,5 km long

Sumaré

⌂ Av. Sumaré, Sumaré,
1,4 km long

cycling in parks

Many parks have bike tracks, like Horto Florestal, Parque Anhangüera, Parque do Carmo, Parque do Ibirapuera and Parque Villa-Lobos (SEE INFO AT PAGE 111).

Parque Municipal das Bicicletas

Located inside a Municipal Olympic Compound of 3 km. Great place for children to learn how to ride a bike!
⌂ Alameda Iraé, 35, Moema
☎ 5088-6544
◷ Everyday, 7 am to 10 pm.
Free entrance.

Bike Repair

Tutto Bike

⌂ Av. Pompéia, 787, Pompéia
☎ 3872-5505
⊕ www.tuttobike.com.br

Ciclovece

⌂ Rua Camargo, 379, Butantã
☎ 3814-1986
⊕ www.ciclovece.com.br

For children and adults

Casa de Pedra – Escalade Gymnasium

Children can celebrate their birthdays. Package deals for companies also available. Holds climbing classes and provides monitors to help during the activities. For children 7 years old and above.

🏠 Rua Venâncio Aires, 31, Perdizes

☎ 3875-1521 / 3873-8178

🕐 Mondays to Thursdays, 6:30 am to 11 pm, Fridays, 6:30 pm to 9 pm, Saturdays, Sundays and Holidays, 2 pm to 8 pm.

🌐 For more locations: www.casadepedra.com.br

Cidade do Livro

Welcome to the magical world of literature! The aims of the Book City are educational as well as cultural, a fabulous way to get your children "hooked" on the pleasures of reading. "Actors" play out day-to-day scenes with an emphasis on teaching the children the values and virtues indispensable in today's world. Themes change constantly and new attractions are invented in order to keep bringing in the "little public". Not only geared towards children between the ages of three and eight, but also towards the older group (9-12). For those, the story gets a little more sophisticated as a mystery is developed, and the group in charge of resolving it gets the help of...? None other than Sherlock Holmes himself!

🏠 Alameda Afonso Schmidt, 877, Santa Terezinha

☎ 6977-8674 / 6959-6179 (visits must be scheduled)

🌐 www.cidadedolivro.com.br

Cidade Portinho Seguro

Inaugurated in May 1998 by Porto Seguro, a Brazilian insurance company, the space occupies 500 square meters dedicated to teaching young children (five to eleven years old) the many different traffic rules and regulations. This is a significant lesson before the new young "drivers" are ready to tackle the real thing. At the end of the presentation, children can use the space to apply their newly acquired skills with their bikes, and therefore become eligible for their very first driving license!

🏠 Rua da Mooca, 1291, Mooca

☎ 3209-6272 / 2162-4022

🕐 Mondays to Fridays, presentations at 8:30 am, 10:30 am and 2:30 pm. Should be scheduled in advance. Free entrance.

🌐 www.portoseguro.com.br (link "cidade portinho seguro")

L&T's best!

Estação Ciência

The Science Station is a huge hangar built at the beginning of the last century and used for industrial purposes. In 1990, when the Science Station came into existence, its purpose was to explain and promote scientific knowledge, to stimulate curiosity and to provide the opportunity to conduct scientific experiments in an environment outside the classroom. In addition to that, the development and accessibility of educational scientific expositions for children, youth and adults contribute to making this venue a most interesting place to visit.

- ⌂ Rua Guaicurus, 1394, Lapa
- ☎ 3673-7022
- ◷ Thursdays to Fridays 8 am to 5:30 pm, Saturdays, Sundays and holidays 9 am to 5:30 pm. Entrance fee applies.
- ⊕ www.eciencia.usp.br

Instituto Butantan

Inaugurated in 1901 as a Therapeutic Serum Institute, today it hosts cultural and scientific activities related to snakes, spiders, lizards, scorpions, and amphibious animals. Composed of three museums, biological, microbiological and historical, it also hosts a wonderful park. Certainly one of the main tourist attractions of São Paulo, especially if you are science-oriented!

- ⌂ Av. Vital Brasil, 1500, Butantã
- ☎ 3726-7222
- ◷ Thurdays to Sundays, 9 am to 4:30 pm. Entrance fee applies.
- ⊕ www.butantan.gov.br

Museu Contemporâneo das Invenções

The Contemporary Museum of Inventions promotes some quite unusual and unique discoveries. The intention is to support scientific and technological innovation.

- ⌂ Rua Dr. Homem de Mello, 1109, Perdizes
- ☎ 3873-3211
- ◷ Mondays to Fridays, 10 am to noon, and 2 pm to 5 pm. Entrance fee applies.
- ⊕ www.inventores.com.br

Parque Lúdico – SESC Itaquera

Composed of three different themed areas, this park encourages a new way of playing by taking advantage of the surrounding environment.

Espaço Aventura: On top of a 20-meter high mountain, treasure is hidden and in order to get there, children have to overcome a series of obstacles.

Bichos da Mata: An area of 330 square meters built with six giant animal sculptures.

Orquestra Mágica: Composed of fifteen big musical instruments. The idea is to motivate the children to enjoy music.

- ⌂ Av. Fernando do Espírito Santos Alves de Matos, 1000, Itaquera
- ☎ 6523-9200
- ◷ Wednesdays to Sundays (holidays included), 9 am to 5 pm. Entrance fee applies.
- ⊕ www.sescsp.org.br

Parque da Mônica

Perhaps the most read comic book character in Brazil, Mônica and her friends come to life in this wonderful park for children. If you are planning to visit, you should call first, as it is not open all the time. A monitor is available on the premises, should you wish to leave your children supervised there for a period of time, in which case a fee is applicable. The park also holds a cinema and theater, as well as many different attractions.

- Shopping Eldorado
  Av. Rebouças, 3770, Pinheiros
- 3093-7766
- Thursdays and Fridays from 10 am to 5 pm, Saturdays and Sundays from 10 am to 8 pm. Entrance fee applies.
- www.monica.com.br

Pipódromo Parque do Tietê

About four or five times a year, the organizers of the website www.pipas.com.br put together an event for kites of all kinds to be "let loose", in this pleasant area inside the Ecological Forest Park of Tietê. A great way of spending a sunny afternoon with the kids.

- Rua Guira Acangatara, 70, Vila Rica
- 6958-3999
- Everyday, from 7 am to 5 pm. Free entrance.
- www.daee.sp.gov.br
  (click on link "parques")

Planetário Mundo Estelar

The Planetarium brings the Universe closer; you are able to see the stars from the north and the south hemispheres. It has two sections; the one for children up to ten years old is quite entertaining, as "actors" give information about the Universe. The other is for adults, full of special effects and scientific details.

- Rua Huet Bacelar, 407, Ipiranga
- 2273-5500
- Saturdays, Sundays and holidays; presentations at 12 am, 2 pm and 4 pm for children, and at 5 pm for teens. Entrance fee applies.
- www.mundoestelar.com.br

Zoológico

The natural landscape of a forest and lake holds over 3,200 animals (from both Brazil and other countries), in a area of 824,529 m^2. Once inside, you can visit the Zoo Safari where animals move around freely. The safari takes place in comfortable vans where environmental educators explain everything about the animals and related habitats along the 4 km trip inside Mata Atlântica.

- Av. Miguel Stéfano, 4241, Água Funda
- 5073-0811
- Tuesdays to Sundays, from 9 am to 5 pm. Entrance fee applies.
- www.zoologico.sp.gov.br

Nightlife

Night in São Paulo is quite active – there is always something going on. You can just go for a drink, listen to music or even practice your dancing steps!
In general, people – especially college students – tend to go out late, at around 10:30 pm, 11 pm, or even later!

Bars

Água Doce Cachaçaria

Appetizers and full menu, popular when games are played on T.V. Live music on weekends.
- Av. Macuco, 655, Moema
- 5056-1615
- www.aguadoce.com.br

Armazém da Vila

Appetizers, live music, dance floor, background music. Focused on samba, pagode and axé.
- Rua Beira Rio, 116, Vila Olímpia
- 3045-3573 / 3845-9192
- www.armazemdavila.com.br

Ásia 70

Appetizers and a full menu, live music, dance floor, background music. 1970s, 1980s and 1990s flashback with Asian decoration.
- Rua Domingos Andrade, Brooklin
- 5506-4903
- www.asia70.com.br

Avenida Club

Weekend bar, with appetizers, live music, dance floor. On Tuesdays, the famous stand-up comedy "Terça Insana" is presented. Every other night a different program is presented.
- Av. Pedroso de Morais, 1036, Pinheiros
- 3814-7383
- www.avenidaclub.com.br

Azucar

Bar with appetizers and full menu. Wednesdays have live music. Dance floor, background music. Cuban music.
- Rua Dr. Mário Ferraz, 423, Itaim
- 3078-3130
- www.azucar.com.br

Bar e Restaurante Vascello

Appetizers and full menu, background music.
- Rua Haddock Lobo, 804, Cerqueira César
- 3083-7033 / 3086-4733

Bar Vivo in Motion

Appetizers, background and live music, dance floor. Focused on electronic music.
- Rua Gomes de Carvalho, 1715, Vila Olímpia
- 3045-1014
- www.barvivo.com.br

Boogie

Appetizers and full menu, live music, dance floor, background music. Focused on disco.
- Rua Alvorada, 515, Vila Olímpia
- 3168-8872
- www.boogie.com.br

Bourbon Street

Bar, restaurant, appetizers and full menu, background and live music. Focused on jazz.

⌖ Rua dos Chanés, 127, Moema
☎ 5561-1643
🌐 www.bourbonstreet.com.br

Buena Vista Club

Bar, appetizers, live and background music, dance floor. Jazz, forró, salsa, MPB (Popular Brazilian Music).

⌖ Rua Prof. Atílio Innocenti, 780, Vila Olímpia
☎ 3045-5245
🌐 www.buenavistaclub.com.br

Canto da Ema

Appetizers, live and background music, dance floor. Focused on forró.

⌖ Av. Brig. Faria Lima, 364, Pinheiros
☎ 3813-4708
🌐 www.cantodaema.com.br

Circus Club

Appetizers and full menu, background music, bingo, entertainers, game machines.

⌖ Av. Ibirapuera, 2601, Moema
☎ 5542-6117
🌐 www.circusclub.com.br

Charles Edwards

Appetizers, background and live music, dance floor. Focused on classic and pop rock.

⌖ Av. Pres. Juscelino Kubitschek, 1426, Itaim
☎ 3078-5022
🌐 www.barcharles.com.br

Coppola Music

Bar, appetizers, live and background music, dance floor. Rock, black music, flashback and 1980s/1990s dance music.

⌖ Rua Girassol, 323, Vila Madalena
☎ 3034-5544
🌐 www.coppolamusic.com.br

Disco

Bar, dance floor, background music. House, electronic music.

⌖ Rua Prof. Atílio Innocenti, 160, Itaim
☎ 3078-0404
🌐 www.clubdisco.com.br

Dublin

Appetizers and full menu, background and live music, dance floor. Focused on pop rock.

⌖ Rua Min. Jesuíno Cardoso, 178, Vila Olímpia
☎ 3044-4194
🌐 www.dublin.com.br

Ébano Bar e Danceteria

Bar and restaurant, appetizers and full menu, background and live music, dance floor. Each night a different music style.

⌖ Av. Hélio Pelegrino, 531, Vila Olímpia
☎ 3842-4445 / 3842-5349
🌐 www.ebanobar.com.br

Frangó Cervejaria

Specializing in beers, serving brands from Germany, Belgium, Holland, Brazil, England, Ireland, Mexico, Japan, Argentina, Uruguay, Scotland and France.

📍 Largo da Matriz Nossa
   Senhora do Ó, 168,
   Freguesia do Ó
☎ 3932-4818
🌐 www.frangobar.com.br

Jacaré Grill

Appetizers, very popular when
games are played on T.V.
📍 Rua Harmonia, 321/337,
   Vila Madalena
☎ 3816-0400
🌐 www.jacaregrill.com.br

Joan Sehn

Appetizers and a full menu,
background music.
📍 Av. Lavandisca, 765, Moema
☎ 5051-9162

Kamaroty Music

Bar, appetizers, live music, dance
floor, background music. Pagode,
axé, pop rock.
📍 Rua Gomes de Carvalho, 560,
   Vila Olímpia
☎ 3845-3232
🌐 www.kamarotymusic.com.br

Lanterna

Bar and restaurant, appetizers
and full menu, background and
live music, dance floor. Rock,
techno and MPB (Popular
Brazilian Music).
📍 Rua Fidalga, 531,
   Vila Madalena
☎ 3031-0483 / 3816-0904
🌐 www.lanterna.com.br

Little Darling

Bar, appetizers, background and
live music, dance floor. Focused

on 1950s, 1960s and 1970s
rock'n'roll.
📍 Av. Iraí, 229, Moema
☎ 5542-9912
🌐 www.littledarling.com.br

Maevva Bar

Appetizers and restaurant
with full menu, background and
live music, dance floor. Pagode,
pop rock, MPB (Popular
Brazilian Music).
📍 Rua Prof. Atílio
   Innocenti, 376, Itaim
☎ 3044-6222
🌐 www.maevva.com.br

Manga Rosa

Bar, background music, dance
floor. Focused on electronic
music for young people.
📍 Rua Guararapes, 1754,
   Brooklin
☎ 5506-1990
🌐 www.clubmangarosa.com.br

Maré Alta Bar & Mar

Bar, restaurant, appetizers and
full menu, background music.
Specializes in sea food.
📍 Rua Quatá, 426,
   Vila Olímpia
☎ 3044-1271 / 3842-0349
🌐 www.barmarealta.com.br

Memphis Dance Club

Appetizer and full menu,
live music, dance floor.
Focused on 1960s and 1970s
rock.
📍 Av. dos Imarés, 295, Moema
☎ 5542-9767
🌐 www.memphis.com.br

Mercearia São Roque

Bar, restaurant, appetizers and full menu, background music.

🏠 Rua Amauri, 35,
Jardim Europa

☎ 3062-2612

🌐 For more locations:
www.merceariasaoroque.
com.br

Mistura Brasileira

Appetizers, live music, dance floor. Focused on MPB (Popular Brazilian Music).

🏠 Rua Padre Estevão Pernet,
112, Tatuapé

☎ 6941-8881

🕙 Only Fridays to Sundays.

🌐 www.misturabrasileira.com.br

Mood Club

Bar, background music, dance floor. Black music and samba.

🏠 Rua Teodoro Sampaio, 1109,
Pinheiros

☎ 3060-9010

🌐 www.moodclub.com.br

Na Mata Café

Restaurant, appetizers and a full menu, dance floor, live and background music. Each night a different music style.

🏠 Rua da Mata, 70, Itaim

☎ 3079-0300

🌐 www.namata.com.br Bar,

Original

Famous for its happy hour and its super cool chopp. Background music.

🏠 Rua Graúna, 137, Moema

☎ 5093-9486

Passatempo Bar e Restaurante

Appetizers and a full menu offered, live music, dance floor. Focused on live MPB (Popular Brazilian Music).

🏠 Rua Jerônimo da Veiga, 446,
Itaim

☎ 3079-5054 / 3167-2297

🌐 www.passatempo-mpb.
com.br

Pueblo de Mexico

Bar, restaurant, appetizers and full menu, background music.

🏠 Rua Min. Jesuíno Cardoso,
104, Vila Olímpia

☎ 3845-2140

🌐 www.pueblo.com.br

Rey Castro

Bar and restaurant, appetizers and full menu, background music, live music, dance floor. Cuban music, salsa, merengue and Latin pop.

🏠 Rua Min. Jesuíno Cardoso,
181, Vila Olímpia

☎ 3044-4383

🌐 www.reycastro.com.br

Rose Bom Bom

Bar, dance floor, background music. Rock, hip-hop, funk, flashback and 1980s rock.

🏠 Rua Luis Murat, 370,
Vila Madalena

☎ 3813-3365

🌐 www.rosebombom.com

Santa Aldeia

Bar and restaurant, appetizers and full menu, background

music, live music, dance floor.
Each night a different music style.

🏠 Rua Beira Rio, 113,
Vila Olímpia

☎ 3845-9235

🌐 www.santaaldeia.com.br

Studio SP

Bar, live music, dance floor,
background music. Focused
on indie music live shows.

🏠 Rua Inácio Pereira da Rocha,
170, Vila Madalena

☎ 3817-5425

🌐 www.studiosp.org

Taag Music

Bar, restaurant, appetizers and a
full menu, dance floor, background
music. Focused on dance music.

🏠 Av. Dr. Cardoso de Melo,
1275, Vila Olímpia

☎ 3845-8343

🌐 www.taagmusic.com.br

Ton Ton Jazz Music Bar

Bar, restaurant, appetizers and
a full menu, background music
and live music, dance floor. Jazz.

🏠 Alameda dos Pamaris, 55,
Moema

☎ 5044-7239 / 5094-0589

🌐 www.tonton.com.br

Villa Country

Appetizers and full menu,
background music, shows with
artists, game room and dance
floor. Focused on country music.

🏠 Av. Francisco Matarazzo,
774/810, Barra Funda

☎ 3868-5858

🌐 www.villacountry.com.br

Yucatan

Appetizers and a full menu,
background music, on weekends
Mexican live music.

🏠 Av. Pres. Juscelino Kubitschek,
393, Itaim

☎ 3846-3505

🌐 www.yucatan.com.br

Zur alten Muehle

Appetizers and full menu,
background music.

🏠 Rua Princesa Isabel, 102,
Brooklin

☎ 5044-4669

Parks

For information on all of the
city's parks:
http://portal.prefeitura.sp.gov.
br/secretarias/meio_ambiente/
parques

Aclimação

🏠 Rua Muniz de Souza, 1119,
Aclimação

☎ 3208-4042

🕐 Every day, from 6 am to 8 pm.

Água Branca – Parque Dr. Fernando Costa

Many different attractions,
just visit the site. Don't miss the
chance to have breakfast on
Saturday and Sunday mornings.

🏠 Av. Francisco Matarazzo, 455,
Água Branca

☎ 3675-7436

🕐 Every day, from 6 am to 6 pm.

🌐 www.parqueaguabranca.sp.
gov.br

Alfredo Volpi (Parque do Morumbi)

Rua Eng. Oscar Americano, 480, Morumbi

3031-7052

Every day, from 6 am to 6 pm.

Burle Marx

Av. Dona Helena Pereira de Moraes, 200, Morumbi

3746-7631

Every day, from 7 am to 7 pm.

Guarapiranga – Parque Alves de Lima

Estrada do Guarapiranga, 575, Ribeirão Pires

5514-6332

Every day, from 6 am to 6 pm.

Horto Florestal

Rua do Horto, 931, Horto Florestal

6231-8555

Every day, from 6 am to 6 pm.

www.hortoflorestal.com.br

L&T 's best!

Ibirapuera

Most probably the best in São Paulo, Ibirapuera offers bike rentals (for adults and children), health advice, running, jogging and walking tracks, mist spots to cool off when the sun gets too hot (something we had never seen before), children's swings, beverages and light snacks. Large trees provide fabulous shade which make the work out extremely pleasant and comfortable. The Biennal of São Paulo is located inside the park, therefore when exhibitions or shows are held, the traffic tends to be quite heavy.

Av. Pedro Álvares Cabral, Ibirapuera

5573-4180

Every day, from 5 am to midnight.

Jardim Botânico

Av. Miguel Stéfano, 3031, Água Funda

5073-6300

www.ibot.sp.gov.br

Jardim Luzitânia

2,8 km bike track.

Av. IV Centenário, 1268, Jardim Luzitânia

Parque Anhangüera

2,7 km bike track.

Av. Fortunata Tadiello Natucci, 1000 (km 24,5 Via Anhangüera), Perus

3917-2406

Every day, from 6 am to 6 pm.

Parque das Bicicletas

(SEE INFO AT PAGE 103.)

Parque do Carmo

8,2 km bike track.

Av. Afonso de Sampaio e Souza, 951, Itaquera

6748-0010

Every day, from 6 am to 6 pm.

Parque da Independência

Av. Nazareth, Ipiranga

2273-7250

Every day, from 5 am to 8 pm.

Trianon – Parque Tenente Siqueira Campos

⌂ Rua Peixoto Gomide, 949, Cerqueira César

☎ 3289-2160

🕐 Every day, from 6 am to 6 pm.

Parque Villa-Lobos

1,6 km bike track.

Bike rental available.

⌂ Av. Prof. Fonseca Rodrigues, 1655, Alto de Pinheiros

☎ 3023-0316

🕐 Every day, from 7 am to 6 pm.

🌐 www.ambiente.sp.gov.br/villalobos

Amusement Parks

Hopi Hari

Has over 40 attractions, beautiful landscape, and over 760,000 m². It includes a rollercoaster that goes underneath the highway and stays open more than 300 sunny days per year. If you are looking for fun and excitement, Hopi Hari is the ideal place to spend a great time.

⌂ Rodovia dos Bandeirantes, km 72,5, Vinhedo

☎ 0300 789 5566

🌐 www.hopihari.com.br

Playcenter

The pioneer amusement park in Brazil, since 1973 it has offered more than 30 attractions for any age. It shares many similarities to most of the big amusement parks in the world, and it is the venue for numerous events and promotions throughout the year.

⌂ Marginal do Tietê, entrance by Rua José Gomes Falcão, 20, Barra Funda

☎ 3350-0199

🌐 www.playcenter.com.br

Wet'n Wild

An aquatic park just outside São Paulo, provides entertainment for the whole family. Next to Hopi Hari.

⌂ Rodovia dos Bandeirantes, km 72, Itupeva

☎ 4496-8000

🌐 www.wetnwild.com.br

Sport Stadiums

One of Brazilian "cults", if we may call it that, is soccer. Brazilians are passionate about the sport and take it extremely seriously. Remember Pelé? Soccer is part of their culture (just as plastic surgery is), and a must-see during your stay in São Paulo. The main teams of the city are São Paulo, Corinthians, and Palmeiras.

In addition to soccer stadiums, São Paulo also has many venues for other sports that have caught the nation's attention, such as Formula 1, volleyball, swimming and gymnastics.

Be careful when discussing soccer and make sure to enquire about the team of the person you are talking to, in order to avoid a fierce disagreement!

Autódromo Municipal de Interlagos

A large race track which is used year round for various types of races. It is the site of many important competitions like the Brazilian Grand Prix of Formula 1 and the Campeonato Paulista de Automobilismo.

📍 Av. Sen. Teotônio Vilela, 261, Interlagos

☎ 5666-8822

🌐 www.autodromointerlagos.com

Estádio do Morumbi – Estádio Cícero Pompeu de Toledo

Considered one of the biggest private stadiums in the world with a capacity of 80,000 people, the stadium was inaugurated on February 10th, 1960. It belongs to the São Paulo Soccer Club.

📍 Praça Roberto Gomes Pedrosa, 1, Morumbi

☎ 3749-8000

Games are played practically year round.

Estádio do Pacaembu – Estádio Municipal Paulo Machado de Carvalho

The stadium was inaugurated on April 27th, 1940, in a neighborhood called Pacaembu, which means, in native Indian language (**tupi-guarani**), "flooded land." In the 1950s, none other than Pelé, the "soccer king" himself, started his career here! If you live nearby, you can become a member for free and have access to the gym and the Olympic swimming pool.

📍 Praça Charles Miller, Pacaembu

☎ 3664-4650

Estádio Municipal de Beisebol

The stadium consists of a baseball field and a gymnasium.

📍 Av. Pres. Castelo Branco, 5446, Bom Retiro

☎ 3221-5105

Ask for authorization in advance to be able to play.

Ginásio do Ibirapuera

Local and international competitions of volleyball, basketball and gymnastics.

📍 Rua Abílio Soares, 1300, Ibirapuera

☎ 3887-3500

restaurants

Brazil is a country blessed with the availability and abundance of the freshest and best ingredients. Immigration has always been common and the influences obvious throughout the years. Whether influenced by Africans with the introduction of *feijoada* (SEE UNDER GLOSSARY AT PAGE 212), the Italians with the import of pasta, pizza, the arts, and the intellects, the Japanese with the intro-duction and development of agriculture (mainly fruits and vegetables as the dietary customs before their arrival were mostly beans, rice and meats, particularly dried meats), Germans with their famous sausages, and Lebanese with their delicious *kibes* and *esfihas* (SEE UNDER GLOSSARY AT PAGE 212), São Paulo has benefited from it all.

All year round one can always encounter a great variety of fruits and vegetables, which usually, in other parts of the world, are only available in season. The same goes for meats, fish or seafood – you can find it all here.

São Paulo is considered by many to rank high amongst the gastronomical cities of the world where continental cuisine with a constant strong influence of Brazilian fusion is becoming increasingly popular. As in many major cities, the restaurant scene is extremely active and changes constantly. New additions appear constantly. A good, helpful beginning could be the "Guia Josimar Melo," published annually, the restaurant section in "Veja SP" weekly magazine, and the "O melhor do Brasil" published annually by *Veja* as well, which lists restaurants and bars all over the country.

Paulistanos take their foods very seriously, and a popular culinary custom, if we may call it that, is to dedicate certain days of the week to certain foods. For example, Sunday is across the board known as "Pizza night,"

a fun, extremely casual outing. Wednesday and Saturday are dedicated to *feijoada*, Thursday and Sunday are pasta days and Friday is fish day.

Attention to eating healthily is the norm, rather than the exception, so one can enjoy his/her meal guilt-free, whatever the venue.

Reservations are strongly recommended and, as you will find out quite quickly, are only taken up to 8:30 pm. *Paulistanos* tend to eat on the late side, a popular habit in the Latin American world. Therefore, should you wish a "quiet night", we suggest that you dine around 8 pm.

> Most restaurants will open on Sundays for lunch and close at 5 pm to yield the space for pizzarias!

American

T.G.I. Friday's
You would think you were back in the U.S.!
🏠 Av. Antonio Joaquim de Moura Andrade, 737, Itaim
☎ 3885-2844
🌐 www.fridays.com.br

Barbecued meat
Although *churrascarias* are common in other parts of South America, Brazil has probably the most restaurants which serve and have *churrascos*. There are two

kinds of *churrascos*: one where the waiters keep coming over with long skewers of meats, poultry, game, etc., called *rodízio*; and the other where you choose your meat, which is then barbecued. Both are great stops when visitors come to town, as they are so different from your regular restaurant! At the former, one can eat till his heart's content and has to actually signal the waiter to stop serving by turning a wheel from green to red. Included in the meal is a hearty salad bar with various dishes of vegetables, pasta and seafood. Dessert is also included in the price. However, side dishes and drinks are extra. Prices are set per person.

Some places will explain in English the various cut of meats.

Barbacoa

A great place to experience the excellent Brazilian *churrasco*.
- Rua Renato Paes de Barros, 65, Itaim
- 3168-5522
- For more locations: www.barbacoa.com.br

Emporium Plaza

- Rua Oscar Freire, 574, Jardins
- 3065-3355
- ww.emporiumplaza.com.br

Fogo de Chão

- Av. Santo Amaro, 6824, Santo Amaro
- 5524-0500
- For more locations: www.fogodechao.com.br

Jardineira Grill

- Av. dos Bandeirantes, 1001, Vila Olímpia
- 3845-0299
- www.jardineiragrill.com.br

Rodeio

The most traditional meat restaurant of Jardins.
- Rua Haddock Lobo, 1498, Jardins
- 3474-1333
- www.churrascariarodeio. com.br

L&T's best!

Vento Haragano

One of the best *churrascos* in town; very pleasant atmosphere even when it is full. Be careful not to go crazy at the salad bar as you'll want to leave plenty of room for the main course!
- Av. Rebouças, 1001, Pinheiros
- 3083-4265
- www.ventoharagano.com.br

Brazilian

Don't wait too long to experience the **feijoada** with all its side dishes. However, a word of advice: make sure you have no dinner plans that evening! (Don't forget a lighter version is also available.)

Bolinha

- Av. Cidade Jardim, 53, Jardim Europa
- 3061-2010
- www.bolinha.com.br

Brasil a Gosto

Very pleasant atmosphere with light Brazilian cuisine, publishes its own book, great for ladies' lunches.

🏠 Rua Prof. Azevedo Amaral, 70, Jardins

☎ 3086-3565

Capim Santo

A choice of dining al fresco or inside. Fusion of Brazilian and international cuisine.

🏠 Alameda Min. Rocha Azevedo, 471, Jardins

☎ 3068-8486

🌐 www.capimsanto.com.br

Carlota

One of the "musts," as soon as you feel settled. Fusion cuisine-exotic, Asian dishes with a Brazilian flair, Carlota is a very busy restaurant where reservations are strongly recommended. Fun to go with a couple of friends to sample the variety of appetizers, but do leave room for dessert.

🏠 Rua Sergipe, 753, Higienópolis

☎ 3661-8670

🌐 www.carlota.com.br

Consulado Mineiro

Pleasant restaurant in front of a pretty square. Focused on *comida mineira*.

🏠 Praça Benedito Calixto, 74, Pinheiros

☎ 3088-6055 / 3064-3882

🌐 For more locations: www.consuladomineiro. com.br

D.O.M. Restaurante

One of the top restaurants in the city with one of the most renowned chefs in São Paulo, Alex Atala. D.O.M. offers **menu de degustação** (tasting menus) as well as the regular "à la carte." Reservations are highly recommended. The couvert dishes are non-traditional and garlic lovers are in for a treat!

🏠 Rua Barão de Capanema, 549, Cerqueira César

☎ 3088-0761

🕐 Closed on Sundays.

🌐 www.domrestaurante.com.br

Dona Lucinha

Focused on Brazilian popular food, mostly *comida mineira*.

🏠 Av. Chibarás, 399, Moema

☎ 5051-2050

🌐 www.donalucinha.com.br

Sabuji

Fusion of contemporary and Brazilian cuisine.

🏠 Rua Sabuji, 40, Jardim Paulistano

☎ 3814-1240

Santa Gula

🏠 Rua Fidalga, 340-fundos, Vila Madalena

☎ 3819-0504

🌐 www.stagula.com.br

Tordesilhas Restaurante

🏠 Rua Bela Cintra, 465, Cerqueira César

☎ 3107-7444

🌐 www.tordesilhas.com

Café bar and Ice cream

Häagen-Dazs
The one and only!
⌂ Rua Oscar Freire, 900, Jardins
☎ 3062-1099
🌐 www.haagendazs.com.br

Mille Foglie
Library and gastronomy space
for cooking classes. Offers space
for rental.
⌂ Rua da Consolação, 3542,
   Jardins
☎ 3083-6777
🌐 www.millefoglie.com.br

L&T's best!

Nespresso Boutique Bar
This chic café & shop is destined to be a new Oscar Freire hotspot. You can have a delicious espresso or buy yourself a fabulous Nespresso machine, and they sell all the pods! When visiting São Paulo after nearly a three month absence, my total joy and surprise was to find this newly-established coffee place. What was even more astonishing, was that, practically at the same time in New York City, Nespresso opened its doors on Madison and 65th Street! Remember our comment about drawing a parallel between **Sampa** and New York? Well, there you are! Need more proof? I don't think so!
⌂ Rua Padre João Manoel,
   1164, Jardins
☎ 3064-9974
🌐 www.nespresso.com

Offellê Gelateria d'Art
Ice cream, coffee, cakes. Takeaway desserts.
⌂ Alameda Lorena, 1784, Jardins
☎ 3088-8127
🌐 www.offelle.com.br

Starbucks Coffee
The long awaited arrival of Starbucks in Brazil is here! They have initially launched two stores in Shopping Morumbi, but we're certain there will be many more to follow!
⌂ Shopping Morumbi
   Av. Roque Petroni Jr., 1089,
   Morumbi
☎ 5181-2100

Suplicy Cafés Especiais
Our version of Starbucks! Differents kinds of coffee. Savour them there or buy to take home. A nice place to meet a friend for that 5 pm tea or cappuccino. Sandwiches, bagels (yes, bagels!) and desserts available.
⌂ Alameda Lorena, 1430, Jardins
☎ 3061-0195
🌐 www.suplicycafes.com.br

French

Bar du Taste-vin
⌂ Alameda Itu, 1415, Cerqueira
   César
☎ 3086-1918
🌐 www.tastevin.com.br

Bistrot Sophia
Contemporary cuisine in a light, airy space. Well located in Jardins and quieter than the rest of the group for lunch.

Rua da Consolação, 3368-A,
Jardins

3081-7698

www.sophiabistrot.com.br

Braverie

A newcomer on the block,
Braverie offers light dishes for
lunch, all very carefully prepared.
Don't leave without picking up
some of their delicious bread,
dessert and home-made coffee!

Rua Joaquim Antunes, 48,
Jardim Paulista

3082-6644

Charlô Bistrô

A nice bistro atmosphere;
the breaded escalope is delicious!
It also caters at the Jockey Club
(SEE INFO AT PAGE **204**).

Rua Barão de Capanema, 440,
Cerqueira César

3088-6790

www.charlo.com.br

Di Bistrot

Another fun, pleasant bistro
where French cuisine is served.
Truly one of our favorites.

Rua Jacurici, 27, Itaim

3079-9098

www.dibistrot.com.br

Freddy

Freddy has this experienced
look that seems to say "we have
been around and we are still
around." One can have a quiet
dinner with attentive service.
English menu provided upon
request. Continental and seafood. Amongst the traditional
dishes you will find frogs, legs
and beef bourgignon.

Praça Dom Gastão Liberal
Pinto, 111, Itaim

3167-0977

Ici Bistrot

We really felt like we were entering
a French bistro in Paris. The menu
is written on a blackboard, the
dishes very French and the
atmosphere super pleasant.

Rua Pará, 36, Higienópolis

3257-4064

www.icibistro.com.br

La Brasserie Erick Jacquin

La Brasserie Erick Jacquin has
it all, from exquisite food and
wines, to the excellent service,
attention to details and pleasant
atmosphere. Delicious oysters,
steak tartare, duck dishes, and
fabulous desserts. You can have
the choice between the front
room, a more casual ambiance
with wooden tables, or the main,
more elegant dining room.
Either one is a fine choice, same
menu offered. Also open
on Sunday nights!

Rua Bahia, 683, Higienópolis

3826-5409

www.brasserie.com.br

Le Coq Hardy

One of the older restaurants
in **Sampa**. You will feel as if you
are entering a winter garden.

Rua Jerônimo da Veiga, 461,
Itaim

3079-3344

www.restaurantelecoqhardy.
com.br

Le Vin Bistrot

Great oysters, shrimp cooked with
pernod and beef bourguignon are
some of our recommendations.

The atmosphere is very cozy, with rooms decorated with old photographs of the owners' family. Another big plus is that it opens on Sundays until midnight!

🏠 Alameda Tietê, 184, Jardins
☎ 3081-3924
For more locations:
🌐 www.levin.com.br

Marcel Restaurante

Marcel, a specialist in all kind of soufflés, has a quiet, pleasant atmosphere. It's smoked salmon and filet au poivre are delicious! For those of you more daring and very "Frenchy," Marcel offers frog legs either as an appetizer or as a main dish. Once more, a great plus is that it opens on Sunday nights as well!

🏠 Rua da Consolação, 3555, Jardins
☎ 3064-3089
For more locations:
🌐 www.restaurantemarcel. com.br

Mercearia do Francês

Mostly French cuisine in a fun, relaxed atmosphere. The Mercearia do Francês has its own signature appetizers which consist of miniature "tapas," great for sharing among friends! With a very pleasant covered terrace, it is also one of the few good restaurants open on Sunday nights in São Paulo.

🏠 Rua Itacolomi, 636 Higienópolis
☎ 3214-1295

Hamburger

Good old hamburger has a new meaning in Brazil, not least because the cuts of meats are different. We would strongly suggest that you to take the plunge and go for the "unknown," for you almost certainly won't be disappointed!

Burguer & Bistro

Taking a vegetarian friend out for dinner and cannot decide which burger to have? Well, the choice is made easier as samplers are offered! A little more chic than the rest of the group.

🏠 Rua Bela Cintra, 1693, Jardins
☎ 3062-0643
🕐 Closed on Mondays.

General Prime Burger

Dealing with your teenager who is getting homesick? Don't hesitate to treat him or her to this cool place where hamburgers and hot dogs reign! Acclaimed chef Sergio Arno came up with the idea for this mix of fast food and high cuisine, which makes General Prime Burger not only a "must" for teenagers but for lovers of a good, tasty meal.

🏠 Rua Joaquim Floriano, 541, Itaim
☎ 3168-0833
🌐 www.primeburger.com.br

Hamburgueria Nacional

A cool place! Not only serves excellent burgers and different sandwiches, but also caters for those of us who pay attention to their waistlines! Fresh salads, tuna and meat are among the items offered. Provides a washroom facility for handicapped diners on the ground floor.

🏠 Rua Leopoldo Couto de Magalhães Jr., 822, Itaim

☎ 3073-0428

Lanchonete da Cidade

Very popular in Jardins, destination for all ages, and only a few steps away from Häagen-Dazs! Delivery service available.

🏠 Alameda Tietê, 110, Jardins

☎ 3086-3399

🌐 www.lanchonetedacidade. com.br

New Dog Hamburger

By the time you have done the rounds, you will realize that we truly are living in a global world!

🏠 Rua Joaquim Floriano, 254, Itaim

☎ 3168-7899

🌐 www.newdog.com.br

The Fifties

Delivery service. Another great hamburger joint.

🏠 Rua Tabapuã, 1100, Itaim

☎ 3168-6068

🌐 www.thefifties.com.br

International

Boa Bistrô e Bem-Estar

Good bistro and well-being, Boa Bistrô, in addition to its good food and healthy drinks, offers massages and relaxation. Worth checking out! Another good spot for eating "outdoors".

🏠 Rua Padre João Manoel, 950, Jardins

☎ 3082-5709

🌐 www.boabistro.com.br

L&T 's best!

Chakras

Getting tired of the hustle and bustle of São Paulo? Need to recharge your batteries to continue your shopping? Well, have we got the place for you! Walk two blocks north of Oscar Freire and step into a serene environment which will transport you to Thailand and where you will be able to savour the dishes "al fresco" without inhaling **Sampa**'s pollution.

Before being seated, you have the option of waiting for your guests or making that urgent last phone call from the bar area. Chakras' menu is more like a little book. Take the time to go through it, as a variety of cuisines are featured.

But that is not all of Chakras' charm! Some Sunday nights the chef will choose a movie that is shown on a big screen and he'll serve a special menu to reflect the theme of the film. Check on their web site for more info.

Should you decide to do a party, Chakras is a wonderful venue for that as well.

🏠 Rua Dr. Melo Alves, 294, Jardins

☎ 3062-8813 / cel. 8382-3579

🌐 www.chakras.com.br

Empório da Anita

Has a small shop where you can buy a few cooking utensils.

🏠 Rua Dr. Melo Alves, 498, Jardins

☎ 3061-3140

Empório Caffé Armani

A great way of taking a break while shopping in this fabulous store. Has a couple of tables outside. Food prepared by the Fasano group. Another great location is in the new section of Shopping Iguatemi.

🏠 Rua Haddock Lobo, 1568, Jardins

☎ 3897-9093

🌐 www.casafasano.com.br

Estação SP Design

Besides the restaurant you will find a "gourmet space" which could be rented should you wish to cook for your friends! Sells gifts, and decorative items.

🏠 Rua Haddock Lobo, 1012, Jardins

☎ 3898-2335

🌐 www.estacaospdesign.com.br

Estación Sur

Argentinian meat restaurant.

🏠 Alameda Joaquim Eugênio de Lima, 1396, Jardim Paulista

☎ 3885-0133

🌐 www.estacionsur.com.br

Fidel

🏠 Rua Haddock Lobo, 834, Jardins

☎ 3088-7850

www.fideljardins.com.br

Figueira Rubaiyat

This restaurant has an outdoor garden that was designed around 130 year old fig tree. Wednesday and Saturday they serve traditional *feijoada* for lunch, besides the regular menu. A must for anyone who does not plan to do much after this copious meal washed down by *caipirinha*! Dishes from the *feijoada* buffet both described in English and Portuguese.

🏠 Rua Haddock Lobo, 1738, Jardins

☎ 3063-3888

🌐 www.rubaiyat.com.br

From The Galley

New in the city and looking forward to meeting nice people? From The Galley is the perfect choice. You will be seated at a long rectangular table and in no time you will be exchanging phone numbers with fellow diners. A new concept in *Sampa*. Two tasting menus offered only: one with four dishes, one with eight. Excellent choice of wines offered at a reduced price. Should you be in the mood for dining "tête-à-tête" this option is also possible in the VIP room, which consists of a comfortable couch and a plasma T.V.! Total privacy, as your waiter will only appear at the touch of the calling button! The menu changes monthly. Great for private parties up to 26.

🏠 Rua Leopoldo Couto de Magalhães Jr., 761, Itaim

☎ 3073-0928

🌐 www.fromthegalley.com.br

In Città

Also caters.

⌂ Rua Dr. Melo Alves, 651,
Jardins

☎ 3063-5707

For more locations:

🌐 www.incitta.com.br

Mercearia do Conde

A fun place for lunch which
tends to be quite crowded.
Good contemporary cuisine
with some different specialties,
including Mexican.
Also carries fun gifts for sale.

⌂ Rua Joaquim Antunes, 217,
Pinheiros

☎ 3081-7204

🌐 www.merceariadoconde.
com.br

Parigi

One of the restaurants of the
Fasano family, Parigi has a dual
menu, French and Italian. Both
offer extremely well-prepared
dishes served in a casual, chic
atmosphere. The escalope of veal
(breaded) is better than those in
Italy. Leave room for the cheese,
as their trolley is one of the best!
Besides the dining room, you
have a choice of sitting in the
enclosed veranda – a rare
opportunity in São Paulo.

⌂ Rua Amauri, 275, Itaim

☎ 3167-1575

🌐 www.casafasano.com.br

Prêt Café

A small, charming place with a
covered outdoor space. Very good
continental food. Feels like home

cooking. Ideal for a relatively
quick lunch, buffet style.
The buffet changes every day.

⌂ Rua Bela Cintra, 2375,
Jardim Paulista

☎ 3085-8544

◷ Closed on Sundays.

Santo Grão

A great, busy place for lunch,
Santo Grão is one of the best
spots to take a break from shopping till you drop. It has a covered
outside patio and an indoor section. That is not all – you can
"join l'utile a l'agreable" and use
one of the two computers available. Serves fabulous cappuccinos
and Sunday brunches as well!

⌂ Rua Oscar Freire, 413, Jardins

☎ 3082-9969

🌐 www.santograo.com.br

Spot

Very popular, Spot is sure to
please any taste. Great for your
college kids who are visiting!

⌂ Alameda Min. Rocha
Azevedo, 72, Cerqueira César

☎ 3283-0946

🌐 www.restaurantespot.com.br

Terraço Itália

A tradicional bar/restaurant with
a full view of the city, live music
and tea served in the afternoon
(SEE ALSO UNDER HISTORICAL MONUMENTS
AT PAGE 21)

⌂ Itália Building
Av. Ipiranga, 344,
forty-first floor, Centro

☎ 3257-6566

🌐 www.terracoitalia.com.br

Z Deli

Are you homesick for your
favorite New York deli? Don't
be, as Z Deli will do the trick!

🏠 Alameda Lorena, 1689, Jardins

☎ 3088-5644

Italian

Cantina do Piero

Italian pasta, seafood, meat.

🏠 Rua Haddock Lobo, 728,
Jardins

☎ 3062-9635 / 3062-6918

🌐 www.cantinadopiero.com.br

Combinati

🏠 Rua Haddock Lobo, 855,
Jardins

☎ 3891-0244 / 3891-0254

🌐 www.combinati.com.br

Gero

Curious to see who is in town?
Want to be seen? Gero is the
place to go. Always packed,
reservations are a must.
It is part of the Fasano group.

🏠 Rua Haddock Lobo, 1629,
Jardins

☎ 3064-0005 / 3064-6317

🌐 www.casafasano.com.br

Gero Caffe

Gero Caffe has its own bustling
clientele, whether for lunch or
dinner.

🏠 Shopping Iguatemi
Av. Brig. Faria Lima, 2232,
Jardim Paulista

☎ 3813-8484

🌐 www.casafasano.com.br

Il Sogno di Anarello

Traditional Italian restaurant.

🏠 Rua Sogno di Anarello, 58,
Vila Mariana

☎ 5575-4266

Piselli

Good Italian neighborhood
restaurant. Brick oven pizza.

🏠 Rua Padre João Manoel, 1253,
Cerqueira César

☎ 3081-6043

🌐 www.piselli.com.br

Pomodori

Looking for a very pleasant,
intimate Italian restaurant? Look
no further, at Pomodori you are in
good hands. Beware, and don't fill
yourself on their antipasto plate,
(which is part of their couvert),
as more delicious dishes are yet
to come! It can also be reserved
for private parties.

🏠 Rua Dr. Renato Paes de
Barros, 534, Itaim

☎ 3168-3123

🌐 www.pomodori.com.br

Sallvattore

The Italian Trattoria "par
excellence", Sallvattore has a great
atmosphere. Extensive menu
with delicious and traditional
pasta dishes, and, yes, pizzas
cooked in a brick oven! Restrain
yourself when Italian-style pizza
bread is placed in front of you,
otherwise you might regret it!

🏠 Rua Salvador Cardoso, 131,
Vila Olímpia

☎ 3078-8686

🌐 www.sallvattore.com.br

Vecchio Torino

Is Italian food one of your favorites? Then Vecchio Torino will be as well! You will be dining in a very elegant atmosphere and will almost instantly savor the excellent cuisine by sampling the "couvert" offered. We suggest you ask for the tasting menu so you can enjoy the talents of Giuseppe, chef and owner, who will come to your table with a big jovial smile to make sure everything is alright. You can even phone in advance and request your favorite dishes!

📍 Rua Tavares Cabral, 119, Pinheiros

☎ 3816-0560

🕐 Closed on Mondays.

Via Blu Restaurant

Fun place for the whole family with good pizzas and traditional pasta dishes. Live music on Friday.

📍 Rua Lopes Neto, 247, Itaim

☎ 3078-8868

🌐 www.viablu.com

Vicolo Nostro

Enjoy your meal by yourself in the bar, beside the fire place or in the restaurant.

📍 Rua Jataituba, 29, Brooklin

☎ 5533-3096

🌐 www.vicolo.com.br

Japanese

As the Japanese community is large in São Paulo, you will find a great number of Japanese restaurants. Most of them are quite good, but of course some have that extra little "something". Some restaurants serve a "sushi rodízio" which can be quite fun. Waiters will keep coming with beautifully laid-out trays of sushi and other goodies, until you say "Please, no more."

Dhaigo

📍 Rua Araçari, 178, Itaim

☎ 3168-2819 / 3167-2086

🌐 www.dhaigo.com.br

Jam Warehouse

An exotic place built of bamboo and straw, features live music.

📍 Rua Lopes Neto, 308, Itaim

☎ 3079-4259

🌐 www.jamwarehouse.com.br

Japengo Shopping Iguatemi

Fun with the kids as you pick up your own ready-made plate from the conveyer belt. A nice break from the food court.

📍 Av. Brig. Faria Lima, 2232, ground floor, Jardim Paulista

☎ 3034-4080

🌐 For more locations: www.japengo.com.br

Jun Sakamoto

📍 Rua Lisboa, 55, Pinheiros

☎ 3088-6019

Kappa Garden

📍 Av. dos Imarés, 542, Moema

☎ 5041-8322 / 5092-3883

Koi

- Alameda Tietê, 360, Jardins
- 3083-4848
- For more locations:
  www.koi.com.br

Kosushi

- Rua Viradouro, 139, Itaim
- 3167-7272
- For more locations:
  www.kosushi.com.br

Mori Sushi

- Rua da Consolação, 3610,
  Jardins
- 3898-2977
- www.morisushi.com.br

Nagayama

Very fresh sushi along with excellent barbecued skewers and one of my favorite "Shabu-Shabu" in **Sampa**.

- Rua Bandeira Paulista, 369,
  Itaim
- 3079-7553
- For more locations:
  www.nagayama.com.br

Nakombi

Casual atmosphere in this place where two VW vans were transformed into food counters.

- Rua Pequetita, 170,
  Vila Olímpia
- 3845-9911 / 3845-1173
- For more locations:
  www.nakombi.com.br

Shintori

- Alameda Campinas, 600, Jardins
- 3283-2455
- www.shintori.com.br

Shundi & Tomodachi

Very creative, the chef always has specials, choice of tasting menus as well. Excellent sushi.

- Rua Dr. Mário Ferraz, 402,
  Vila Olímpia
- 3078-6852
- www.shundietomodachi.
  com.br

Sushimassa (Sushibar)

- Rua Haddock Lobo, 895,
  Jardins
- 3083-7306
- Closed on Sundays.

Lebanese

One of the biggest foreign communities in São Paulo, the Lebanese have greatly influenced all aspects of Brazilian culture. Arabic food is plentiful, from the very casual to more sophisticated. Little cafés are scattered all over the city; don't be fooled by their modest looks, as the quality is quite good and the food authentic.

Very good Lebanese caterers are available should you decide to go ethnic! In addition to specialized food stores, most supermarkets sell arabic ingredients, prepared foods and desserts!

Abu-zuz

A very casual place in the heart of the downtown business district. Don't be "put off" by the lack of "décor," just go there and enjoy the authentic Lebanese cuisine and delicious sandwiches. Perfect choice if pressed for time!

Rua Miller, 622/624, Brás

3315-9694

Almanara

Almanara serves one of the best grilled filet mignon on skewers (Shish Kebab) as well as other Lebanese delicacies! It does get pretty crowded, therefore try and go on the early side. All locations maintain the same standards.

Rua Oscar Freire, 523, Jardins

3085-6916

For more locations:
www.almanara.com.br

Arábia

Rua Haddock Lobo, 1397, Jardins

3061-2203

For more locations:
www.arabia.com.br

Arguile

Alameda Santos, 1187, Jardins

3287-3291

www.arguile.com.br

Baalbek

Alameda Lorena, 1330, Jardins

3088-4820

Brasserie Victoria

Av. Pres. Juscelino Kubitschek, 545, Itaim

3845-8897

www.brasserievictoria.com.br

Casa Garabed

Catching a late flight and worried about where to eat? Not a problem – Casa Garabed closes at 9 pm, is on the way to Guarulhos International Airport and will serve you a fabulous Lebanese meal in a clean, unpretentious atmosphere. Arrive early and take your time!

Rua José Margarido, 216, Santana

6976-2750

www.casagarabed.com.br

Folha de Uva

Rua Bela Cintra, 1435, Jardins

3062-2564

www.folhadeuva.com

Jaber

"Lanchonete" type where you can sit, it does great meat pies and provides take away. Its *esfihas* are among the best, as they're always recommended by "Veja" magazine's yearly guide of top restaurants.

Rua Morgado de Mateus, 173, Vila Mariana

5083-7083

For more locations:
www.jaber.com.br

Miski Restaurante e Rotisserie

An all round high-quality Lebanese restaurant, Miski offers a full take out service. On Wednesdays and Saturdays, in addition to the regular a la carte, they serve a limited buffet, with the traditional "Mouloukhie," a green vegetable soup served with chicken, rice and meat. Worth a try!

Alameda Joaquim Eugênio de Lima, 1690, Jardins

3884-3193

Tâmara

⌂ Alameda Santos, 1518, Jardins
☎ 3288-1248

Tenda do Nilo

Excellent home cooking, Tenda do Nilo is a cozy restaurant run by two very joyful sisters, who greet you as if they have known you all your life. Has its regular clientele, so don't be surprised if the wait is a little long. But trust us, it is well worth it! Specials every day. Dishes available for take out, with some notice.

⌂ Rua Coronel Oscar Porto, 638, Paraíso
☎ 3885-0460
◔ Closed on Sundays and dinners.

Light Food

Forneria San Paolo

Serves sandwiches and regular meals, probably one of the most casual of the Fasano group.

⌂ Rua Amauri, 319, Itaim
☎ 3078-0099
⊕ www.casafasano.com.br

Oliviers & Co

Light food for lunch, it has a wonderful display of virgin oils, spices, etc. A delight to whoever enjoys cooking, and adjacent to L'Occitane (SEE UNDER BEAUTY AT PAGE 140)

⌂ Rua Bela Cintra, 2023, Jardim Paulista
☎ 3088-9008
⊕ For more locations: www.oliviers-co.com.br

Mediterranean

A Bela Sintra

The "new" version of Antiquarius, A Bela Sintra has very much the feel of a cool N.Y. restaurant.

⌂ Rua Bela Cintra, 2325, Jardins
☎ 3891-0740 / 3891-1090
⊕ www.abelasintra.com.br

Amadeus

Mainly seafood, Amadeus has a very pleasant atmosphere.

⌂ Rua Haddock Lobo, 807, Jardins
☎ 3061-2859 / 3088-1792
⊕ www.restauranteamadeus. com.br

L&T's best!

Antiquarius

In our view, Antiquarius is a real treat. The atmosphere, the decor, the food and the service are amongst the best São Paulo has to offer. It serves traditional Portuguese cuisine with a continental flair. If you are in no mood for *bacalhau* (cod), try the duck risotto. Make sure you leave room for dessert, as, they too, are not to be missed! With an excellent choice of wines, Antiquarius is a must for any special occasion or just for "impressing your visitors from out of town!" By the way, should you wish, an English menu is supplied upon demand.

⌂ Alameda Lorena, 1884, Jardins
☎ 3064-8686
⊕ www.antiquarius.com.br

Don Curro

Spanish food, paella.

⌂ Rua Alves Guimarães, 230,
Pinheiros

☎ 3062-4712

⊕ www.restaurantedoncurro.
com.br

Oba Restaurante

Spanish food.

⌂ Rua Dr. Melo Alves, 205, Jardins

☎ 3086-4774

Pizza

Most pizza places will also
cater a pizza party at your place
– complete with pizza oven,
waiters & sodas!

A Tal da Pizza

⌂ Rua Meandro, 430,
Granja Viana

☎ 4612-0198

⊕ http://restaurantes1.com.br/
ataldapizza/

Camelo

One of the most traditional thin
crust pizzas, it also delivers.

⌂ Rua Pamplona, 1873,
Jardim Paulista

☎ 3887-0702

⊕ For more locations:
www.pizzariacamelo.com.br

Casa Bráz

Considered the best pizza in São
Paulo – medium crust. Delivers.

⌂ Rua Graúna, 125, Moema

☎ 5561-1736 / 5561-0905
For more locations:

⊕ www.casabraz.com.br

Casa da Pizza

Delivery service.

⌂ Rua Brasília, 90, Itaim

☎ 3077-0010

⊕ www.casapizza.com.br

La Gloria

⌂ Av. Macuco, 685, Moema

☎ 5051-5329

⊕ www.lagloriapizzabar.com.br

Leona

Close to Congonhas Airport.
Features live music, three floors
and delivers in the same
neighborhood.

⌂ Rua Constantino de Souza,
582, Campo Belo

☎ 5096-3000

⊕ www.leonapizzabar.com.br

Pizzaria Cristal

⌂ Rua Prof. Artur Ramos, 551,
Jardim Paulistano

☎ 3031-0828

Pizzaria Zi Tereza

⌂ Av. Vereador José Diniz, 3401,
Campo Belo

☎ 5044-8436

Primo Basílico

The hot spot on Sunday nights.
Delivery service.

⌂ Alameda Gabriel Monteiro da
Silva, 1864, Jardim Paulistano

☎ 3082-8027

Santa Pizza

⌂ Rua Harmonia, 117,
Vila Madalena

☎ 3816-7848

⊕ www.santapizza.com.br

templates for weekends

One of the toughest things to do when moving to a new city is to find fun and interesting programs for the weekend. Inevitably, every time we moved, no matter which continent or city we were in, my husband would turn to me and ask: "What are we doing, any plans this weekend?," expecting, of course, an affirmative answer.

More so, I was given the glorious title of "social director." Never mind trying your best to "get by" throughout the week, the fact of the matter is you've got to think of something in order to keep everyone happy. If you have children, somehow things are a little easier, as they get to make friends and start socializing early in the game.

The beauty about living in São Paulo is that you don't have to go away for the whole weekend; you can take day trips and enjoy the change of scenery, which is quite striking as soon as you exit the city. We have put together a few options within a reasonable distance of **Sampa**, and a few further away. Please keep in mind that traffic, especially on the way back on Sundays, is quite heavy.

Your best guide to any outing (*passeio*) is **Guia 4 Rodas**' "Fim de semana", published by Abril. Also please regularly check newspapers' and magazines' weekly guides (SEE UNDER MAPS AND GUIDES AT PAGE 68). Don't wait till you become fluent in Portuguese as this will truly help you learn!

We felt that in addition to all of the options below, we should recommend a few places which require taking a plane. Brazil wouldn't be Brazil without the Foz do Iguaçu (Falls of Iguaçu), Salvador in Bahia, Rio de Janeiro, Búzios and the Amazon, of course, to name a few places you must see (SEE TRAVEL AGENCIES AT PAGE 137).

Flights within Brazil are numerous. Keep in mind that, whenever there is a holiday, a minimum night's stay is required and you will find that prices often go up. It is not a bad idea to stay in the city, as São Paulo gets very quiet over certain holidays, such as *Carnaval*, and this is a delight. A good idea when you are planning an overnight stay is to pack a box of tissues, as for some reason hotels rarely provide them!

Weekends out of town

ARAÇARIGUAMA
Rancho 53
40 minutes from São Paulo, with access by Rodovia Presidente Castelo Branco, km 53. If you would like to really impress your visitors, especially if you have just moved in, take them there for lunch. For a "Fado" (typical Portuguese dance) presentation,

make sure to book at least two weeks in advance. Only locals know this place, which serves the traditional Portuguese fish *bacalhau* (cod) in many different ways.

🏠 Rua Nossa Senhora da Penha, 1, Bairro Honda, Araçariguama

☎ 11 4136-1381

ATIBAIA

A short 67 km from São Paulo, Atibaia is easily accessible by Rodovia Fernão Dias. Known for its strawberries, its equestrian ranches (Hípica Nashville and Estância Park Atibaia) and its production of artisanal carpets, Atibaia has beautiful scenery and is a quiet serene town. A great outing for your out-of-town visitors. A hotel outside Atibaia worth checking out is Unique Garden in Mairiporã (Estrada Laramara, 3500, tel. 11 4486-8700, www.uniquegarden.com.br). A good place for lunch is Restaurante Francês (Rodovia Fernão Dias, km 7, Vargem, tel. for reservation: 11 4598-4429).

🌐 www.atibaia.com.br

BROTAS

For extreme sports such as rafting, cascading, tree-top walking, horseback riding. There are 35 waterfalls in the area. A good idea would be to have a travel agency prepare the whole trip for you.

🌐 www.brotas.com.br

CAMPINAS

One of the biggest urban cities in Brazil and one of the important economic centers in South America, not least due to the University of Campinas (Unicamp), which plays an important role in the life of the city.

🌐 www.campinas.sp.gov.br

CAMPOS DO JORDÃO

You will feel transported to Europe! Charming small mountain town which gets crowded during the winter months of July and August. In July, don't miss the classical music festival. Make sure you buy your tickets way in advance, as this is a very popular event. As for your stay, try the traditional Grande Hotel Campos do Jordão (tel. 12 3668-6000, www.sp.senac.br/hoteis).

🌐 www.camposdojordao.com.br

EMBU DAS ARTES

Small town about 45 minutes out of São Paulo, it has weekly artisanal fairs (SEE ANTIQUE MARKETS AT PAGE 74). Some antique shops, art galleries and rustic furniture. In the mood for German or Brazilian food? Try Restaurante O Garimpo (Rua da Matriz, 136, tel. 11 4704-6344, www.ogarimpo.com).

🌐 www.embu.com.br

The town is alive during the weekends; most shops are closed on Mondays.

GUARUJÁ

Although one and a half hours from **Sampa**, on a warm summer day Guarujá is a good spot, should you wish to lunch facing the sea. One of its major attractions is a huge aquarium, with over 700 different fish species. Try the delicious fish at Rufino's (Av. Miguel Stefano, 4795, tel. 13 3351-5771) or at Dalmo Bárbaro (Av. Miguel Stefano, 4751, tel. 13 3351-9298, www.dalmobarbaro.com.br).

🌐 www.guaruja.com.br

HOLAMBRA

149 km out of São Paulo, easily accessible by Rodovia dos Bandeirantes and Rodovia Dom Pedro I, this is the place to go with the whole family. A small city which was colonized by Dutch immigrants, Holambra produces 35% of the flowers sold in the country and hosts an extremely beautiful fair called Expoflora, which starts the last week of August and goes till the third week of September. During the year, visit its floral shops and experience the true Dutch cuisine.

🌐 www.holambra.tur.br

ILHA DO CARDOSO

308 km away from **Sampa**. For true nature lovers who do not care much about luxury. Bird-watching, monkeys, turtles, fish. Ten beaches, treks, 1,800-meter high mountains, waterfalls. From here you can take an excursion to Cananéia (www.cananet.com.br), where the bay dolphins get close to swimmers. On Cardoso Island you can stay at Pousada Ilha do Cardoso (www.cananet.com.br/pousadailhadocardoso), a very simple place. In Cananéia, you can stay at Costa Azul Club (tel. 13 3851-1489) or Hotel Marazul (tel. 13 3851-1407).

ITAPECERICA DA SERRA
Viktoria Garten

37 km away from São Paulo, a charming hotel with numerous facilities and different kinds of alternative therapies and stress treatment.

🏠 Estrada Benedito Pereira de Borba, 1340, Itapecerica da Serra

☎ 11 4147-1467

🌐 www.viktoriagarten.com.br

ITATIBA
Hotel Fazenda Dona Carolina

About 86 km away from São Paulo. An old coffee farm, the Fazenda Dona Carolina has been turned into a charming hotel. Rooms are very well appointed with the Portuguese colonial flair. Good international cuisine. Swimming and recreational activities such as horseback riding, tennis, cycling and fishing.

🏠 Estrada Manoel Stefani, km 39,5 da Rod. Itatiba-Bragança

☎ 11 4534-9100

🌐 www.donacarolina.com.br

ITU

About 100 km from São Paulo, accessible by Rodovia Presidente Castelo Branco. Definitely worth a visit, Itu is a nice little town with some antique shops and a German restaurant, Steiner, which opened in 1902, and has been in the hands of the family for four generations. Its most famous dish is the filet parmesan, which attracts people from other cities and causes line-ups over the weekends! It's so big it is enough to feed a batallion! This might be a reflection of what the city is famous for: everything is big here. Check out the phone booth, you won't be able to miss it. Anytime a *Paulista* sees something huge the question is: "Does this come from Itu?"

🌐 www.itu.com.br

Alberto Coimbra Antiguidades e Demolições

📍 Praça Padre Anchieta, 80, Centro
☎ 11 4013-0443

Antiquário e Bar Passado & Presente's

📍 Rua Bom Jesus, 72 / Praça Padre Anchieta, Centro
☎ 11 4022-0828

Bar do Alemão Steiner

If you go here for lunch, it is advisable to arrive on the "early side", to avoid a 50-minute wait.

📍 Rua Paula Souza, 575, Centro
☎ 11 4022-4284
🌐 www.bardoalemaodeitu.com.br

Fazenda Capoava

Close to Itu, about 97 km from São Paulo, Fazenda Capoava has many activities to enjoy.

📍 Estrada do Pedregulho, Bairro do Pedregulho
☎ 11 4023-0903
🌐 www.fazendacapoava.com.br

Fazenda Santo Antonio da Bela Vista

📍 Estrada do Jacu, 118
☎ 11 4023-1335 (reservation required)
🌐 www.belavistafazenda.com.br

JUQUITIBA

This would be the ideal place to go should you want to experience river rafting. Located about 74 km from São Paulo. Accessible by Rodovia Régis Bittencourt.

🌐 www.juquitiba.com

LITORAL NORTE

The beauty and relative proximity to São Paulo make the Litoral Norte (North Coast) an extremely popular destination during the summer months (December-February). You can rent a condo or a house equipped with a pool for the month of January. Try to avoid, at all costs, coming back the eve of the first school day, as the traffic is truly unbearable. Remember that the sun in this part of the world is not what you might be used to, so a very high factor sun lotion is recommended.

Also have available an insect repellent and an anti-itch cream should you get bitten.

The North Coast has a spread of beautiful beaches. Starting from Bertioga, you will go through many beach towns, amongst them Juqueí, Barra do Sahy, Barra do Una, all the way until you reach Ilhabela. We strongly recommend spending at least one night as it takes about 3 hours to reach Juqueí. It is a quaint little town which reminded me a lot of "Juan-les-Pins" in the South of France. Many good restaurants, good beach shopping, but most of all a clear, clean ocean, with an unbelievably warm temperature during the summer months. A pure delight and the best way to recharge your batteries! Whenever you have the opportunity, try to explore all the beaches.

MOGI-MIRIM
Solar das Andorinhas
Farmhouse-type hotel for relaxing. Has a water park, golf field, sauna, game room and game fields.
- Rodovia Campinas-Mogi-Mirim, km 121
- 19 3757-2700
- www.solardasandorinhas.com.br

MONTE VERDE
177 km from São Paulo. Accessible by Rodovia Fernão Dias until Camanducaia, then another 32 km of unfortunately poorly-paved roads, and the last 14 not paved at all! Strongly advisable to use a 4 x 4, or to avoid a rainy day. The poor roads are on purpose in order to avoid crowds. An ideal outing for cold days, as you can savour the fondues, raclettes and chocolates. Various attractions, such as horse-back riding, walking trails, excursions in jeeps, and... ice-skating! Many good hotels, such as Kuriuwa (tel. 35 3438-1959, http://kuriuwahotel.com.br).
- www.monteverdemg.com.br

The temperature here can go down as far as -10°C.

PARATI
305 km by Rodovias Ayrton Senna and Carvalho Pinto, then take Rodovia dos Tamoios until Caraguatatuba, following Rodovia Rio-Santos. Parati, in the state of Rio de Janeiro, was founded in the 16th century. It is a colonial style village by the sea, with cobble-stones and lots of cozy restaurants and handicraft shops. An international literary event takes place there every year (www.flip.org.br), gathering many important writers from around the world. The best beaches are a bit far off, like Ponta Negra, do Sono and dos Antigos. If you are a fan of scuba-diving, the bay of Parati is one of the best in the country. You can also rent a boat and go around the islands. Another option, should you get seasick, is to go trekking on the Golden Trail which was built in the

18th century, with the purpose of bringing gold from the mines of Minas Gerais to be sent to Portugal through the port of Parati. A pousada worth checking out is Pardieiro, owned by famous actor Paulo Autran (tel. 24 3371-1370, www.pousadapardieiro.com.br).
🌐 www.paraty.com.br

PENEDO

283 km from São Paulo, between the states of Rio de Janeiro, São Paulo and Minas Gerais. Access by Rodovias Ayrton Senna, Carvalho Pinto and Dutra. Penedo was founded by Finnish immigrants who created the first Brazilian sauna, called Finnish sauna. The Nordic culture has left imprints in the local architecture, gastronomy and culture. A very interesting place for excursions to Morungaba, Visconde de Mauá, and Itatiaia, which is an ecological reserve and the oldest park in Brazil. Stay at the hotel Pequena Suécia (tel. 24 3351-1094, www.pequenasuecia.com.br).
🌐 www.penedo.com

SÃO ROQUE
Quinta dy Engenho

Traditional ranch house, set in extensive grounds in the hills above a small town. It is a very friendly place, run by the family, that gives excellent service and pays great attention to detail. The house has been tastefully redeco-rated while still keeping its character. The rooms are large and comfortable, and the restaurant serves excellent food and has a fine atmosphere. Close to the house are gardens, a swimming pool with a bar, and a building housing an "ofuro," which has a view down the valley, and is highly recommended for a relaxing experience. This is a terrific venue to just get away from it all, to take the family for a break, or for a romantic weekend. For business people, the house has conference facilities and can accommodate large parties.

📍 Estrada da Fonte,
   Vila Darci Penteado
☎ 11 4714-0760
🌐 www.quintadyengenho.
   com.br

SÃO FRANCISCO XAVIER

157 km away from São Paulo. A recommended venue for couples who wish to spend a quiet, simple weekend amidst what is left of the "Mata Atlântica" forest, which covers the chain of mountains along the Atlantic coast. One can trek from São Francisco Xavier to Monte Verde. Two different treks available take about 2 hours. You can stay at Pousada A Rosa e o Rei, located 15 km from the village, with its very natural style, or at Serra do Luar or Chapéu de Palha. The whole region of São Francisco and Penedo has excellent trout to catch or to eat.

Things to do at the weekend in **Sampa**

1. Take the metro with the kids to **Liberdade** (SEE UNDER NEIGHBOR-HOODS AT PAGE 32), check out the shops and have some divine sushi!

2. Take the children for a real American brunch at **Sofitel Hotel** (Rua Sena Madureira, 1355, Ibirapuera, tel. 5087-0800, www.accorhotels.com. br). There's a separate dining area for kids with monitors to watch them while Mom & Dad enjoy a Bloody Mary! Drive down to Ibirapuera Park, check out the latest exhibit at the MAM or, if the sun is shining, just enjoy the park.

3. Go to **Cia. Dos Bichos** off Raposo Tavares, at Estrada da Capuava, 2990, tel. 4703-3548, www.ciadosbichos.com.br. A mini farm that includes a petting zoo and a restaurant – it's fun for the whole family! Then have a pizza at the famous **A Tal da Pizza** (see page 129) Rua Meandro, 430. Granja Viana, Cotia, S.P. Tel. (11) 4612-0198

4. Go to the snake museum at **Butantã** and then have Chinese food at **Ton Hoi**. Av. Professor Francisco Morato, 1484. Tel. 3721-3268 www.tonhoi.com.br

5. Have waffles at **Santo Grão** (SEE UNDER RESTAURANTS AT PAGE 114), while you check the *Vejinha* magazine for theaters, movies and events going on, in and around São Paulo.

6. Get up early, drive to the **São Paulo Zoo** (SEE OUTINGS AT PAGE 103) and enjoy the animals. But don't snack, for you will be lunching at the famous churrascaria **Fogo de Chão** (SEE RESTAURANTS AT PAGE 114). Make sure you have no dinner plans that night!

7. Put on your most comfortable walking shoes, park at Rua Fidalga, have lunch at **Martin Fierro** or **Jacaré art**. Then visit galleries Fortes Vilaça and Millan Antonio (SEE ART GALLERIES AT PAGE 90).

8. Do not eat any breakfast. Take the metro to **Mercado Municipal** (SEE UNDER HISTORICAL MONUMENTS AT PAGE 21). For an added adventure, have "brunch as you go," sampling all the delicacies they have to offer (*mortadela* sandwiches, *pastéis de bacalhau*). Visit all the stands and buy your groceries for the week. Recruit your kids to carry your bags and reward them with a fresh pineapple on a stick!

9. Take the metro to the **Pinacoteca** (SEE UNDER MUSEUMS AT PAGE 94), enjoy the exhibits, and have a coffee outside facing Parque da Luz. If you still have some energy left, visit the Estação da Luz and have lunch at the Mercado Municipal.

10. Have brunch at either the Emiliano, Fasano or the Renaissance Hotel. Visit **Luisa Strina Art Gallery** on Oscar Freire, walk down to Dan Gallery on the corner of Estados Unidos and Haddock Lobo, continue to Galeria Nara Rosler and Thomas Cohn (SEE ART GALLERIES AT PAGE 90).

11. On Sunday, check out the **flea market** next to **MASP**, have lunch at the Figueira and continue to the antique fair at MuBE (SEE ANTIQUES AT PAGE 74).

12. Rent a small sailboat at **Interlagos** and have brunch at the Transamerica Hotel.

13. Go to **Casa da Fazenda** (Av. Morumbi, 5594, tel. 3742-2810) for lunch and make an afternoon of it. A great place to go with the family as they have monitors to play with the children and usually something fun going on in the gazebo.

14. Have lunch at **Charlô** or **Merceria** at the **Jockey Club** (SEE E QUESTRIAN CLUBS AT PAGE 204). Place some bets and let the kids play in the playground in front of the race track.

travel agencies

GPS Turismo
🏠 Rua Oscar Freire, 2066, Jardins
📞 3088-1311
🌐 www.gpsturismo.com.br

Prime Tour
A very high-end agency which designs trips within Brazil and overseas. With 17 years of experience, Prime Tour is a member of the Virtual Group since 1999, whose members are amongst the best luxury travel agencies in the world. Nothing is spared and satisfaction is guaranteed as the profile of each client is studied in great detail in order to provide an unforgettable vacation!
🏠 Av. Paulista, 171, fifth floor, Paraíso
📞 3178-4760
🌐 www.primetour.com.br

Teresa Perez
Teresa Perez prides itself in organizing the most interesting trips overseas (from São Paulo) with an emphasis on attention to details, finding exquisite accommodations, and making sure that her customers come back over and over again for more!
🏠 Av. Brig. Faria Lima, 1982, thirteenth floor, Jardim Paulista
📞 3365-4000
🌐 www.teresaperez.com.br

Top Level
A full, reliable service for private clients and corporative accounts. Lynne Logullo, an American who has lived here for over 30 years, can attend to all your travel needs. She is extremely efficient, paying attention to all details from hiring a bodyguard to providing an English speaking guide. Expertise in handling travel plans to any destination in the world including, of course, Brazil.
🏠 Rua Barão do Triunfo, 464, first floor, Brooklin
📞 5536-9300
🌐 www.topleveltur.com.br

Personal

beauty

Beauty Supplies

Gianini's

⌂ Rua São Florêncio, 196, Penha
☎ 6684-1634
🌐 www.gianini.com.br

Ikesaki

Three whole floors of cosmetics, perfumes and beauty stuffs for a good price.
⌂ Rua Galvão Bueno, 37, Liberdade
☎ 3346-6944
🌐 www.ikesaki.com.br

Day Spa

Clínica Amarynthe

Inside Daslu store.
⌂ Av. Chedid Jafet, 131, third floor, Vila Olímpia
☎ 3841-8250
🌐 www.amarynthe.com.br

Kyron Day Spa

⌂ Shopping Iguatemi
   Av. Brig. Faria Lima, 2232, Jardim Paulistano
☎ 3095-3000
🌐 www.kyron.com.br

Hairdressers

Most beauty salons offer facials, hair removal and make-up services. Although some customers do not book in advance, appointments are strongly recommended.

L&T's best!

Ash

Beto da Silva had a dream which he was able to transform into reality (something quite challenging to do in **Sampa**), and that was to open his very own, unique beauty salon in São Paulo. However, this is not your typical beauty salon– it is more like something you would see either in Los Angeles or in Asia. From the minute you step into this old house – kept intact on the outside but totally remodelled on the inside, except for the elevator, which is genuinely an antique –, you feel you are transported into another world.

The atmosphere is indeed unique: besides the very clean and crisp decor and the separate wing for men, you will find a beautiful garden where one can relax enjoying a glass of Moet et Chandon or a light snack. Beto has managed to get the very best professionals from all areas of the beauty industry. From hairdressing to manicure, pedicure, facials and massages, to name a few. A perfect gift to give to someone who needs pampering, and who would like to get away from the "hustle and bustle" of São Paulo.
⌂ Rua Colômbia, 229, Jardim Paulista
☎ 3085-1648

Iracema Cabeleireiros
🏠 Rua Padre João Manoel,
740, Jardins
☎ 3082-2935

Jacques Janine
🏠 Rua Augusta, 2799, Jardins
☎ 3082-6133 / 3064-5805
🌐 For more locations:
www.jacquesjanine.com.br

Jean Louis David
🏠 Rua Haddock Lobo, 608, Jardins
☎ 3898-1132
🌐 jeanlouisdavidhaddock.com.br

M.G. Hair Design
🏠 Rua Estados Unidos, 1838,
Jardins
☎ 3061-1499 / 3068-9035

Studio
🏠 Shopping Iguatemi
Av. Brig. Faria Lima, 2232,
Jardim Paulista
☎ 3094-2640

Perfume stores and make-up
Beauty products for the face and body.

Anna Pegova
Beauty products and treatments.
🏠 Alameda Lorena,1582, Jardins
☎ 3081-2402
🌐 For more locations:
www.annapegova.com.br

Gaudi
Presents, perfumes, crystal.
🏠 Rua Normandia, 97, Moema

☎ 5535-6500
🌐 www.gaudila.com.br

L´Occitane en Provence
Boutique and spa. Soaps, lotions, creams, colognes, dried herbs, candles and gifts.
🏠 Rua Bela Cintra, 2023, Jardins
☎ 3088-9008
🌐 For more locations:
www.loccitane.com.br

Mac
A replica of the stores abroad, but don't forget, at higher prices.
🏠 Shopping Iguatemi
Av. Brig. Faria Lima, 2232,
third floor, Jardim Paulista
☎ 3815-5011
🌐 www.maccosmetic.com

Victor Perfumes Cosméticos
🏠 Rua Augusta, 2829, Cerqueira
César
☎ 3082-3956

Oruam
🏠 Rua Barão de Itapetininga, 88,
store 8, Centro
☎ 3256-5703
🌐 For more locations:
www.oruam.com.br

Sete Cosmetics
🏠 Alameda Lorena, 1879, Jardins
☎ 3063-5780
🌐 For more locations:
www.setecosmetics.com.br

Top Internacional
🏠 Rua Oscar Freire, 979, Jardins
☎ 3064-0383

Podologist

Rosi Severo

One of the best podologists, Rosi is extremely professional. After her pedicure, you will want to be in sandals constantly!

☎ cel. 9916-0354

education

Nursery schools

These are all bilingual schools.

Away with Words

🏠 Rua Mourato Coelho, 87, Pinheiros

☎ 3081-2455

🌐 www.awaywithwords.com.br.

Global Me

🏠 Rua Colômbia, 66, Jardins

☎ 3085-9662

🌐 www.globalme.com.br

Kid's Corner

St. Paul's Church.

🏠 Rua Comendador Elias Zarzur, 1239, Alto da Boa Vista

☎ 5523-7121

Playpen

🏠 Praça Prof. Américo de Moura, 101, Cidade Jardim

☎ 3812-9122

🌐 www.playpen.com.br

Talk Kids

🏠 Rua Bento de Andrade, 84, Ibirapuera

☎ 3886-9010

🌐 www.talkkids.com.br

Tots and Teens

🏠 Rua Nove de Julho, 283, Alto da Boa Vista

☎ 0800 11 38 38 / 5548-2828

🌐 www.totsandteens.com.br

Wings to Fly

🏠 Rua Chabad, 71, Jardins

☎ 3062-6517 / 3083-6592

🌐 www.wingstofly.com.br

Private schools

American

Chapel International School

(Escola Maria Imaculada)

🏠 Rua Vigário João Pontes, 537, Chácara Flora

☎ 2101-7400

🌐 www.chapelschool.com

Graded School

🏠 Av. Giovanni Gronchi, 4710, Morumbi

☎ 3747-4800

🌐 www.graded.br

Pan American Christian Academy

🏠 Rua Cássio de Campos Nogueira, 393, Jardim das Imbuias

☎ 5928-9655

🌐 www.paca.com.br

British

St. Francis College

🏠 Rua Bélgica, 399, Jardim Europa

☎ 3082-7640

🌐 www.stfrancis.com.br

St. Nicholas School

British school for kids from 2 to 18 years old. Also provides adequate Brazilian studies for Ensino Fundamental & Ensino Médio.

🌐 Rua do Emissário, 333, Pinheiros
☎ 3814-1355
🌐 www.stnicholas.com.br

St. Paul's School

British curriculum.

🌐 Rua Juquiá, 166, Jardim Paulistano
☎ 3085-3399
🌐 www.stpauls.br

French
Lycée Pasteur

🌐 Rua Vergueiro, 3799, Vila Mariana
☎ 5574-7822
🌐 www.flp-sp.com.br

Spanish
Colégio Miguel de Cervantes

🌐 Av. Jorge João Saad, 905, Morumbi
☎ 3779-1800
🌐 www.cmc.com.br

German
Colégio Humboldt

🌐 Av. Eng. Alberto Kuhlmann, 525, Interlagos
☎ 5685-6664
🌐 www.humboldt.com.br

Colégio Porto Seguro

🌐 Rua Floriano Peixoto Santos, 55, Morumbi
☎ 3749-3250
🌐 www.portoseguro.org.br

Escola Suíço-Brasileira

🌐 Rua Visconde de Porto Seguro, 391, Alto da Boa Vista
☎ 5548-6672
🌐 www.esbsp.com.br

Brazilian
Colégio Dante Alighieri

Curriculum includes Italian class.

🌐 Alameda Jaú, 1061, Jardins
☎ 3179-4400

Colégio Pio XII

🌐 Rua Colégio Pio XII, 233, Morumbi
☎ 3759-5050
🌐 www.pioxiicolegio.com.br

Colégio Pueri Domus

Brazilian and American school.

🌐 Rua Verbo Divino, 993-A, Chácara Santo Antônio
☎ 5182-2155
🌐 For more locations: www.pueridomus.br

Dutch
Escola Holandesa

🌐 Rua Job Lane, 1030, Jardim Petrópolis - Alto da Boa Vista
☎ 5522-9811
email: nedschoolsp@uol.com.br

Italian
Escola Italiana Eugenio Montale

🌐 Rua Dr. José Gustavo Busch, 75, Parque Morumbi - São Paulo
☎ 3759-5959

Private tutors

Besides language schools, which are numerous, you can have a tutor come to your home for a private lesson, if you wish to learn faster, and in a more comfortable setting. The lessons at home are much more productive, as the learning is customized. The ideal situation is to find teachers who speak more than one language besides Portuguese, though it is not needed. Keep in mind that a good rapport between teacher and student is crucial. Before making a decision, interview them and ask about their methods, in order to determine what will work best for you. Do not forget that most companies already have on staff a chosen teacher who might just be a perfect fit! The language schools offer "at home" services as well, but at higher costs, therefore it is more beneficial to recruit independently.

Airamaia
Private portuguese classes.
☎ 3225-9897 / cel. 9398-8322

Connie Gonzalez
Interpreter – Portuguese, English and French.
☎ cel. 9335-8606
🌐 connieworld@terra.com.br

Gisele Damha
Portuguese and English.
☎ cel. 9245-7228
🌐 gidamha@yahoo.com.br

Maria Augusta Machado
English, Spanish, French and Portuguese.
☎ cel. 7123-3408
🌐 sequeiramam@gmail.com

Specialty schools

Art and Craft classes
Atelieart
Different painting techniques, from patina to marmorization. Mosaic classes also available.
📍 Rua Manoel da Nóbrega, 673, Paraíso
☎ 3885-5656
🌐 www.atelieart.com.br

Ateliê Olaria Paulistana
Ceramic painting and clay modelling classes.
📍 Rua Mourato Coelho, 1433, Vila Madalena
☎ 3031-5294
🌐 www.olariapaulistana.com.br

Barro Blanco Artesanato
Ceramic painting classes.
📍 Rua Alves Guimarães, 108, Pinheiros
☎ 3085-8649

Ki Ki Kits
Patchwork, painting on wood, doll making, and embroidery.
📍 Av. Brig. Faria Lima, 2152, first floor, Jardim Paulista
☎ 3031-6195 / 5686-1022
🌐 www.kikikits.com.br

Lygia Mello Franco
Needlepoint classes.
📍 Rua Diogo de Quadros, 235, Brooklin
☎ 5182-3357
🌐 www.anacordeiro.com.br

Quadrifoglio
Offers painting classes on canvas,

fabric, ceramic, glass, also mosaic.
◉ Rua Normandia, 25, Moema
☎ 5094-1864
⊕ www.quadrifoglioarte.com.br

Language schools
FOR TRANSLATION SEE PAGE **64**.

Berlitz
◉ Rua Joaquim Floriano,
   1052, Itaim
☎ 3089-5290
⊕ For more locations:
   www.berlitz.com.br

Alliance Française
◉ Rua Bela Cintra, 1737, Jardins
☎ 3062-9013
⊕ For more locations:
   www.aliancafrancesa.com.br

Alumni
◉ Rua Padre João Manoel,
   319, Jardins
☎ 3067-5322
⊕ For more locations:
   www.alumni.org.br

Music lessons
Núcleo de Ensino Musical
◉ Rua José Maria Lisboa, 921,
   Jardins
☎ 3889-9084
⊕ www.music-center.art.br

fitness

Fitness clubs
Paulistanos are very serious about
their physical fitness and one is
spoiled for choice, as fitness clubs
are numerous. The large clubs ask
for a yearly medical exam which
can either be done on the premises or at your own doctor. You
might find this a nuisance, but
let us assure you the time spent
is well worth it. Physical trainers
are available upon request and
keep an eye on what is going on
in the gym. They are ready to
help, so don't be shy to ask. Some
will even offer services at home,
as gyms in residential buildings
are quite common. Classes in gyms
are held daily, just ask for the time-
table. Pilates, a strengthening and
stretching exercise, is very popular
and you will find some of the best
teachers in this city!

It is customary to pay your
monthly classes at the beginning of each month. Should
you travel frequently and wish
to keep your time slots, you
are allowed to pay half of
the class fee, called "taxa."
Should you miss a class and
inform the club within 24
hours, you can re-schedule
it. This is called a "reposição."
No more than two repos
a month are allowed. These
rules are strictly enforced.

Med Pilates
Also offers sessions of RPG,
for posture correction.
◉ Rua do Viradouro, 63,
   tenth floor, Itaim
☎ 3079-9858
⊕ www.medpilates.com.br

Tennis Atlântica

Another wonder in São Paulo where you least expect it. Tucked between good-looking homes in a quiet street, you will find a super club with one court! No membership or initiation fee required! Just book your time, pay your monthly lessons and hit that ball!

- Rua Atlântica, 227, Jardins
- 3085-7106

The Pilates Studio Brasil

- Inside Competition
  Rua Oscar Freire, 2066, Jardins
- 3081-1157
- For more locations:
- www.pilates.com.br

Fitness Centers

Companhia Athletica

- Shopping Morumbi
  Av. Roque Petroni Jr., 1089,
  superior floor, store 101/102
- 5188-2000
- For more locations:
  www.ciaathletica.com.br

L&T's best!

Competition

Competition has a fabulous Pilates studio and you don't need to belong to the club in order to attend Pilates classes, as both are run separately!

- Rua Oscar Freire, 2066,
  Jardim América
- 3061-0647
- For more locations:
  www.competition.com.br

First Personal Studio

- Rua da Consolação,
  3249, Jardins
- 3063-3646
- www.firstpersonalstudio.com.br

Fórmula

- Shopping Eldorado
  Av. Rebouças, 3970, second
  underground floor, store
  2001, Pinheiros
- 3094-3100 / 2197-7333
- For more locations:
  www.formulaacademia.com.br

Reebok Sports Club

- Av. Duquesa de Goias, 800
  Morumbi
- 3759-7878
- www..reebokclub.com.br

health

We debated long and hard on whether we should include this section in our guide, as we all know that it is a huge responsibility to recommend doctors in general. However, we strongly felt that it would be indispensable for you who have just arrived to have a short list of English-speaking medical professionals whom we personally think are worth recommending. Please remember that this is our personal opinion (as is everything else in this guide).

It is always a good idea to carry a photo ID with you as it is often required before being allowed entrance to the large office buildings and gaining clearance. Brazil's good reputation as far as plastic surgery is concerned also extends to other areas of medicine. We find the care and attention here to be excellent, despite the difficulty in sometimes finding doctors who speak English.

If your doctor has an anglo-saxon name, that does not necessarily imply that he/she speaks the queen's language!

Chinese Medicine

Dr. Marcello Jovchelevich
🏠 Alameda Tietê, 626, Jardins
☎ 3081-7350

Dentists

Dr. Newton Paulo Bosco Cardoso
🏠 Rua Afonso Braz, 525, room 111, Vila Nova Conceição
☎ 3845-3904
🌐 www.newclinic.com.br

Dr. Sergio Mauro Giorge
🏠 Rua Joaquim Floriano, 72, sixth floor, room 61, Itaim
☎ 3707-1178 / 3707-1178

Dr. Estela Aranha
Children's specialist.
🏠 Rua Mariana Corrêa, 58, Jardim Paulista
☎ 3062-0010 / 3062-4661

Dermatologists

Clínica Ligia Kogos de Dermatologia
🏠 Av. Brasil, 485, Jardim Paulista
☎ 3052-3551

Dr. Evandro A. Rivitti
🏠 Rua Cincinato Braga, 59, room 1-F2, Paraíso
☎ 3285-2653 / 3285-2664

Dr. Nuno Osório
For all your concerns, including laser resurfacing. English spoken fluently by Dr. Osório and some of his staff. Keeps abreast of the latest technology.
🏠 Rua Dr. Eduardo de Souza Aranha, 99, eleventh floor, Itaim
☎ 3849-1888

Valéria Marcondes de Oliveira
Dr. Valéria will answer all of your skin problems, issues and questions. Speaks English, and participates in conferences abroad.
🏠 Rua Almirante Pereira Guimarães, 192, Pacaembu
☎ 3672-5911

Endocrinologist

Dr. Ana Paula A. C. Costa
Dr. Ana Paula specializes in obesity problems and esthetic medicine. Contemplating plastic surgery? Before deciding, a visit to Dr. Ana Paula Costa is well

worth it! She has a very professional staff and is fluent in English.

🏠 Av. Pacaembu, 1782,
Pacaembu

☎ 3801-1550

🌐 www.draapcosta.com.br.

Gastro

Dr. Carlos Domene

Gastro surgeon, fluent in English, Dr. Domene treats each patient with professionalism, care and attention.

🏠 Av. Arnolfo de Azevedo, 208, Pacaembu

☎ 3864-5002

General Practitioner

Dr. Roberto Zeballos

🏠 Av. Brasil, 1368, Jardins

☎ 3064-8597

Gynaecologists, Obstetricians

Clínica Célula Mater / Dr. Carlos E. Czeresnia

English spoken. The clinic assists woman of all of ages, teenager to senior.

🏠 Alameda Gabriel Monteiro da Silva, 802, Jardim Paulistano

☎ 3085-4099

🌐 www.celulamater.com.br

Clínica IMEG / Dr. Eduardo Motta

🏠 Rua Iguatemi, 192,

third floor, Itaim

☎ 3168-5311

Dr. Marcelo Zugaib

🏠 Av. Brasil, 299,
Jardim Paulista

☎ 3887-3253

Dr. Lucila Evangelista

SEE HOSPITAL BELOW.

Inside of Hospital Israelita Albert Einstein and at Clínica Célula Mater, Ste 1104.

☎ 3747-3104

Hospital

Hospital Albert Einstein

🏠 Av. Albert Einstein, 627/701,
Morumbi

☎ 3747-1233

🌐 www.einstein.br

Hospital Samaritano

🏠 Rua Conselheiro
Brotero, 1468,
Higienópolis

☎ 3821-5300 / 3821-5300

🌐 www.samaritano.org.br

Hospital Santa Cruz

🏠 Rua Santa Cruz, 398,
Vila Mariana

☎ 5080-2000

🌐 www.hospitalsantacruz.com.br

Hospital São Luiz

🏠 Rua Dr. Alceu de Campos
Rodrigues, 95, Itaim

☎ 3040-1100

🌐 For more locations:
www.saoluiz.com.br

Hospital Sírio Libanês
🏠 Rua Adma Jafet, 91,
   Bela Vista
☎ 3155-0200 / 3155-090
🌐 www.hsl.org.br

Laboratories

Specialized clinics for blood and urine tests as well as all image exams (ultrasounds, colonoscopies, etc.) labs are very convenient and user friendly. Is is advisable to call ahead to schedule an appointment and confirm which location offers the exam you intend to do. Have your CPF and RNE handy as these are required for making the appointment. The turnaround time is very quick and results are available online or can be sent to your home by messenger. Most have special areas just for children.

Some laboratories provide at home and/or office services as well.

Delboni Medicina Diagnóstica
🏠 Av. Brasil, 762,
   Jardim América
☎ 3049-6999
🌐 For more locations:
   www.delboniauriemo.com.br

Fleury Medicina Diagnóstica
Will keep records of all past exams done there, which comes in handy. They have vaccines.

🏠 Av. Brasil, 1891,
   Jardim América
☎ 3179-0822 24-hour
🌐 For more locations:
   www.fleury.com.br

URP
🏠 Av. Paulista, 491,
   Paraíso
☎ 3882-7777 call center
🌐 www.urp.com.br

Nutritionists

NUTRITIONISTS ARE USUALLY ENCOUNTERED IN ENDOCRINOLOGISTS CLINICS AS WELL AS "WELL BEING" (BEM-ESTAR) CLINICS. SEE PAGE 152.

Opticians

Dax Ótica
🏠 Alameda Lorena, 1652,
   Jardins
☎ 3062-4130
🌐 For more locations:
   www.oticadax.com.br

Ótica Amarelinha
Nice selection of both imported and domestic frames. Efficient and speedy service.
🏠 Alameda Lorena, 1304,
   store 1, Jardins
☎ 3081-5492 / 3064-4686
🌐 www.amarelinha.com.br

Ótica Mitani
🏠 Rua Augusta, 2178,
   Cerqueira César
☎ 3083-2287
🌐 www.mitani.com.br

Ótica Ventura

Own designed frames.
🏠 Alameda Gabriel Monteiro da
Silva, 1010, Jardim Paulistano
☎ 3081-1939
🌐 For more locations:
www.oticaventura.com.br

Wanny Optical Sunglasses

🏠 Alameda Lorena,1628, Jardins
☎ 3063-0515

Ear, Nose and Throat

Prof. Dr. Pedro Luiz Mangabeira Albernaz

🏠 Av. Brig. Faria Lima, 2639,
room 31/32, Itaim
☎ 3032-2198

Ophthalmologists

Dr. Alexander de Almeida

Fluent in English and French,
shares his practice with his wife.
🏠 Rua Padre João Manoel, 450,
first floor, Jardins
☎ 3085-0365

Dr. Mauro Plut

🏠 Rua Mato Grosso, 128,
Higienópolis
☎ 3259-7177

Orthopedists

Clínica da Coluna Axis

🏠 Av. Pedroso de Morais, 2330,
Alto de Pinheiros

☎ 3813-9686
🌐 www.axisclinica.com.br

Dr. Claudio Santili

🏠 Rua Mato Grosso, 306,
room 1212, Higienópolis
☎ 3871-5592

Dr. Luiz A. Mestriner

Renowned orthopedic surgeon.
🏠 Rua dos Otonis, 709,
Vila Clementino
☎ 5572-3699

Pediatricians

Dr. Eduardo Juan Troster

Pediatrician & intensive care,
speaks English.
🏠 Av. Europa, 887, Jardim Europa
☎ 3083-6007 / 3081-1309

Dr. Antonio Carlos de Souza Aranha

Specializes in homeopathy.
🏠 Rua Regina Badra, 576,
Alto da Boa Vista
☎ 5687-3799

Dr. Hermann Grinfeld

Pediatrician & neonatologist.
🏠 Rua Hungria, 664, room 64,
Jardim Europa
☎ 3812-2400

Dr. Jorge I. Huberman

🏠 Av. Jandira, 257, room 4,
Moema
☎ 5056-8818

Dr. Sergio Spalter

Homeopathic & allopathic
pediatrics.

⊙ Rua Escobar Ortiz, 203,
Vila Nova Conceição
☎ 3842-9194

Dr. Dominque Orkov

Pediatrician & neonatologist.
⊙ Rua do Rocio, 423, room 610,
Vila Olímpia
☎ 3044-5908

Pain Specialist

Dr. José Eduardo Fukugava

⊙ Rua Guarará, 529, room 111,
Jardim Paulista
☎ 3052-3838

Pharmacies

Quite often your doctor can tell you the equivalent name (corresponding medicine) of the medicine you require, that you will find available in São Paulo. Ask for your discount card. Medicine can also be ordered and delivered. 24-hour service.

Droga Raia

⊙ Av. Brig. Faria Lima, 1727,
Jardim Paulista
☎ 3237-5000
⊕ For more locations:
www.drogaraia.com.br

Drogaria Onofre

⊙ Av. Rebouças, 2890, Pinheiros
☎ 3097-9449 / 3111-6533
⊕ For more locations:
www.onofre.com.br

Drogaria São Paulo

⊕ For locations check:
www.drogariasaopaulo.com.br

Farmácia Pague Menos

⊙ Av. Rebouças, 2736, Pinheiros
☎ 3086-2002

Physiotherapist

Mônica

RPG, Pilates. Sore muscles? Problems with posture? Mônica will solve your problems.
☎ cel. 9192-7791

Plastic Surgeons

Clínica Pedro Vital Netto

⊙ Rua Bento de Andrade,
216, Ibirapuera
☎ 3885-6022

Dr. Fábio Carramaschi

Fluent in English and French.
⊙ Rua Dr. Eduardo de S. Aranha,
387, thirteenth floor, Itaim
☎ 3040-3355
⊕ www.fabiocarramaschi.med.br

Dr. José Yoshikazu Tariki

⊙ Rua Afonso Braz, 473, room
171, Vila Nova Conceição
☎ 3842-0353

Dr. Ricardo Marujo

⊙ Rua Dr. Alceu de Campos
Rodrigues, 229, room 203,
Vila Nova Conceição
☎ 3845-7899

Prescription drugstores

The "farmácia de manipulação" offers a distinctive service, which entails making, on demand, most types of remedies, vitamins, and creams prescribed by doctors, dermatologists, etc., in addition to carrying homeopathic products. Some of them sell organic food, honey and body massage creams.

Center Fórmula

🏠 Rua Dr. Melo Alves, 762, Jardins

☎ 3083-7538

🌐 For more locations:
   www.centerformula.com.br

Farmácia Buenos Aires

🏠 Rua Sergipe, 120, Higienópolis

☎ 3829-8100

Farmácia Equilíbrio

🏠 Rua Desembargador do Vale, 248, Pompéia

☎ 3675-1431

🌐 For more locations:
   www.equilibrio.com.br

Urologists

Dr. Anuar Maluli

🏠 Av. República do Líbano, 732, Ibirapuera

☎ 3887-6266

Prof. Dr. Sami Arap

🏠 Rua Dona Adma Jafet, 50, room 33, Bela Vista

☎ 3255-2933 / 3255-2647

Well-Being Clinics

Ana Villela

Services carried out in the comfort of her home. Very clean and pleasant atmosphere, Ana is often recommended by plastic surgeons.

☎ 3031-1326

Luiza Sato

Suffering from back pain? Need a well-deserved break from opening and sorting out all those boxes? Eager to recharge your batteries? Have we got the place for you! Enter the serene zen world of Luiza Sato, where the only sounds heard are those of nature and waterfalls. After sipping a soothing cup of green tea, let yourself be pampered by Luiza's professional team. You will be in the hands of therapists specializing in Shiatsu and other methods of total relaxation. The only drawback is that you will want to go back for more!

At their new location, Rua Pelotas, 388, tel. 5083-5413, you will find the newly relocated beauty salon "Tres Jolie", where you will be able to continue your day of pampering.

🏠 Rua Joaquim Antunes, 161, Jardim Paulistano

☎ 3081-8320 / 3081-8322

🌐 For more locations:
   www.luizasato.com.br

Zentai

Shiatsu-massage, lymphatic

drainage and acupuncture.

🏠 Rua Maria Pêra, 32, São Judas

☎ 5589-8170

🌐 www.zentai.com.br

Vaccination Clinics

Going somewhere exotic, but forgot to get the necessary shots? No problem! This can be done at Guarulhos International Airport (Cumbica)or Congonhas airport just before boarding! Be careful, though, for sometimes the vaccine requires more than one shot, with an interval in between. In general, vaccines should be taken 10 days before a flight. Destinations that require vaccines can be found on the following website www.anvisa.gov.br.

> Some pediatricians will administer vaccines at their own office, but many others prefer to send patients to a clinic that specializes in vaccinations.

Cedipi

🏠 Rua Joaquim Eugênio de Lima, 1338, Jardim Paulista

☎ 3887-6111

🕐 Monday to Friday, 8 am to 6 pm; Saturday, 8 am to 3:30 pm.

🌐 www.cedipi.com.br

Fleury Medicina Diagnóstica

SEE LABORATORIES AT PAGE 149.

Hospital Albert Einstein

SEE HOSPITAL AT PAGE 148.

relocation companies

L&T's best!

Junqueira & Junqueira

Lucia Rocha Junqueira has been in the professional relocation business for eleven years, is well experienced with international companies and is totally fluent in English. Her small, but excellent, company prides itself in the high quality of service and attention to every detail!

🏠 Av. Diógenes Ribeiro de Lima, 2005, cj. 82 F, Alto de Pinheiros

☎ 3021-9950 / 3021-7287

🌐 For more locations: www.junqueiraejunqueira.com.br

Larm Brazil

🏠 Av. Piracema, 600, Barueri

☎ 11 4193-1006

🌐 www.larm.com.br

VP Relocation

All you have to do is go to the site and read! You are in for a very pleasant surprise. Extremely professional, VP Relocation goes that extra step in personalized service and in providing what is crucial in making the relocation experience as easy and as stress-free as possible. Some of the staff are "ex-pat." Who better would know what one goes through!

🏠 Av. Paulista, 2444, cj. 33/34, Jardins

☎ 3159-0097

🌐 www.vprelocation.com.br

Shops & Stores

baby equipment

São Paulo has plenty of baby equipment stores and you will no doubt get to know most of them, as babies (as you are well aware) always need something new! Today you can find almost every imported product here; however, if you can bring things from abroad (strollers, high chairs, car seats), you will save yourself a lot of money – the prices can be up to four times as much as you would pay in the States.

Alô Bebê
🏠 Rua Cunha Gago, 479,
    Pinheiros
☎ 3813-0045
🌐 For more locations:
    www.alobebe.com.br

Babylândia
Infant & children's furniture.
🏠 Av. Ibirapuera, 3266,
    Indianópolis
☎ 5093-6401
🌐 For more locations:
    www.babylandia.com.br

Best Baby
SEE PAGE 162.

Etna
SEE PAGE 80.

Hercules / Ecobaby
A full line of imported and local infant & children's equipment.
🏠 Av. Sumaré, 535, Perdizes
☎ 3871-2134
🌐 www.lojashercules.com.br

L&T's best!
Per Bambini
Upscale furniture for infants and children. A good idea would to be to walk up and down this street, as it is full of shops of kid's furniture.
🏠 Rua Min. Jesuíno
    Cardoso, 121, Vila Olímpia
☎ 3845-0849
🌐 http://perbambini.com.br

Rug For Kids
Custom and ready-made rugs.
🏠 Rua Costa Carvalho, 138,
    Alto de Pinheiros
☎ 3813-0982
🌐 www.rugsforkids.com.br

Tok & Stok
SEE HOME AT PAGE 72.

bookshops and magazine stands

Easily found in shopping malls, or as separate stores. Some are extremely specialized and have individual sections dealing with specific subjects.

Bookshops
You can order a book if not found in the store. The bigger bookstores have stationery and music sections as well.

Fnac
Computers and accessories, foreign books and magazines, DVDs, CDs, cards, cellphones and cameras.

Rua Pedroso de Morais, 858,
Pinheiros
4501-3000
For more locations:
www.fnac.com.br

The bookstore sells tickets
for shows in the city
until 8 pm.

Haddock Lobo Books & Magazines

Newspapers, books,
imported magazines.
Rua Haddock Lobo,
1503, Jardins
3082-9449
www.haddocklobo.com.br

Laselva

Probably the first bookstore
you will see when arriving in
Sampa, as it is present in both
the city's international airports,
as well as in other locations.
Shopping Iguatemi
Av. Brig. Faria Lima, 2232,
Jardim Paulista
3813-9041
For more locations:
www.laselva.com.br

Livraria Cultura

One of São Paulo's best bookstores. Sells newspapers, books,
imported magazines. Also promotes literary events.
Conjunto Nacional
Av. Paulista, 2073,
Cerqueira César
3170-4033
For more locations:
www.livrariacultura.com.br

Livraria da Vila

Books, CDs, DVDs.
Rua Fradique Coutinho, 915,
Vila Madalena
3814-5811
For more locations:
www.livrariadavila.com.br

Livraria Saraiva

Books, magazines, CDs, DVDs.
Shopping Brascan Century Plaza
Rua Joaquim Floriano, 466,
Itaim
3078-7887
For more locations:
www.livrariasaraiva.com.br

Livraria Siciliano

For locations:
www.siciliano.com.br

Magazine Stands

Foreign and domestic magazines.
Get to know the one closest to
your residence, so that you can
reserve your favorite magazines!

Banca Cerqueira César

International newspapers
and magazines.
Rua Padre João Manoel,
826, Jardins
3064-3806

Banca Rocha

Italian and Spanish newspapers.
Rua da Consolação,
3447, Jardins
3083-7285

Banca Star

International newspapers
and magazines.
Rua Haddock Lobo,
1395, Jardins
3060-8456

Banca Vilaboim

International newspapers and magazines.

- 🏠 Praça Vilaboim, 49-A, Higienópolis
- ☎ 3667-2107

Book Repairs

Vecchio Libro

Classes given in book restoration, bookbinding and creating albums. Also provides cleaning of personal libraries at home. Interesting and stimulating with a big advantage, very limited amount of Portuguese (if any) is necessary in order to follow the classes!

- 🏠 Rua Oscar Freire, 1921, Jardim América
- ☎ 3062-0593
- 🕐 Monday to Friday, from 9 am to 8 pm.

Brazilian crafts and stones

Arte Tribal

Brazilian native art and handmade objects.

- 🏠 Rua Augusta, 2795, Jardins
- ☎ 3081-8170
- 🌐 www.artetribal.com.br

Galeria Arte Brasileira

- 🏠 Alameda Lorena, 2163, Jardins
- ☎ 3062-9452
- 🌐 www.galeriaartebrasileira. com.br

Legep

Brazilian stones and gifts.

- 🏠 Av. Washington Luiz, 4407, Santo Amaro
- ☎ 5561-6255
- 🌐 www.legep.com.br

candle shops

Candella Velas

Candles, torches, floating lighting and special projects.

- 🏠 Rua Horácio Lafer, 334, Itaim
- ☎ 3168-3193
- 🌐 www.candella.com.br

Mist

- 🏠 Rua Estilo Barroco, 760, Chácara Santo Antônio
- ☎ 5182-0241 / 5182-8689

cars

You can find many car dealerships / *concessionárias de veículos* scattered all over São Paulo. You may want to inquire about bullet proofing (*blindagem*). Check websites for locations:

Chevrolet GM

- 🌐 www.gm.com.br

Citroën

- 🌐 www.meucitroen.com.br

Fiat

- 🌐 www.fiat.com.br

Ford

- 🌐 www.ford.com.br

Honda
🌐 www.honda.com.br

Land Rover
🌐 www.landrover.com.br

Mitsubishi
🌐 www.mitsubishi.com.br

Renault
🌐 www.renault.com.br

Volkswagen
🌐 www.volkswagen.com.br

Car Rental / *Locadoras*

Avis Brasil
📍 Rua da Consolação, 382, Consolação
☎ 3259-6868
🌐 For more locations: www.avis.com.br

Locablin
📍 Rua Prof. José Leite e Oiticica, 530, Brooklin
☎ 5535-5912 / 5533-2005
🌐 www.locablin.com

Localiza
📍 Centro Empresarial Av. Maria Coelho de Aguiar, 215, store 57, Santo Amaro
☎ 2122-8093
🌐 For more locations: www.localiza.com

Totality Import
📍 Av. Nove de Julho, 5345, Itaim
☎ 3168-1133
🌐 www.totalblindados.com.br

Garages – Car Service

Auto Elétrico e Mecânica ITALS
📍 Rua Oscar Freire, 433, Cerqueira César
☎ 3088-2247 / 3063-3844

JBarboza
📍 Rua Estilo Barroco, 781, Brooklin
☎ 5183-5543 / 5181-3018

Special cars
A good tip is to go up and down Rua Colômbia, in the Jardins, where many imported cars and motorcycles stores are gathered.

Audi Caraigá
📍 Rua Colômbia, 659, Jardim América
☎ 3896-6000
🌐 www.caraiga.com.br

Autostar BMW
📍 Rua Colômbia, 810, Jardim América
☎ 3061-5177
🌐 www.autostar.com.br

Harley-Davidson Concept
Choppers for those "born to be wild". Or just for those who want to check out the most well-known american motorcycle.
📍 Rua Colômbia, 157, Jardim América
☎ 3069-1200
🌐 For more locations: www.harley-davidson.com.br

Jaguar

⌂ Rua Colômbia, 799,
   Jardim América
☎ 3069-1200
🌐 For more locations:
   www.jaguarcars.com.br

Mercedes Comark

⌂ Rua Colômbia, 785,
   Jardim América
☎ 2122-0900
🌐 www.comark.com.br

Nissan Itavema

⌂ Rua Colômbia, 784,
   Jardim América
☎ 3061-9000
🌐 For more locations:
   www.itavema.com.br

L&T 's best!

Private Collections

Exceptional antique cars –
a great father day's gift!
⌂ Rua Javaés, 184, Bom Retiro
☎ 3361-4900
🌐 www.privatecollections.
   com.br

cigar stores

Carry most brands of cigars, cig-
arettes and smoking accessories –
a good places to find last-minute
gifts and little gadgets!

Caruso Tabacaria

⌂ Alameda Lorena, 1575,
   Jardins
☎ 3062-5975
🌐 For more locations:
   www.tabacariacaruso.com.br

Davidoff Tabacaria

⌂ Alameda Lorena, 1821,
   Jardins
☎ 3083-7344
🌐 For more locations:
   www.davidoffbrasil.com.br

Lenat Tabacaria

⌂ Rua Oscar Freire, 1174, Jardins
☎ 3082-5062
🌐 For more locations:
   www.lenat.com.br

clothing and apparel

Athletic wear

Brazilians attach a tremendous
importance to fitness, so having
the proper outfit is "de rigueur."
In addition to the traditional
stores, fitness centers and gyms
carry the necessary gear. Most
gyms have a space that sells
nutritious foods, where you can
sit and enjoy a light snack. The
selection of shops carrying international brands is quite good,
and will help you get that indispensable item until your next
trip overseas.

Adidas Store

⌂ Rua Oscar Freire, 1057, Jardins
☎ 3061-9646
🌐 For more locations:
   www.adidas.com.br

Decathlon

⌂ Rua Duquesa de Goiás, 381,
   Real Parque, Morumbi
☎ 2167-0800
🌐 www.decathlon.com.br

For Sport

Clothes, shoes, sports accessories.

📍 Rua Vieira Maciel, 19,
   Ibirapuera

☎ 3887-9928

🌐 For more locations:
   www.forsport.com.br

Nike

A nice selection of Nike products,
Oscar Freire's store also carries
children's sizes.

📍 Rua Oscar Freire, 969, Jardins

☎ 3068-0044

🌐 For more locations:
   www.nike.com.br

Speedo

📍 Rua Augusta, 2521, Jardins

☎ 3063-5211

🌐 For more locations:
   www.speedo.com.br

Tennis Point

Specializes in tennis accessories.

📍 Rua Dr. Renato Paes
   de Barros, 428, Itaim

☎ 3168-2017

🌐 www.tennispoint.com.br

The Puma Store

📍 Rua da Consolação, 3452,
   Jardins

☎ 3891-0711

🌐 For more locations:
   www.puma.com

Track and Field

📍 Rua Oscar Freire, 959,
   Jardins

☎ 3048-1277

🌐 For more locations:
   www.tf.com.br

Bathing Suits

A unique phenomenon in Brazil
is the sale of bathing suits all year
round due to the mild climate,
even in winter. Rest assured that
despite the common knowledge
that Brazilian bikinis are tiny
(and they sure are) you will find
the "proper" coverage. Just
remember to go up one size!

Cover ups for the beach can
be custom made.

Água de Coco

📍 Rua Oscar Freire,
   1181, Jardins

☎ 3061-3367

🌐 For more locations:
   www.aguadecoco.com.br

L&T's best!

Jo de Mer

By the time you reach Jo
de Mer on Oscar Freire, you
will have seen many of Brazil's
best bikinis. Save some energy
and breath for this last one –
it is worth it!

📍 Rua Oscar Freire, 329, Jardins

☎ 3081-4232

🌐 www.jodemer.com.br

Lenny

Their entire line of bathing suits
and bikinis have matching cover
ups – pants, skirts, wraps (one
of the most forgiving cuts!).

📍 Rua Escobar Ortiz, 480,
   Vila Nova Conceição

☎ 3846-6594

🌐 For more locations:
   www.lenny.com.br

Poko Pano
🏠 Alameda Lorena, 1650,
Jardins
☎ 3082-0799
🌐 For more locations:
www.pokopano.com.br

Rosa Chá
🏠 Rua Oscar Freire, 977, Jardins
☎ 3081-2793
🌐 For more locations:
www.rosacha.com.br

Salinas
🏠 Rua Oscar Freire,
1072-B, Jardins
☎ 3082-9715 / 3082-3775
🌐 For more locations:
www.salinas-rio.com.br

Children's Clothing and Shoes

Alô Bebê Mega Store
All you need for kids and babies,
toys, clothes.
🏠 Av. Giovanni Gronchi, 5000,
Morumbi
☎ 3744-1001 / 3742-2990
🌐 For more locations:
www.alobebe.com.br

Baby Basics
Newborn – 6 years old.
🏠 Rua Adolfo Tabacow, 192, Itaim
☎ 3167-7643
🕐 Only from Monday to Friday.
🌐 www.babybasics.com.br

Balangandã
A really cute store that carries
the original designs.

Boys and girls, newborn to 10
years old. Also has a small
selection of toys.
🏠 Rua Oscar Freire, 240, Jardins
☎ 3082-6830
🌐 www.balangandakids.com.br

Bb Moderno
Clothes for 0-6 years old and
decoration for children's rooms.
🏠 Rua Dr. Andrade Pertence, 179,
Vila Olímpia
☎ 3849-0223
🌐 For more locations:
www.bbmoderno.com.br

Best Baby
Your one-stop shopping store for
imported equipment and toys.
A nice selection of Brazilian-
made baby clothing from newborn to 8 years old.
🏠 Rua Dr. Melo Alves, 413,
Jardins
☎ 3083-6444
🌐 www.bestbaby.com.br

Chicco
Exclusively Chicco products
from Italy. The stores carry
the whole line of toys, equipment and clothes.
🏠 Rua Oscar Freire, 1082,
Jardins
☎ 3085-5710
🌐 For more locations:
www.chicco.com

Clo Figueiredo
Ready-to-wear and custom-
made baby bedding, clothing
and maternity nighties! A lot
of the clothing items are hand-

made, a rarity nowadays. Also, some interesting and innovative decorative items, such as personalized family tree frames!

⌂ Rua Paes de Araújo, 129, Itaim

☎ 3167-5657

Daslu

SEE FORMAL WEAR AND EVENING GOWNS AT PAGE 170.

L&T's best!

Dona Borboleta

An adorable little store in Jardins that carries baby gifts, children's furniture & linens, and even offers afternoon tea for little ones on Fridays, from 3 pm to 6 pm!

⌂ Alameda Franca, 1332, house 4, Jardins

☎ 3086-2026

🕓 Saturdays, only from 10 am to 2 pm.

Green

Brazilian brand of children's clothing and shoes, with lots of cute matching sets.

⌂ Rua Bela Cintra, 2165, Jardins

☎ 3088-2986

🌐 For more locations: www.greenbymissako.com.br

Jacadi

Imported French clothing for boys and girls.

⌂ Rua Bela Cintra, 1870, Jardins

☎ 3082-1138

🌐 www.jacadi.com

Miniature

Fun and alternative clothes for boys and girls. Ask them about their party planning as well! Also beautiful dresses for weddings.

⌂ Rua Prof. Atílio Innocenti, 63, Itaim

☎ 3078-2858

🕓 By appointment on Saturdays.

Minou Minou

Imported and Brazilian clothing and shoes for boys and girls from 2-12 years old.

⌂ Rua Dr. Melo Alves, 438, Jardins

☎ 3082-5092

Monne

A small-scale Brazilianized version of Ralph Lauren.

⌂ Rua Dr. Melo Alves, 357, Jardins

☎ 3081-0864

🌐 For more locations: www.boutiquemonne.com.br

Paola da Vinci

Imported French clothing for boys and girls. Also bath and bed items.

⌂ Rua Haddock Lobo, 1700, Jardins

☎ 3086-3863

🌐 For more locations: www.paoladavinci.com.br

Petit Bateau

Imported French items. Check upstairs for sales items.

⌂ Rua Bela Cintra, 2159, Jardins

☎ 3081-2112

🌐 www.petitbateau.com

Tartine et Chocolat

Imported French items.
Keep an eye out for their sales.
🏠 Rua Haddock Lobo, 1353,
   Jardins
☎ 3064-5146 / 3064-0520
🌐 www.tartine.com.br

Va Lutin

Brazilian made, French-
style clothing.
🏠 Rua João Lourenço, 323,
   Vila Nova Conceição
☎ 3849-7185
🕐 Saturdays, only from
   10 am to 2 pm.
🌐 www.vallutin.com.br

Children's Shoe Stores

Casa Tody

One of the most traditional
children's shoe stores in São Paulo
– even it's decor remains as if
unaltered by time. A great place
for school and party shoes!
🏠 Rua Augusta, 2634, Jardins
☎ 3088-2164

Geox

SEE SHOES AT PAGE 176.

Noa Noa

A dream of a shop! They've got
it all, from sports, to school, to
party shoes. And for adults too!
🏠 Shopping Iguatemi
   Av. Brig. Faria Lima, 2232,
   Jardim Paulista
☎ 3812-8493
🌐 For more locations:
   www.noanoa.com.br

Shulko

National & imported brands.
Lots of cute styles you don't
see at the other shops; different
from the norm.
🏠 Rua Maestro Elias Lobo, 1051,
   Jd. Paulista
☎ 3051-7313

Dry Cleaners

5àSec

Large chain of dry cleaners –
can be found all over São Paulo.
🏠 Alameda Tietê, 281, Jardins
☎ 3063-1678
🌐 For more locations:
   www.5asec.com.br

Bonne Cleaners

Recommended by some of
the best stores in Jardins, this
upscale dry cleaner uses only
imported products to clean
your most delicate garments.
🏠 Rua Peixoto Gomide,
   1098, Jardins
☎ 3258-1010

Dry Clean USA

🏠 Rua Itacolomi, 636,
   Higienópolis
☎ 3237-3322
🌐 For more locations:
   www.drycleanusa.com.br

By Clean Lavanderia

Wet or dry, they clean as
recommended.
🏠 Rua Domingos de Morais,
   814, loja 40, Vila Mariana
☎ 5579-3798
🌐 www.byclean.com.br

Lav-Lav

Specializes in leather, also evening gowns.

- Rua Estados Unidos, 2066, Jardins
- 3062-2436
- www.vallutin.com.br

Washtec Sumaré

Wash, dye and customize clothes and leather. Specializes in helmets and motorcyclists' clothing.

- Rua João Ramalho, 971, Sumaré
- 3871-9193
- www.washtecsumare.com.br

Elegant and Casual Wear

It is quite easy to dress in São Paulo, as long as you own a cool pair of jeans. All you have to do is pair it up with any of your favorite tops. Jeans are a very popular item and can be locally made. They will take you from morning to night, summer to short winters.

There are numerous fashion shops scattered in all districts – the choice is quite endless. In doing our survey, we tried to keep this diversity in mind and want you to have an option, as far as pricing is concerned. A good way to start, is to familiarize yourself with the different boutiques before you actually start buying.

Soon, you will be able to zero in on what stores serve your needs best. Staff are always ready to help your decision, despite the language barrier.

In some major shopping malls (Iguatemi, for example), as well as at the unique Daslu, you will find familiar imported designers and products. Now go on and enjoy the relaxed and Brazilian carefree way of dressing up!

Ask for the *cartão* (business card), and write down the name of the saleslady who helped you, as it will facilitate further future interaction.

OSCAR FREIRE

Sampa's version of Rodeo Drive, Madison Avenue and Sloane Street. Take a taxi, ask to be dropped at the corner of Oscar Freire and Melo Alves. (Should you decide to drive, many parking lots are available on Oscar Freire, and the stores will stamp your ticket.) Walk east as far as Rua Peixoto Gomide, which has a number of São Paulo's hottest young designers. Check both sides of the street and walk North and South one block on Bela Cintra, Haddock Lobo, Melo Alves and Peixoto Gomide. When you're done, you will have seen the best selection of shopping Brazil has to offer.

Many of these stores are also located in some shopping malls. On the following pages, a few of our favorite stores.

Adriana Barra

Hip, retro designs. She is part of a group of hot young designers in São Paulo. Casual, easy to wear clothes with a Brazilian flair. Uses lots of groovy prints. Located in a neat enclave – take the time to check it out.

- Rua Peixoto Gomide, 1801, house 5, Jardins
- 3062-0387
- www.adrianabarra.com.br

Annelise de Salles / Maguy Did It / Ucha

Three talented designers recently opened this store to house their respective lines of fabulous clothing & accessories for women & children. Annelise goes for the delicate, romantic fashion; Maguy Etlin, for inventive, handmade accessories; while Ucha Meirelles stays chic and comfortable.

- Rua Peixoto Gomide, 1749, Jardins
- 3062-7659

Cris Barros

Hip, great cuts.

- Rua Oscar Freire, 295, Jardins, and at Daslu!
- 3082-3621
- www.crisbarros.com.br

Emannuelle Junqueira

She makes beautiful dresses for weddings, evenings & parties.

- Rua Peixoto Gomide, 1805-C, Jardins
- 3083-4593
- www.emannuellejunqueira. com.br

Francesca Giobbi

Original, chic and comfortable designer shoes.

- Rua Peixoto Gomide, 1757, Jardins
- 3060-8595
- www.francescagiobbi.com.br

Gisele Nasser

High end clothing.

- Rua Oscar Freire, 232, house 4, Jardins
- 3082-0315
- www.giselenasser.com.br

Isabela Capeto

- Rua da Consolação, 3358, Jardins
- 3898-1878
- www.isabelacapeto.com.br

Isabella Giobbi

High-end design, ready to wear, original designs, carries accessories as well.

- Alameda Lorena, 1426, Jardins
- 3061-2001

Vibi Leardi

Passing by, one would never guess that this charming enclave holds four shops, amongst them the work of the very talented shoe and jewellery designer, Virginia Leardi. Once again, this is the beauty of São Paulo – an enigmatic city where tucked-away discoveries make it so very interesting. All original designs.

- Rua Peixoto Gomide, 180, Jardins
- 3081-8729

OUR OTHER TIPS

Acquastudio
Bathing suits and cover ups.
☍ Rua Oscar Freire, 903, Jardins
☎ 3062-8252
🌐 www.acquastudio.com.br

Andrea Saletto
Very well-made,
sophisticated designs.
☍ Rua Oscar Freire, 1072, Jardins
☎ 3088-5418
🌐 www.andreasaletto.com.br

Animale
Casual clothes, costume jewellery,
leather bags, shoes for women.
☍ Rua Bela Cintra, 164, Jardins
☎ 3064-8476
🌐 For more locations:
www.animale.com.br

Arestta
Women's clothing.
☍ Alameda Lorena, 2093, Jardins
☎ 3063-4586
🌐 For more locations:
www.arestta.com.br

Banca de Camisetas
There are many types of T-shirts
to choose from: romantic, casual, humorous, serious, and
better still, for the whole family.
How cool is it to go around
wearing the same T-shirt as
your teenager (who might think
you are too square!).
☍ Rua Harmonia, 322,
Vila Madalena
☎ 3817-5281
🌐 For more locations:
www.bancadecamisetas.com.br

Blow Up
Casual clothes, costume jewellery,
leather bags, shoes for women.
☍ Rua Oscar Freire, 801, Jardins
☎ 3081-2447

Browns
Similar to Brooks Brothers.
☍ Alameda Lorena, 1889, Jardins
☎ 3081-2331

Canal Concept
☍ Rua Oscar Freire, 987, Jardins
☎ 3083-2511
🌐 For more locations:
www.canalconcept.com.br

Christian Dior
I don't think C.D. needs an
introduction! Clothes, costume
jewellery, leather bags, shoes,
watches, lingerie for women.
☍ Rua Haddock Lobo, 1589,
Jardins
☎ 3061-9299
🌐 www.dior.com

Comentário Visual
Clothes and items for home
decoration.
☍ Rua Oscar Freire, 899, Jardins
☎ 3085-0263

Daslu
SEE FORMAL WEAR AND EVENING GOWNS
AT PAGE 170.

Diesel
The jeans boutique *par excellence*.
☍ Rua Oscar Freire, 1009, Jardins
☎ 3082-4937
🌐 For more locations:
www.diesel.com

Extra's & G's

Sizes 46 to 56 for women.
🏠 Av. dos Eucaliptos, 660, Moema
☎ 5044-1267

Fil du Fil

Knitted clothes for children
and women.
🏠 Av. Bem-te-vi, 153, Moema
☎ 5093-9838

Guaraná Brasil

🏠 Alameda Lorena, 1599, Jardins
☎ 3061-0182
🌐 For more locations:
  www.grupoguaranabrasil.
  com.br

Huis Clos

Very hip, Huis Clos is sure to
please today's woman on the go!
Great for different evening wear.
🏠 Rua Oscar Freire, 1105, Jardins
☎ 3088-7370
🌐 For more locations:
  www.huisclos.com.br

Jeans Hall

Huge selection of American and
European jeans. Their motto?
It's not enough for the jeans
to be perfect, they have to
be perfect on you!
🏠 Shopping Iguatemi
  Av. Brig. Faria Lima, 2232,
  Jardim Paulista
☎ 3814-8243
🌐 www.jeanshall.com.br

Le Lis Blanc

Casual and work clothes,
costume jewellery, leather bags,
shoes for women.

🏠 Rua Oscar Freire, 809, Jardins
☎ 3083-2549
🌐 For more locations:
  www.lelis.com.br

Lita Mortari

Casual, chic and dressy clothes,
costume jewellery, leather bags,
shoes for women.
🏠 Rua Oscar Freire, 679,
  Jardins
☎ 3063-1585
🌐 For more locations:
  www.litamortari.com.br

Louis Vuitton Brasil

See Leather at page 173.

Marcia Mello

Accessories, clothes, shoes.
🏠 Alameda Lorena, 1626, Jardins
☎ 3064-0689
🌐 For more locations:
  www.marciamello.com.br

Marco Lab

Great workout clothes.
🏠 Rua Lisboa, 568, Pinheiros
☎ 3088-1460

Maria Bonita Extra

Easy to wear and chic clothing.
Carries costume jewellery, leather
bags, and shoes for women.
🏠 Rua Oscar Freire, 705, Jardins
☎ 3063-3609 / 3088-4877
🌐 For more locations:
  www.mariabonitaextra.com.br

Mercearia

Your teenage daughter will fall
in love with Mercearia. Just watch
out for that credit card of hers!

🏠 Rua Oscar Freire, 1053, Jardins
☎ 3064-1419
🌐 For more locations:
   www.mercearia.com.br

Ondée
The best of the major
Brazilian stylists.
🏠 Alameda Lorena, 1646, Jardins
☎ 3082-8383 / 3063-0161

One up
Good for teenagers.
🏠 Rua Oscar Freire, 935, Jardins
☎ 3081-3438
🌐 For more locations:
   www.oneupfashion.com.br

Raia de Goeye
Founded by two Brazilian
women who design ultra-hip
clothing. Carries costume jewellery, leather bags and shoes.
They even designed a line for
C&A "a la target." It also has
a corner at Daslu.
🏠 Rua Adolfo Tabacow, 261,
   Itaim
☎ 3079-2772
🌐 www.raiadegoeye.com.br

Richard's
See men's / women's wear at page 174.

Rock Lily
🏠 Alameda Lorena, 1598,
   Jardins
☎ 3082-6897

Rox and Dreams
Accessories, clothes.
🏠 Alameda Lorena, 1635, Jardins
☎ 3088-4292

Sampaka
🏠 Av. Rouxinol, 578, Moema
☎ 5536-0350

Stroke
See men's / women's wear at page 174.

Thorrè
Casual, easy to wear clothes
with some imported items.
🏠 Rua Peixoto Gomide, 1801,
   house 1, Jardins
☎ 3061-0369

United Colors of Benetton
🏠 Alameda Lorena, 1683, Jardins
☎ 3088-5422
🌐 For more locations:
   www.benetton.com

Versace
Italian designer of clothes,
leather bags, women's shoes,
linen clothes, home furnishings,
home accessories.
🏠 Rua Bela Cintra, 2209, Jardins
☎ 3088-8602
🌐 www.versace.com

Zion
Casual chic women's wear, carries accessories as well.
🏠 Alameda Lorena, 1648, Jardins
☎ 3081-1109
🌐 www.zionstore.com.br

Embroidery work

Mercerie Bordados
🏠 Shopping Iguatemi
   Av. Brig. Faria Lima, 2232,
   third floor, Jardim Paulistano
☎ 3816-2534

Fabric stores (for clothes)

Firenze Tecidos
🏠 Rua Augusta, 2781, Jardins
☎ 3088-2022
🌐 www.firenzetecidos.com.br

GJ Tecidos Finos
Highend fabrics. Aside from the store in the 25 de Março neighborhood, it also has an e-commerce service, for sales online.
🏠 Ladeira Porto Geral, 73, first floor, Centro
☎ 3325-0000
🌐 www.gjtecidos.com.br

Mittus
🏠 Rua Augusta, 2483, Jardins
☎ 3062-5255

Tecelagem Francesa
🏠 Alameda Tietê, 20, Jardins
☎ 3088-7700

For the expecting Mom
Whether you're trying to get pregnant or are already pregnant, or even just thinking about it, São Paulo is a great place to be! The doctors are absolutely top notch, the services (lab & scans) are excellent and the private hospitals are on par with some 4-star hotels. The only thing I had problems with in São Paulo when I was pregnant was finding maternity clothes that fit – but if you don't gain 55 lb/20 kg during your pregnancy (like I did!), you won't have to worry about this –

you'll find very cute, very chic maternity clothes. Also, this useful website has lots of addresses: www.afamiliacresceu.com.br

Mammy Gestante
🏠 Rua João Lourenço, 613, Vila Nova Conceição
☎ 3845-2216 / 3845-9832
🌐 For more locations: www.mammygestante.com.br

Maria Barriga
🏠 Rua Aspicuelta, 145, Vila Madalena
☎ 3814-4228
🌐 For more locations: www.mariabarriga.com.br

Place des Mamans
Casual chic maternity wear, carries accessories as well.
🏠 Rua Haddock Lobo, 1340, first floor, Jardins
☎ 3083-5355

Zazou
🏠 Rua Prof. Atílio Innocenti, 952, Vila Olímpia
☎ 3846-6511
🌐 For more locations: www.zazou.com.br

Formal Wear and Evening Gowns
In general, Brazilian men are "under dressed" compared to their female companions. Although black tie is not "de rigueur" for men, women tend to wear long gowns more frequently than usual. It is not uncommon to find

women quite elegantly dressed at dinner parties, despite the lack of use of ties for men, or even when the dress code is known as *traje informal* (informal dress code). Don't panic if you have not found the appropriate long garment, as it is quite easy to have something made at a fraction of the price it would cost overseas. Tailors and seamstresses are plentiful and quite capable. Some holidays have a "specific" dress code, which is followed quite strictly. Christmas is known to be celebrated in red, and New Year's Eve is "all white." That includes men, women and children. As for return policies: much stricter than what you're probably used to. Stores in general will only issue credit notes with a limited time frame. Be aware of this, as your unused credit will expire.

> Due to the reverse in seasons, winter clothing is mostly available from March to August; sizes usually follow the European Index. For ex., a 36 is the equivalent of a 2 in the U.S.A., and a 38 to a 4-6, etc. We recommend, however, that you try everything, as cuts are different and sizes vary from shop to shop.

Arthur Caliman

Elegant evening wear.
- Rua João Cachoeira, 1246, Itaim
- 3045-5351
- www.arthurcaliman.com.br

Black Tie

Rent and sale of evening wear for women, men, kids. Also, costumes and bridal wear.
- Av. Rebouças, 2823, Jardim Paulistano
- 3067-4600
- For more locations: www.blacktie.com.br

Candy Brown Habillées

We will stress, one more time, that anything can be done in São Paulo as far as dressing up! An American who has lived here for a number of years, Candy has been very successful in capturing and combining elegance and style in formal wear. She custom makes garments in any fabric, color, or pattern you require. Dresses, tops, pants and skirts are on display and the choice is extremely varied. Candy has also gone one step further and designs wedding dresses! Some have been featured in magazines.
- Rua Prof. Filadelfo de Azevedo, 521, house 3, Vila Nova Conceição
- 3051-8851 / 3885-6195

Carlos Miele

Now internationally known, this *Paulista* designer makes gorgeous feminine gowns. Jewellery, shoes and bags also available.
- Rua Bela Cintra, 2232, Jardins
- 3065-7700
- www.carlosmiele.com.br

Christian Dior

SEE ELEGANT AND CASUAL WEAR AT PAGE **165**.

L&T's best!

Daslu

Your ultimate shopping experience, a unique South American mega store only accessible by car (as opposed to public transportation). Daslu carries an endless variety of imported and domestic products from clothing (men, women and children) to ordering your own helicopter or boat "en passant" to the wine cellar, the electronics section, the home decoration area... or the fabulous kids department! They carry everything from babies to teens – they even have a Baby Gap corner!

Plan a day there: first, pamper yourself in the hands of the super-qualified spa staff and enjoy one of the four (but very different) eating spots! A delicious continental buffet at Leopoldina, where reservations are strongly required, a sushi bar, a casual snack enclave, (which serves the equivalent of "high tea" after 4 pm) and a small, intimate pastry shop which serves English tea with all its trimmings! A genuine must in São Paulo!

Note: Daslu accepts all methods of payment (cash, credit cards, personal checks), and even has an automated HSBC ATM machine for your convenience on the premises!
- ⌂ Av. Chedid Jafet, 131, Vila Olímpia
- ☎ 3841-4000
- 🌐 www.daslu.com.br

If you are lucky enough to be in São Paulo during the *liquidação* (sale), it would be strongly advisable to get there around 9:30 am, on the first day if possible, as the lines go around the block and everything goes in the blink of an eye! Prices are slashed in half...

Emporio Armani

A marvellous elegant boutique, Emporio Armani has a great collection from casual, to dressy, to formal. Don't worry if you can't make up your mind quickly. Instead, let us recommend you take a break, have either a coffee or even lunch in the restaurant adjacent to the shop, ponder on what to buy and... go for the kill!
- ⌂ Rua Haddock Lobo, 1550, Jardins
- ☎ 3897-9090
- 🌐 For more locations: www.emporioarmani.com

Gloria Coelho

Inventive designs & wonderful cut, her clothes look great on!
- ⌂ Rua Bela Cintra, 2173, Jardins
- ☎ 3085-6671
- 🌐 For more locations: www.gloriacoelho.com.br

Hats & Veils Sabrina

Rental for black tie affairs.
- ⌂ Av. Ceci, 428, Planalto Paulista
- ☎ 5055-9177 / 5055-7752
- 🌐 For more locations: www.sabrinachapeus.com.br

Reinaldo Lourenço

Ready to wear and evening collection, one of **Sampa's** hottest designers. Cutting edge casual wear and beautifully-cut formal gowns. Reinaldo reconstructs vintage fashion, merging past and future in his work.

- Rua Bela Cintra, 2167, Jardins
- 3063-1795 / 3085-8150
- For more locations:
  www.reinaldolourenco.com.br

Salvatore Ferragamo

An international brand which we believe does not need any introduction recently opened its very own store in São Paulo. Clothes, accessories, shoes and bags. Only fitting, it is available at Daslu as well.

- Rua Haddock Lobo, 1583, Jardins
- 3081-5324
- www.ferragamo.it

Só a Rigor

Rent and sale of evening gowns, costumes for costume parties, shoes and bags for women, clothing for men, children and brides. Costume jewellery available for rent or sale.

- Av. Rebouças, 2445, Jardins
- 3064-3818
- www.soarigor.com.br

Suely Caliman

Elegant formal and party dresses. Carries costume jewellery as well.

- Rua Bela Cintra, 1833, Jardins
- 3060-8236
- www.suelycaliman.com.br

Fur Storage

Luiz Mori

Sells and repairs fur.

- Rua Barata Ribeiro, 190, room 54, Bela Vista
- 3257-0248 / 3120-6203

Leather

Inovathi Acessórios

Bags for men and women, luggage.

- Av. dos Maracatins, 1646, Moema
- For more locations:
  www.inovathi.com.br

Louis Vuitton Brasil

The name says it all! Leather items, both elegant and casual wear.

- Rua Haddock Lobo, 1587, Jardins
- 3088-4126
- For more locations:
  www.louisvuitton.com

Prima Donna Acessories

Costume jewellery, leather bags.

- Alameda Lorena, 2055, Jardins
- 3064-0048
- For more locations:
  www.primadonnaaccessories.com

Lingerie

You will find in every neighborhood many small lingerie shops where you will find the basics, available in different brands. From bras, panties, p.j.'s, to stockings and socks.

Corpo e Arte

Good basic cotton underwear.

🏠 Rua Oscar Freire, 957, Jardins

☎ 3081-1277

🌐 For more locations:
www.corpoearte.com.br

Fruit de la Passion

🏠 Alameda Lorena, 1774, Jardins

☎ 3064-3334

🌐 For more locations:
www.fruitdelapassion.com.br

Lolita Sensualité

A newcomer on the block, Lolita will tend to all of your needs and dreams! A visit to the second floor might be quite interesting!

🏠 Rua Dr. Melo Alves, 490, Jardins

☎ 3063-0715

Rosa Shock

Men, women, children.

🏠 Av. Bem-te-vi, 199, Moema

☎ 5092-2376

Verve

A nice Brazilian lingerie shop with products made in Rio de Janeiro.

🏠 Alameda Lorena, 1924, Jardins

☎ 3083-7431 / 3083-2635

🌐 www.verve.com.br

Men / Women's Wear

Carmin

🏠 Rua Oscar Freire, 1007, Jardins

☎ 3088-0559

🌐 For more locations:
www.carmim.com.br

Club Chocolate

A restaurant as well, a cool, airy place in São Paulo where CD music mixes with the sound of parrots. Club Chocolate is a little different from your usual store or restaurant. Particularly nice for a girl's lunch out with the ladies. Please do not forget to check the top floor reserved for "women only."

🏠 Rua Oscar Freire, 913, Jardins

☎ 3084-1500

Fause Haten

🏠 Alameda Lorena, 1731, Jardins

☎ 3081-8685 / 3068-8642

Inova

Casual wear for men and women.

🏠 Alameda Lorena, 1564, Jardins

☎ 3085-5884 / 3061-3555

Richards

Our version of Banana Republic.

🏠 Rua Oscar Freire, 1129, Jardins

☎ 3062-6784

🌐 For more locations:
www.richards.com.br

Stroke / Sbarco

Knitwear clothes and jeans.

🏠 Alameda Lorena, 2066, Jardins

☎ 3064-8560

🌐 For more locations:
www.stroke.com.br

TNG

🏠 Rua Augusta, 2598, Jardins

☎ 3083-7350

🌐 For more locations:
www.tng.com.br

Triton

Hip and funky casual wear.

🏠 Rua Oscar Freire, 993, Jardins

☎ 3085-9089

🌐 For more locations:
www.triton.com.br

Zara

The Spanish emporium offers the hippest styles at excellent prices!

🏠 Shopping Ibirapuera
Av. Ibirapuera, 3103, Moema

☎ 2101-1970

🌐 For more locations:
www.zara.com.br

Zoomp

🏠 Rua Oscar Freire, 995, Jardins

☎ 3064-1556

🌐 For more locations:
www.zoomp.com.br

Men's Wear

Hobi Club

🏠 Alameda Lorena, 1979, Jardins

☎ 3063-9577

🌐 www.hobiclub.com.br

Otto Design for Men

🏠 Shopping Iguatemi
Av. Brig. Faria Lima, 2232,
first floor, store C-20
Jardim Paulistano

☎ 3032-5045

🌐 www.ottodesignformen.com.br

Paul & Shark Yachting

🏠 Rua Haddock Lobo, 1491,
Jardins

☎ 3061-2588

🌐 www.paulshark.com.br

Timberland

Clothes and shoes for men.
Also women's shoes.

🏠 Rua Oscar Freire, 1106, Jardins

☎ 3898-2687

🌐 For more locations:
www.timberland.com.br

Seamstresses

Ateliê Luciana Chehin

🏠 Rua Afonso Braz, 656, room
93, Vila Nova Conceição

☎ 3044-6611

Espaço da Moda

Luiza is one of São Paulo's best kept secrets; take her a photo of a dress from a magazine and she'll copy it exactly. Her expert workmanship is worth the price! By appointment only.

🏠 Av. Pompéia, 475,
Pompéia

☎ 3673-2973

Modista Vera Lúcia

🏠 Rua Augusta, 2299, store 7,
Jardins

☎ 3085-9055

Shoes

Please keep in mind that shoe sizes in São Paulo differ from those you are accustomed to, and even from store to store. It is, therefore, advisable to go by what feels comfortable.

ATHLETIC

SEE ATHLETIC WEAR AT PAGE 160.

CHILDREN

SEE CHILDREN'S SHOE STORES AT PAGE 164.

MEN
Geox
Athletic and casual shoes for men. Women and children's shoes as well.
- Rua Oscar Freire, 1143, Cerqueira César
- 3083-3313
- www.geox.com

Shoestock
Discount shoe warehouse. Men's, women's and children's shoes.
- Av. Bem-te-vi, 221, Moema
- 5044-4513
- www.shoestock.com.br

WOMEN
Arezzo
Always has the latest styles.
- Rua Oscar Freire, 808, Jardins
- 3081-4929
- For more locations: www.arezzo.com.br

Banana Price
Discount shoe warehouse. Shoes and bags.
- Alameda Lorena, 1604, Jardins
- 3081-3786 / 3081-3460

Cervera Alpargateria
"Eco-friendly" shoes, made of rope, *juta* and fabric.
- Rua Oscar Freire, 1262, Jardins
- 3086-0735
- For more locations: www.cervera.com.br

Constança Basto
Shoes and bags for women. Different styles, from casual chic to the very dressy.
- Shopping Iguatemi
  Av. Brig. Faria Lima, 2232, store X-87, third floor, Jardim Paulista
- 3813-6545
- www.constancabasto.com

Elisa Atheniense
Bags and shoes.
- Alameda Lorena, 1632, Jardins
- 3081-0600
- www.elisaatheniense.com.br

Francesca Giobbi
SEE ELEGANT AND CASUAL WEAR AT PAGE 165.

Franziska Hubener
Classic and basic shoes and purses which, although "made in Brazil", look very "international", at a lower cost.
- Shopping Iguatemi
  Av. Brig. Faria Lima, 2232, store A-19/20, Jardim Paulista
- 3814-3575 / 3815-4611
- www.franziskahubener.com.br

J.Wlad
Offers a nice selection of women's shoes for all occasions, including unusual flats which, depending on the outfit, could be worn both during the day and at night.
- Rua Oscar Freire, 926, Jardins
- 3064-1006
- For more locations: www.jwlad.com.br

L&T 's best!

Jorge Alex

One of the largest single shoe stores in São Paulo, Jorge Alex has it all, from casual to elegant, to the very dressy. Carries accessories as well. Be prepared to spend some time browsing through the whole store before starting your selection. Ideally you should hit this store late morning or early afternoon to avoid rush hour at the end of the day. Well-priced too! Also for men and children.

⌂ Rua Alfredo Pujol, 1269, Santana

☎ 3321-7700

🌐 www.jorgealex.com.br

Kila

⌂ Rua da Consolação, 3153, Jardins

☎ 3081-1416

SHO & PURS

Imported shoes and handbags.

⌂ Shopping Iguatemi
Av. Brig. Faria Lima, 2232, third floor, Jardim Paulista

☎ 3031-4950

Verano Calçados

⌂ Av. Bem-te-vi, 232, Moema

☎ 5094-0249

🌐 www.calcadosverano.com.br

Yellow Cake

⌂ Rua Dr. Mário Ferraz, 329, Itaim

☎ 3078-6800

🌐 For more locations:
www.yellowcake.com.br

Shoe repairs

Oficinas Poppy

Besides shoe repair, it also offers key cutting, an electrician, and plumbing services.

⌂ Alameda Min. Rocha Azevedo, 1195, Jardins

☎ 3082-3087

Sapataria do Futuro

Shoe and clothes repair, embroidery on linens. Very professional, and a high quality of service.

⌂ Alameda Lorena, 1517, Jardins

☎ 3062-2623

🌐 For more locations:
www.sapatariadofuturo.com.br

Tailors

Arturo Minelli

⌂ Rua Coronel Firmo da Silva, 298, Sumaré

☎ 3862-6356 / 3672-0589

🌐 www.arturominelli.com.br

Ismael Alfaiate

⌂ Rua Oscar Freire, 540, Jardins

☎ 3062-6075

Leonardo Ufficio di Moda

⌂ Alameda Franca, 1213, Jardins

☎ 3062-7202 / 3085-9795

🌐 www.leonardoalfaiate.com.br

Teen Wear

In general we find that Brazilian teenage girls tend to be more sophisticated in the way they dress. That being said, we have not found that many places geared strictly towards teenage girls – or boys, for that matter. However, here are a few suggestions we feel confident will please your eager young lady at home. As for the young gentlemen, they are by nature easier to please, and their way of dressing has become a universal phenomenom, so there is plenty of good shopping for them in São Paulo!

Doc-Dog
⌂ Alameda Lorena, 1998, Jardins
☎ 3063-3343
⊕ For more locations:
   www.docdog.com.br

Flor
⌂ Alameda Lorena, 1974, Jardins
☎ 3063-5979
⊕ www.flor.net

Guaraná Brasil
SEE ELEGANT AND CASUAL WEAR AT PAGE 165.

Maria Garcia
⌂ Rua Oscar Freire, 1105, Jardins
☎ 3062-0140
⊕ For more locations:
   www.mariagarcia.com.br

Mercearia
SEE ELEGANT AND CASUAL WEAR AT PAGE 165.

Planet Girls
⌂ Rua Oscar Freire, 1148, Jardins
☎ 3081-5787
⊕ For more locations:
   www.planetgirls.com.br

Rip Curl
⌂ Rua da Consolação, 3338, Jardins
☎ 3063-5103
⊕ www.ripcurl.com

Star Point Surf Shop
⌂ Alameda Lorena, 1968, Jardins
☎ 3898-0567
⊕ For more locations:
   www.starpoint.com.br

Trimming

Augusta Aviamentos
⌂ Rua Augusta, 2871, Jardins
☎ 3062-7874

Aviamentos Lorena
⌂ Alameda Lorena, 1630, Jardins
☎ 3081-6601

Bazar Gatinho
⌂ Alameda Tietê, 219, Jardins
☎ 3082-2926

Rendas e Fricotes
⌂ Rua Joaquim Antunes, 132, Pinheiros
☎ 3082-0330
⊕ www.rendasefricotes.com.br

Tricolândia Aviamentos
⌂ Rua Pamplona, 1222, Jardins
☎ 3887-5614
⊕ For more locations:
   www.tricolandia.rg3.net

Watches and clocks repairs

SEE JEWELLERY ALSO, PAGE 192.

Shyrene
Restoration of antique clocks.
⌂ Rua Augusta, 2203, store 4, Jardins
☎ 3088-2331

digital and photo

Computer
SEE ALSO FAST SHOP (PAGE 81), FNAC (PAGE 156), LOJAS AMERICANAS (PAGE 181) AND KALUNGA (PAGE 200).

Dell
Sales and repairs, will come to you.
☎ 0800 701 1268
🌐 www.dell.com.br

Mac Mouse
Macintosh only. Also does repairs.
⌂ Rua Estados Unidos, 737, Jardim Paulista
☎ 6889-7799
🌐 www.macmouse.com.br

Photographic and digital services

Foto Hobby
⌂ Carrefour at Rua Pamplona, 1704, Jardim Paulista
☎ 3884-7696

Kimagen
⌂ Av. Prof. Alfonso Bovero, 494, Sumaré
☎ 3864-2117

Reticências
⌂ Alameda Gabriel Monteiro da Silva, 1325, Jardim Paulistano
☎ 3062-7970

Top Color
⌂ Rua Augusta, 2496, Jardins
☎ 3061-2675

Printing

Alphagraphics
Laminating, prints on T-shirts, photocopies, binding. It also designs, if requested, business cards, invitations, IDs for security passes, and offers other services.
⌂ Av. Brig. Faria Lima, 2941, Jardim Paulista
☎ 3078-4900
🌐 www.farialima.alphagraphics. com.br

Brasil Laser Color – Prints & Co.
Printing and copying of manuscripts, business cards, invitations, IDs for security passes, laminating. Also printing on tissue.
⌂ Shopping Iguatemi
Av. Brig. Faria Lima, 2232, upper floor, Jardim Paulista
☎ 3812-1523

Casa 8
Printing of business cards, invitations, menus.
⌂ Rua Bela Cintra, 1787, Jardins
☎ 3061-3600
🌐 www.casa8.com.br

Convite
Invitations, cards, personal paper products.
- Shopping Iguatemi
  Av. Brig. Faria Lima, 2232, third floor, Jardim Paulista
- ☎ 3812-2450

Crafteria da Ná
Personalized cards and printing.
- ☎ cel. 9128-5040

Cristina Armentano
Personalized stationery available.
- Rua Bastos Pereira, 71, Vila Nova Conceição
- ☎ 3884-1616
- ⊕ www.cardsandco.com.br

Frick-n-Sticker
Services by phone and online.
- Rua Bastos Pereira, 71, Vila Nova Conceição
- ☎ 3744-5069
- ⊕ www.fricksticker.com.br

Paper House
Good selection of imported stationery. Will print personalized business cards.
- Rua Oscar Freire, 281, Jardins
- ☎ 3082-4022
- ⊕ www.paperhouse.com.br

discount stores

Rua 25 de Março
SEE NEIGHBORHOODS AT PAGE 32 FOR MORE INFORMATION.

In the center of São Paulo, Rua 25 de Março is where you can find a variety of things at discount prices. Some of those stores have special days to sell retail, and some require that you buy in bulk. It is the best place to fill gift bags for a birthday party or to find ideas for Halloween costumes. In addition to the regular stores, you will find street vendors (camelôs). A good beginning is to visit the site www.xxv.com.br and www.25demarco.com.br

Ali Eyewear
Glasses for reading, sunglasses, over-the-counter without prescription.
- Shopping 25 de Março
  Rua 25 de Março, 1081, store TA-7, Centro
- ☎ 3228-1062

Anico
Toys, costume jewellery, school supplies.
- Rua 25 de Março, 949/953, Centro
- ☎ 3229-3629

Casa Nobre Comercial
Toys, ornaments, household and imported items.
- Rua 25 de Março, 1078/1084, Centro
- ☎ 3227-9300

Comercial Gomes e Filhos
Gifts, toys (including educational toys and items for the beach), knapsacks, household and imported items.
- Rua 25 de Março, 885/987, Centro
- ☎ 3227-4522
- ⊕ www.comecialgomes.com.br

Estrela América do Sul

Gifts and household items.

⌂ Rua 25 de Março, 792, Centro

☎ 3313-6782

Gordo Brinquedos

Party items, toys and umbrellas.

⌂ Rua Lucrécia Leme, 816,
stores 9/10 (on a side street off
Rua 25 de Março), Centro

☎ 3326-7383

Megastores

In general, São Paulo's megastores offer the best prices for household products, sodas, bottled water, etc. Checking them out first before going to your local store might make your husband happy!

Carrefour

A mega French company, Carrefour offers the same products as Extra on an "upper scale." Here, you can find fresh meats, fish and sea food – even wonderful oysters from Santa Catarina state!

> Another option is the *Sacolão*-market held at Carrefour, usually on Wednesdays and Thursdays. Fruits and vegetables of the same price can be mixed together in one bag. Great way of saving, getting exactly what you need and not throwing away food!

⌂ Rua Pamplona, 1704, Jardins

☎ 3882-0077

🌐 For more locations:
www.carrefour.com.br

Extra

In addition to regular supermarket products, carries electrical domestic products, clothing and outdoor items (for camping, etc.). Similar to Walmart in the U.S.A.

⌂ Rua João Cachoeira, 899, Itaim

☎ 3047-0100

🕐 24 hours a day.

🌐 For more locations:
www.extra.com.br

Lojas Americanas

A variety of items, including small electrical domestic appliances, housewares, CDs, DVDs, toys, packaged food, school supplies. It's a big chain, with stores scattered all over the city and in some major shopping centers; however, stores vary in size, therefore merchandise variety and availability also varies accordingly.

⌂ Shopping Jardim Sul
Av. Giovanni Gronchi, 5819,
stores 122-B/122-C, Morumbi

☎ 3743-7865

🌐 For more locations:
www.americanas.com.br

Sam's Club

Last, but not least, the good old chain that we all know. Quite similar to its namesake overseas, Sam's Club has the same requirements (need to be a member) and attends to most of your household and grocery needs!

⌂ Rua Benedito Fernandes, 270,
Santo Amaro

☎ 2165-6200 / 2165-6221

🌐 For more locations:
www.samsclub.com.br

flower shops

Remember, beautiful exotic flowers and plants are more than a decoration, they also contribute to making our homes warm and more personal!

A Estufa
Gardens, projects, plants.
- Rua Wisard, 53, Vila Madalena
- ☎ 3814-2300
- 🌐 www.aestufa.com.br

Bem me Quer
Gardens, projects, plants.
- Rua da Consolação, 3417, Jardins
- ☎ 3088-5450
- 🌐 www.bemmequer.com.br

L&T's best!

CEAGESP / CEASA
On Tuesdays and Fridays you will find an unbelievable variety of regular and exotic plants, flowers and trees, at extremely reduced prices. Be ready, however, to be there by 6 am, as the best and freshest plants are sold very quickly. From 8:30-9:30 am you can get good deals, as the stands are closing!
Be sure to check out the Easter and Christmas stands. Fresh fruit can also be found here (SEE FRESH PRODUCTS, MEATS AND FISH AT PAGE 185).

D.S. Flores decoração
- Av. Dr. Arnaldo, 680, box 8, Sumaré
- ☎ 3151-3673

Escarlate Flores e design
Garden's, projects, plants.
- Rua Haddock Lobo, 927, Jardins
- ☎ 3085-1704
- 🌐 www.escarlateflores.com.br

Flavia Rocco
- Rua Dr. Clóvis de Oliveira, 216, Butantã
- ☎ 3722-2220
- 🌐 www.flaviarocco.com.br

Flores e Detalhes
- Rua Anacetuba, 89, Itaim
- ☎ 3168-2625

Floricultura Jardim do Itaim
- Rua Jesuíno Arruda, 592, Itaim
- ☎ 3079-7928

Fortaleza Flores Ltda.
Flowers and plants for special occasions and events.
- Rua da Consolação, 3311, Jardins
- ☎ 3081-4669 / 3083-2014
- 🌐 www.fortalezaflores.com.br

Les Jardins Français
Flowers and plants for special occasions and events.
- Alameda Lorena, 1206, Jardins
- ☎ 3088-6310 / 3082-7811

Secret Garden
Gardens accessories and ornaments.
- Alameda Franca, 1055, Jardins
- ☎ 3081-8876
- 🌐 www.secretgarden.com.br

Silvana Flores
🏠 Av. Dr. Arnaldo, 684, box 10,
Sumaré
☎ 3120-5747

Uni Flores
Sales only by Internet or by
phone. Bouquets sent all over the
country.
☎ 3708-5555
🌐 www.uniflores.com

food and beverage

Caterers
One is, once again, spoiled for
choice, and no matter what kind
of party you may give, São Paulo
will have a catering service for
you. You can have different types
of cuisines catered (typical
Brazilian, Lebanese, Japanese,
continental, etc.). Depending on
the caterer, waiters and cleaning
help can either be part of the
deal, or contracted separately.

Baalbek
Very good, informal Lebanese
restaurant provides take out
(no delivery).
🏠 Alameda Lorena, 1330, Jardins
☎ 3088-4820

Buffet França
Space available for rent. Caters
large and small parties. Your
event can also be organized
wherever you choose.
🏠 Av. Angélica, 750, Higienópolis
☎ 3662-6111
🌐 www.buffetfranca.com.br

Casa Fasano
Two fabulous locations for
private parties and events.
🏠 Rua Haddock Lobo, 1644,
Jardins
☎ 3089-9400
🏠 Rua Leopoldo Couto de
Magalhães, 912, Itaim
(which is their new home)
🌐 www.fasano.com.br

Charlô
SEE RESTAURANTS AT PAGE 114.

Dona Antonia
No rental space available there,
only catering service provided.
🏠 Rua Padre Eugênio Lopes,
562, Morumbi
☎ 3721-0882

Fred Frank
Their kitchen space can
be rented for events, with
a limit of 30 people. There is
no limit on parties held in
your home, or in any other
public space. Cooking lessons
provided there, or in your
own kitchen!
🏠 Rua Papanga, 18,
Alto de Pinheiros
☎ 3023-6155
🌐 www.fredfrank.com.br

Marie Ghattas El Khoury
Lebanese catering service by
phone order. Fancy authentic
home cooking? Look
no further.
🏠 Rua Comendador Ismael
Guilherme, 124, Ibirapuera
☎ 5571-1690

O Leopolldo

The Grupo Leopolldo has a number of very well-respected restaurants (Leopolldina at Daslu, Bar des Arts & Terraço Daslu), all of which are available for private parties & events.

🏠 Rua Prudente Corrêa, 432, Jardim Paulista

☎ 3817-6363

Paola Di Verona

Restaurant, rotisserie and brasserie. Tables by reservation. No delivery service.
Italian specialities.

🏠 Rua Barão de Capanema, 468, Jardins

☎ 3067-4454

🌐 www.paoladiverona.com.br

Paula Mesquita

No space available for rent here, but your event can be organized wherever you choose, whether it is a small friendly dinner or a larger cocktail party.
Some pasta dishes available for take out.

🏠 Av. Barão de Campos Gerais, 773, Morumbi

☎ 3759-0809

🌐 www.paulamesquita.com.br

Delivery services

You can have things delivered (just like in the old days), e.g. milk, bread, mineral water, meat, fish and fruit. Obviously, having things delivered fresh to your door costs more, but you pay for the convenience and the service.

A Boa Terra

Organic fruits and vegetables.

☎ 19 3647-1321 / 3647-1192

🌐 www.aboaterra.com.br

Antonio Mitne

Fruit delivery.

☎ cel. 9976-6074 / cel. 9710-4873

Camarão Orgânico Primar

Organic shrimps.

☎ 3735-0324

🌐 www.primarorganica.com.br

Disk Pães Francisco

Bread delivery in Jardins and Itaim.

☎ 5928-3471

Emy Frutas

🏠 Rua Pássaros e Flores, 183, Brooklin

☎ 5097-9857 / 5097-9859

L&T's best!

Fish Marcello

Not only one of the best suppliers of daily fresh fish (except for Sundays and Mondays), Marcello is fluent in English. What a rare treat to know exactly what it is that you are ordering! Remember the fish in Brazil are different from the ones you are used to. However, with the help of Marcello, you can easily learn more and find types that you like.

☎ cel. 7819-2249

Frutas Bibi

Fruit delivery.

☎ cel. 9977-4501 / cel. 9917-8490

MEGASTORE AND SUPER-MARKET DELIVERY:
- 🌐 www.carrefour.com.br
- 🌐 www.emporiosantamaria.com.br
- 🌐 www.extra.com.br
- 🌐 www.paodeacucar.com.br
- 🌐 www.samsclub.com.br
- 🌐 www.santaluzia.com.br/default.asp
- 🌐 www.walmartbrasil.com.br

Fresh products, meats, and fish

Though São Paulo offers many different options, we are certain that once you find your preferred way of shopping it will become quite addictive, and will enable you to adjust to your new life even quicker. You will find friendly vendors, and don't be surprised if they give you the option of "phoning-in" your orders to be delivered. Many of us have met our favorite fish guy and/or butcher that way! Many of the fresh fruits found in markets exist in the frozen sections of supermarkets, and also come in a concentrated juice form. It is this pulp which is often used in desserts, ice-creams, jams and sauces. You just have to add water to the concentrated product.

CEAGESP / CEASA

The freshest fruit & fish at great prices! You will find here the famous flower market as well.
- 🏠 Av. Dr. Gastão Vidigal, 1946, Vila Leopoldina
- ☎ 3643-3700
- 🕐 Every day from dawn till night, but only for those who wish to buy in large quantities. Small quantities can be purchased only on Wednesdays, from 4 pm to 10 pm, at Gate 7, Saturdays, from 6 am to noon, and Sundays, from 7 am to 1 pm, at Gate 3.
- 🌐 www.ceagesp.gov.br

Mercado Municipal
SEE HISTORICAL MONUMENTS AT PAGE **21**.

Street markets

Local street markets, *feira livre* are the places to buy fresh food products – from fruits, vegetables, meats and seafood to spices, condiments, dairy products and more. The weekly neighborhood *feiras* have it all. These are held in the same location at the same time, on the same days. Should your time be limited, you will find the *quitanda* (small stores) in different neighborhoods quite practical.

Grocery Shops

Bombay Herbs & Spices
- 🏠 Alameda Min. Rocha Azevedo, 856, Jardins
- ☎ 3083-3999
- 🌐 www.bombayfoodservice.com.br

Casa Garabed
Delicious Armenian specialities
(SEE RESTAURANTS AT PAGE **114**).

Casa Santa Luzia

An extremely upscale supermarket with outstanding quality, it gets better and better with the addition of new products and items (both imported and domestic). There is a whole upstairs section of "light/ non-fat products", and quick "coffee pit-stop," an ever-growing organic area, a wine and liquor section and much, much more.

📍 Alameda Lorena, 1471, Jardins

☎ 3897-5000

🌐 www.santaluzia.com.br

Empório Santa Maria

Prepared foods, dairy, desserts, liquor and wines, canned and imported products, fresh breads and bagels, two eating spots (one of them a sushi bar), home section, and of course, delivery service.

📍 Av. Cidade Jardim, 790, Jardim Europa

☎ 2102-7700

🌐 www.emporiosantamaria. com.br

> Having a bite to eat, but afraid you might get bored? The international magazine stand across from the exit doors will keep you entertained!

In Città

SEE RESTAURANTS AT PAGE 114.

Maxifour Lebanon Market Center

Arabian specialities.

📍 Rua Júlio Ribeiro, 66, Brás

☎ 6099-0000

🌐 www.maxifour.com.br

Oliviers & Co. La table

Specializes in olive oil. Very pleasant place to have a light lunch.

📍 Rua Bela Cintra, 2023, Jardins

☎ 3088-9008

🌐 For more locations: www.oliviers-co.com.br

Pão de Açúcar

A fine supermarket which has a multitude of branches. Some of them share similarities with Santa Luzia. Depending on the location, as sizes of the branches vary, some branches stay open 24 hours a day. Imported products, shopping done through the Internet and delivery service available.

📍 Alameda Gabriel Monteiro da Silva, 1351, Jardim Paulistano

☎ 3082-9562

🌐 For more locations: www.paodeacucar.com.br

Saddi Center

Arabic specialities, cooking articles.

📍 Rua Guarará, 76, Jardim Paulista

☎ 3885-7755

🌐 www.saddicenter.com.br

St. Marche

A relatively recent addition to São Paulo's high quality supermarket shopping, St. Marche has ambitious plans. Look out for them, as before you know it, there will be a store close to you! Fresh produce, meats, a great selection of dairies and pastries. Worth a visit, as you will be going back for more. Delivery service available.

Av. Comendador Adibo Ares, 275, Morumbi

3744-5464 / 3643-1000 (delivery)

For more locations: www.marche.com.br

HEALTH FOOD AND NATURAL PRODUCTS

You can also find health food products at many gym shops (SEE FITNESS CLUBS AT PAGE 145).

Bio Loja Alternativa

Also a vegetarian restaurant.

Rua Maranhão, 812, Higienópolis

3825-8499

www.bioalternativa.com.br

Empório Siriuba

A beautiful café and store featuring all-natural dried goods, fruits and vegetables. It also provides classes on healthy nutrition and "well-being cuisine."

Alameda Franca, 1590, Jardins

3081-4303

Closed on Mondays.

www.emporiosiriuba.com.br

Mundo Verde

Alameda Santos, 2219, Jardins

3064-2015

For more locations: www.mundoverde.com.br

Nutrishop

Delivery service.

Rua Oscar Freire, 2066, store 3, Jardins

3061-5771

PASTRY SHOPS

Confeitaria São Gabriel

Besides a numerous variety of delicious breads and pastries, it serves the very, very best *mille feuille*-period. Worth every bite.

Av. São Gabriel, 416, Itaim

3885-8878

Dengosa Pães e Doces

Nice place for a typical *Paulistano* breakfast: coffee and milk with toasted bread and butter.

Rua Dr. Melo Alves, 281, Jardins

3061-2919

Doceria Cristallo

Brazilian desserts, good coffee, a very popular place wherever it is located – and there are plenty of them in São Paulo.

Rua Oscar Freire, 914, Jardins

3082-1783

For more locations: www.cristallo.com.br

Galeria dos Pães

A super selection of breads and morning pastries, a mini market, and a quick pit stop for soups and sandwiches.

Rua Estados Unidos, 1645, Jardins

3064-5900

24-hour service

www.galeriadospaes.com.br

Lílian Aiach Tock

Homemade cookies. Phone-order delivery only.

3884-1568

L&T's best!

Pâtisserie Douce France

Authentic, wonderful, mouth-watering French pastry and other foods. Will take orders. Will do mini sizes. On traditional holidays, they prepare the corresponding cake *Bûche de Noël* for Christmas, and *Galette des Rois* for the Epiphany; genuine, with its crown! Don't go there on an empty stomach, for you won't be able to resist the goodies. But if temptation is unbearable, it's ok to comfortably sample it all there!

📍 Alameda Jaú, 554, Jardins

☎ 3262-3542

🌐 For more locations:
www.patisseriedoucefrance.com.br

Specialty Shops

Butchers, fish stores, prepared foods, chocolate stores and others.

Before the holidays, most shops will have extended business hours, will be open on Sundays and will have a selection of gift baskets at different prices, in addition to carrying items reflecting the upcoming celebration.

BUTCHERS
Carneiro & Cia

Exotic meats, excellent fresh lamb, prepared foods and some kitchen appliances. Accepts orders.

📍 Rua Barão de Capanema, 541, Jardins

☎ 3062-5500

🌐 www.carneiroecia.com

Carnes Maria Carolina

They will find you the cut that you need. Home delivery.

📍 Rua Adalívia de Toledo, 72, Morumbi

☎ 3758-4859

Casa de Carnes Parisiene

📍 Rua Padre João Manoel, 574, Jardins

☎ 3081-9684

Wessel

Supplies many fine restaurants, such as the cool General Prime Burger (SEE RESTAURANTS AT PAGE 114).

📍 Av. Brig. Faria Lima, 2383, Jardim Paulista

☎ 3032-3310

🌐 www.wessel.com.br

CHOCOLATE
Cacau Show

📍 Rua Augusta, 2349, Jardins

☎ 3083-4225

🌐 For more locations:
www.cacaushow.com.br

Chocolat du Jour

The coolest stuff for Christmas, Easter and every occasion. Excellent chocolate!

📍 Rua Haddock Lobo, 1672, Jardins

☎ 3062-3857

🌐 For more locations:
www.chocolatdujour.com.br

Genebra Chocolates
⌂ Rua Haddock Lobo, 938,
   Jardins
☎ 3088-5718
🌐 For more locations:
   www.chocolatesgenebra.com.br

Kopenhagen
Quite good. Has a coffee bar to
sustain your stamina! Boutiques in
some shopping malls.
⌂ Rua Augusta, 2437, Jardins
☎ 3062-9394
🌐 For more locations:
   www.kopenhagen.com.br

Neuhaus
⌂ Alameda Lorena, 1898, Jardins
☎ 3088-7117
🌐 For more locations:
   www.neuhaus.com.br

FISH STORE
Horizonte Azul
Always fresh, on-time delivery.
⌂ Rua Tabapuã, 423, Itaim
☎ 3168-5983 / 3078-0695 /
   3161-2199

Peixaria Pacífico
⌂ Rua Fernando de Albuquerque,
   288, Consolação
☎ 3237-0740 / 3256-2082 /
   3256-2399

TK Pescados
Delivery order, located at the
free market at Rua Barão de
Capanema (fish section) in
Jardins, on Thursdays.
☎ 3721-4414 / cel. 8364-8365
   (Marcelo) / cel. 9986-8941 (Célia)

TEA SHOP
Tee Gschwendner Shop
Wide selection of imported
German teas with a handsome
selection of teapots, mugs & cups.
⌂ Shopping Iguatemi
   Av. Brig. Faria Lima, 2232,
   third floor, Jardim Paulista
☎ 3816-5359
🌐 For more locations:
   www.teegschwendner.de

WINE SHOPS
Just as *Paulistanos* are spoiled in
the food department, the same
applies for wines. After all, both
go quite well together! Wine
shops have different suppliers and
therefore the selection varies. For
the wine lover in you, a fabulous
opportunity to get to know the
fantastic wines of South America
(Argentina and Chile) and exper-
iment with small vintages not yet
exported overseas. Take advantage, as wine from this part of the
world is rapidly gaining ground!

Prosecco is a very popular
drink at ladies' lunches.

Casa Do Porto
⌂ Alameda Franca, 1225, Jardins
☎ 3061-3003
🌐 www.casadoporto.com

Enoteca Fasano
Will take orders by phone –
delivers all over Brazil.
⌂ Rua Amauri, 1568, Itaim
☎ 3074-3959
🌐 www.enotecafasano.com.br

Expand

Wide selection of imported wines. It has franchises in some of the country's biggest cities.

⌂ At Daslu
  Rua Chedid Jafet, 131,
  second floor, Vila Olímpia
☎ 3841-4577
🌐 For more locations:
  www.expandgroup.com.br

Gran Cru

⌂ Rua Bela Cintra, 1799, Jardins
☎ 3062-6388
🌐 www.grandcru.com.br

Terroir – Bar des Arts

⌂ Rua Pedro Humberto, 9, Itaim
☎ 3168-2200
🌐 For more locations:
  www.terroirvinhos.com.br

Toque de Vinho

⌂ Rua João Moura, 531, Jardins
☎ 3083-2669

World Wine Grupo Pastina

⌂ Rua Padre João Manoel,
  1269, Jardins
☎ 3085-3055
🌐 For more locations:
  www.worldwine.com.br

Wine Cellar

Niper Refrigeração

Specializes in climatized wine cellars.

⌂ Rua Rubem de Souza,
  473/475, Vila Inglesa
☎ 5563-0677 / 5563-0787
🌐 www.niper.com.br

Water

Different from what you are probably accustomed to, in Brazil it is not advisable to drink water directly from the taps/faucets. Even though São Paulo provides good water for bathing and cleaning, for drinking water it is important to have a water filter or have mineral water delivered in gallons. There are many water delivery shops scattered all over the city. Also, when buying a fridge, check, as some of them come with a water filter already installed. This is a good option to have for automatic ice making.

WATER DELIVERY
Águas Petrópolis Paulista

⌂ Rua Péricles, 376,
  Jardim Petrópolis
☎ 5044-5824
🌐 www.petropolispaulista.com.br

WATER FILTER
Filtros Europa

⌂ Av. Brig. Luiz Antonio, 2013,
  by the parking lot of Extra
  Supermercado, Bela Vista
☎ 3171-1825
🌐 www.europa.com.br

Purificador de Água Brastemp

Brastemp provides the water filter and a monthly service package to make sure everything is working properly.

🌐 www.brastemp.com.br

gift stores

Wedding gifts

FOR MORE OPTIONS, SEE DECORATION
AND UTILITIES AT PAGE 74.

In Brazil, wedding gifts are
bought and delivered before
the wedding. There is
no one-year rule here!

Cecília Dale
SEE LINEN STORES AT PAGE 82.

Cia. de Copos
Specializes in crystal glasses.
🏠 Av. Brig. Faria Lima, 2704,
   Jardins
☎ 3819-4588
🌐 For more locations:
   www.ciadecopos.com.br

Cleusa Presentes
Wedding registry.
🏠 Rua Estados Unidos, 2031,
   Jardim Paulistano
☎ 3089-7000
🌐 For more locations:
   www.cleusapresentes.com.br

Frederic Chopin Presentes
Silver, china, crystal.
🏠 Rua Oscar Freire, 909, Jardins
☎ 3061-0777
🌐 www.fredericchopinpresentes.
   com.br

Gaudi
Presents, perfume, crystal.
🏠 Rua Normandia, 97, Moema
☎ 5535-6500
🌐 www.gaudila.com.br

Hob & Nob
Gifts, candles, artificial flowers.
🏠 Rua Dr. Melo Alves,
   508, Jardins
☎ 3083-4086
🌐 www.hobnob.com.br

Home Marché
🏠 Rua Lopes Neto, 15, Itaim
☎ 3078-8815
🌐 www.homemarche.com.br

Le Paquet
🏠 Rua Oscar Freire, 937, Jardins
☎ 3062-1510
🌐 www.lepaquet.com.br

LS Selection
Ornaments.
🏠 Rua João Cachoeira, 152, Itaim
☎ 3168-3303
🌐 www.lsselection.com.br

Presentes Mickey
🏠 Rua Oscar Freire, 931, Jardins
☎ 3088-0577
🌐 For more locations:
   www.mickey.com.br

Roberto Simões Casa
Wedding registry.
🏠 Alameda Lorena, 1466, Jardins
☎ 3082-2922
🌐 For more locations:
   www.robertosimoescasa.
   com.br

Secrets de Famille
Home furnishing and gifts.
🏠 Rua Haddock Lobo, 1260,
   Jardins
☎ 3083-7949
🌐 www.secretsdefamille.com.br

Suxxar

Domestic supplies.

⌂ Praça Panamericana, 51,
Alto de Pinheiros

☎ 3032-0188

🌐 For more locations:
www.suxxar.com.br

Vista Alegre do Brasil

Portuguese china.

⌂ Rua Oscar Freire, 893, Jardins

☎ 3064-8976

🌐 www.vistaalegre.com.br

Zona D

⌂ Alameda Gabriel Monteiro da
Silva, 783, Jardim Paulistano

☎ 3088-0399

🌐 For more locations:
www.zonad.com.br

jewellery

Costume jewellery and accessories

Brazilian women take great pride
in their physical appearance,
and accessories play a major role
in the "look." Costume
jewellery is extremely popular
and varies greatly in price. It is
a nice alternative to wearing the
"real thing," as you do not have
to worry about theft or loss.
In addition to the regular stores,
you will find at hairdressers,
or through the usual word of
mouth, many designers who are
eager to show their stock, or who
are more than willing to custom
make pieces for you. Make sure,
though, to allow plenty of time

when placing an order, despite
the assurance of the vendor to
deliver the product in no time. A
good idea would also be to check
regularly on the order placed –
it never hurts!

Acessórios Modernos

Costume jewellery, leather bags,
women's shoes, hats, belts, sunglasses, scarves.

⌂ Rua da Consolação,
3391, Jardins

☎ 3083-0011

L&T's best!

Edna D'Bezerra

A megastore with a "sky is the
limit" attitude to jewellery.
So exquisitely well done, that
sometimes it is hard to tell if
the pieces are costume or the
real thing! Definitely worth
a visit, especially if you would
like to impress your friends!

⌂ Rua Oscar Freire, 583,
Jardins

☎ 3063-2949

🌐 www.ednabezerra.com.br

Francesca Romana

One of the nicest fashion jewellery shops around, Francesca
Romana has constantly new
and attractive designs which are
hard to resist. Her collection
changes every season. If you
don't find your size or if you
prefer a specific design in a different semi-precious stone,
all you do is order it! Great for
picking up presents and taking
your out-of-town guests to.

🏠 Rua Oscar Freire,
  1149, Jardins
☎ 3061-1868 / 3081-4648
🌐 For more locations:
  www.francescaromana.com

> FR has overseas stores as
> well, mainly in Mexico and
> New York City. She special-
> izes in costume jewellery;
> however, she also carries
> limited additional items,
> such as sandals and bags.

Mona
Costume jewellery,
women's clothes.
🏠 Av. Bem-te-vi, 177, Moema
☎ 5096-7048

Prima Donna Accessories
Costume jewellery, leather bags.
🏠 Alameda Lorena, 2055, Jardins
☎ 3064-0048
🌐 For more locations:
  www.primadonnaaccessories.
  com

Jewellery Stores
From the fancy to the affordable,
São Paulo will have the right
place for your jewellery needs!
This also includes places to buy
stones unmounted, such as the
one I go to, in the city center.

Amsterdam Sauer
🏠 Av. São Luís, 29,
  first floor, Centro
☎ 3231-5358
🌐 For more locations:
  www.amsterdamsauer.com

Antonio Bernardo
Master goldsmith, Antonio
Bernardo creates rare and
exquisite pieces in white & yellow gold, and more recently,
in sterling silver.
🏠 Rua Bela Cintra, 2063, Jardins
☎ 3083-5622
🌐 www.antoniobernardo.com.br

Boutique Cartier
🏠 Rua Haddock Lobo,
  1567, Jardins
☎ 3081-0051
🌐 www.cartier.com

H. Stern
We don't think H. Stern needs
an introduction, as it truly
is the Brazilian jewellery store
"par excellence!"
🏠 Rua Oscar Freire, 652, Jardins
☎ 3068-8082
🌐 For more locations:
  www.hstern.com.br

JM Lapidações
Brazilian stones and jewellery.
🏠 Rua Barão de Itapetininga,
  125, room 41, Centro
☎ 3218-7878
🌐 www.jmlapidacao.com.br

Mont Blanc
🏠 Rua Oscar Freire, 740, Jardins
☎ 3068-8811
🌐 www.montblanc.com

Vivara
🏠 Rua Oscar Freire, 855, Jardins
☎ 3085-3887
🌐 For more locations:
  www.vivara.com.br

Jewellery and watche repair

Galucci

Also repairs costume jewellery.

📍 Shopping Iguatemi
   Av. Brig. Faria Lima, 2232,
   third floor, Jardim Paulista

☎ 3034-2360 / 3813-7888

🌐 For more locations:
   www.galucci.com.br

movie rental stores

2001 Vídeo

Good collection, also sells DVDs.

📍 Av. Paulista, 726,
   Cerqueira César

☎ 3251-1044

🌐 For more locations:
   www.2001video.com.br

Blockbuster

📍 Rua Henrique Schaumann,
   203, Pinheiros

☎ 3061-3445

🌐 For more locations:
   www.blockbuster.com.br

HM Home Video

Good collection of rarities.

📍 Praça Vilaboim, 20,
   Higienópolis

☎ 3826-8696

music

Music Stores, CD & DVD

You can also find CDs and DVDs
at bookshops such as Fnac and
Saraiva (SEE BOOKSHOPS AT PAGE 157).

Banana Music

📍 Alameda Lorena, 641, Jardins

☎ 3085-8877

🌐 www.bananamusic.com.br

Neto Discos

Specializes in MPB – Popular
Brazilian Music.

📍 Rua Augusta, 1478, Jardins

☎ 3141-2929

Toka CDs

📍 Rua Augusta, 2795, Jardins

☎ 3063-3638

🌐 www.tokacds.com.br

Musical Instruments

A good tip is to go up and down
Rua Teodoro Sampaio, as you will
find many shops specializing in
musical instruments. On Saturdays,
you can also visit the antique fair
at Praça Benedito Calixto (SEE
ANTIQUE MARKETS AT PAGE 74) and have
an *acarajé* (SEE GLOSSARY AT PAGE 212)
with coconut water by the food
tents while you take a rest from
browsing the stalls for bargains.

Batucadas 1000

Brazilian exotic instruments,
drum school.

📍 Rua Teodoro Sampaio, 836,
   Pinheiros

☎ 3062-2000

🌐 www.batucadas1000.com.br

Hendrix

📍 Rua Teodoro Sampaio, 719,
   Pinheiros

☎ 3898-2900

🌐 www.hendrixmusic.com.br

Made in Brazil
☉ Rua Teodoro Sampaio, 777,
   Pinheiros
☎ 3061-3131
⊕ www.madeinbrazil.com.br

Tango
☉ Rua Teodoro Sampaio, 713,
   Pinheiros
☎ 3064-0600

pets

Pet Shops and Vets

Cobasi
A megastore for your pets' needs,
with products and services.
☉ Rua Manoel Velasco, 90,
   Alto de Pinheiros
☎ 3831-8303
⊕ For more locations:
   www.cobasi.com.br

Etc. & Cão Pet Shop
Bath, food, vet services.
Product delivery service.
☉ Rua da Consolação,
   3354, Jardins
☎ 3061-5426

Filhotes & Fricotes
Pet products. Vets, including
Dr. René Simonatto.
☉ Shopping Iguatemi
   Av. Brig. Faria Lima, 2232,
   third floor, Jardim Paulista
☎ 3816-3388

Pet Emporium
☉ Rua Canário, 796, Moema
☎ 5055-5666

Stillus
Vet services (Dr. Erika A. Ishida),
pet medication, accessories, bath
and "hotel" facilities.
☉ Rua Estilo Barroco, 401,
   Chácara Santo Antônio
☎ 5181-3493

Dog walkers

Daniel Moreira
Only in Granja Julieta, Brooklin,
Chácara Santo Antônio and Alto
da Boa Vista neighborhoods.
☎ 5184-1672 / cel. 9443-2310

Eleandro Castro
dos Anjos
Only in Jardins.
☎ 3104-2621 / cel. 9853-3856

Waldomiro Galdêncio
Farias Neto (Miro)
Only in Jardins.
☎ cel. 9841-2981

shopping centers

Quite similar to the shopping
malls overseas, the shopping centers in São Paulo are numerous
and range from the very affordable to the ultimate in luxury.
A most convenient "one-stop,"
especially during the first weeks
of your stay, in order to familiarize yourself with the quality and
diversity of the different brands
available. Valet parking is common, as it is in most restaurants.
Many centers have the same
stores and offer the same variety

of services. Shoe repairs, dry cleaners, drugstores, pharmacies, supermarkets (most often, of course, on a smaller scale), electronics, household appliances, printing, linen, clothing, fitness stores, hairdressers – to name just a few. And of course, last but not least, the fabulous food courts (and sometimes an excellent selection of restaurants), where most cuisines are available. Worried about dragging your children there? Don't! Some even provide children's entertainment areas and movie theaters. Worried about running out of cash? Not a problem! ATM facilities available on the premises. Washroom facilities are attended to on a regular basis, and are some of the cleanest public facilities we have ever encountered!

Most stores, upon your first visit, will want to do your *cadastro* (file). You might feel as if applying for a job, but be patient, as this is done once and these few minutes spent will later prove to be well worth it in avoiding confusion in delivery and in eliminating any mistakes in the issuance of a receipt (*nota fiscal*) for reimbursement.

Please do keep in mind that any imported item will be priced high – sometimes considerably higher – than you would find at home.

One of the biggest advantages of shopping in Brazil is the ability to either pay the total sum all at once or to pay in several installments. If you choose the former method of payment (cash, check, or credit card), you are generally entitled to a 5% discount.

Shopping Anália Franco

An elegant shopping center just outside São Paulo.

🏠 Av. Regente Feijó, 739, Tatuapé

☎ 6643-4360

🕐 Every day, from 10 am to 10 pm. On Sundays and holidays, leisure and food court are from 11 am to 8 pm, and stores from 2 pm to 8 pm.

🌐 www.shoppinganaliafranco. com.br

Shopping Aricanduva

🏠 Av. Aricanduva, 5555, Vila Matilde

☎ 3444-2000

🕐 Every day, from 10 am to 10 pm. On Sundays and holidays, stores are open from 2 pm to 8 pm.

🌐 www.aricanduva.com.br

Shopping Butantã

🏠 Av. Prof. Francisco Morato, 2718, Butantã

☎ 3723-3900

🕐 Every day, from 10 am to 10 pm. On Sundays and holidays, leisure and food court are from 11 am to 8 pm, and stores from 2 pm to 8 pm.

🌐 www.shoppingbutanta.com.br

Shopping Center Lapa

- Rua Catão, 72, Lapa
- 3675-2011
- Mondays to Saturdays, from 9 am to 9:30 pm, stores stay open until 9 pm. Closed on Sundays and holidays.
- www.shoppingcenterlapa. com.br

Shopping Center Light

Next to Viaduto do Chá, one of São Paulo's historical monuments

- Rua Coronel Xavier de Toledo, 23, Centro
- 3257-2299
- Mondays to Fridays, from 10 am to 9 pm. Saturdays, from 10 am to 7 pm. Closed on Sundays and holidays.
- www.shoppinglight.com.br

Shopping Center Norte

- Travessa Casalbuono, 120, Vila Guilherme
- 6224-5959
- Every day, from 10 am to 10 pm. On Sundays and holidays, stores stay open from 2 pm to 8 pm.
- www.centernorte.com.br

Shopping Center Penha

- Rua Dr. João Ribeiro, 304, Penha
- 6942-8222
- Mondays to Saturdays, from 10 am to 10 pm. On Sundays and holidays, from noon to 10 pm, with stores open from 2 pm to 8 pm.
- www.shoppingpenha.com.br

Shopping Continental

- Av. Corifeu de Azevedo Marques, 6300, Parque Continental, Osasco
- 3769-3769
- Every day, from 10 am to 10 pm. On Sundays and holidays, leisure and food court open at noon, and stores from 2 pm to 8 pm.
- www.continentalshopping. com.br

Shopping D

- Av. Cruzeiro do Sul, 1100, Canindé
- 3311-9333
- Mondays to Saturdays, from 10 am to 10 pm. On Sundays and holidays, from noon to 8 pm, with stores open from 2 pm to 8 pm.
- www.shopd.com.br

Shopping D&D

A perfect place to go, if furniture and household items are what you are looking for. Connected to Nações Unidas Convention Center, which also carries its own shopping center with a delicious and elegant food court.

- Av. das Nações Unidas, 12555, Brooklin
- 3043-9000
- Mondays to Fridays, from 10 am to 10 pm. Saturdays, from 10 am to 8 pm. On Sundays and holidays, from 10 am to 7 pm, with leisure and food court open from noon to 7 pm, and stores from 2 pm to 7 pm.
- www.ded.com.br

Shopping Eldorado

This is one of the most popular shopping centers, and is worth a visit. Recently its movie theater underwent major refurbishment, becoming one of the best in the city, with high quality image and sound.

- ⌂ Av. Rebouças, 3970, Pinheiros
- ☎ 3819-0688
- ☉ Every day, from 10 am to 10 pm. On Sundays and holidays, stores are open from 2 pm to 8 pm.
- ⊕ www.shoppingeldorado. com.br

Shopping Frei Caneca

The shopping center for the young-spirited, favored by a hip and alternative clientele.

- ⌂ Rua Frei Caneca, 569, Cerqueira César
- ☎ 3472-2000
- ☉ Monday to Saturday, from 10 am to 10 pm. On Sundays and holidays, from noon to 10 pm, with stores open from 2 pm to 8 pm.
- ⊕ www.freicanecashopping. com.br

Shopping Ibirapuera

Affordable shops, where some great buys can be found. It has a major Saraiva megastore, where book lovers can spend hours.

- ⌂ Av. Ibirapuera, 3103, Moema
- ☎ 5095-2300
- ☉ Every day, from 10 am to 10 pm. On Sundays and holidays, stores are open from 2 pm to 8 pm.
- ⊕ www.ibirapuera.com.br

L&T's best!

Shopping Iguatemi

The most luxurious and complete of the whole group, in terms of clothing, Iguatemi is the home of Vuitton, Tiffany, Burberry, Emporio Armani, as well as Zara! The movie theaters allow you to choose your seat when purchasing the ticket.

- ⌂ Av. Brig. Faria Lima, 2232, Jardim Paulista
- ☎ 3048-7344
- ☉ Mondays to Saturdays, from 10 am to 10 pm. Sundays and holidays, from 2 pm to 8 pm.
- ⊕ www.iguatemisaopaulo. com.br

Shopping Interlagos

- ⌂ Av. Interlagos, 2255, Interlagos
- ☎ 3471-8888
- ☉ Mondays to Fridays, from 10 am to 10 pm. Saturdays, from 9 am to 10 pm. Sundays and holidays, from 2 pm to 8 pm.
- ⊕ www.interlagos.com.br

Shopping Jardim Sul

After Iguatemi and Morumbi, Jardim Sul should be checked out.

- ⌂ Av. Giovanni Gronchi, 5819, Morumbi
- ☎ 3779-3900
- ☉ Mondays to Saturdays, from 9:45 am to 10 pm. On Sundays and holidays, from noon to 10 pm, with stores open from 2 pm to 8 pm.
- ⊕ www.jardimsul.com.br

Shopping Lar Center

- Av. Otto Baumgart, 500, Vila Guilherme
- 6224-5959
- Every day, from 10 am to 10 pm, On Sundays and holidays, stores are open from 2 pm to 8 pm.
- www.larcenter.com.br

Shopping Market Place

Across from Shopping Morumbi, extremely convenient if you have some personal shopping to do.

- Av. Dr. Chucri Zaidan, 902, by Morumbi Bridge, Brooklin
- 3048-7000
- Every day, from 10 am to 10 pm. On Sundays and holidays, stores are open from 2 pm to 8 pm.
- www.marketplace.com.br

Shopping Metrô Santa Cruz

- Rua Domingos de Morais, 2564, Vila Mariana
- 3471-8000
- Monday to Saturday, from 10 am to 10 pm. Sunday and holidays, from 10:30 am to 10 pm, with leisure and food court open at 11 am, and stores from 2 pm to 8 pm.
- www.shoppingmetrostacruz. com.br

Shopping Metrô Tatuapé

- Av. Radial Leste, next to Tatuapé metro station
- 6192-9444
- Every day, from 10 am to 10 pm. On Sundays and holidays, stores are open from 2 pm to 8 pm.
- www.shoppingtatuape.com.br

Shopping Morumbi

Comes second after Iguatemi on the "luxury scale." Also well-known international stores. Across the street from Shopping Market Place.

- Av. Roque Petroni Jr., 1089, Morumbi
- 5189-4500
- Every day, from 10 am to 10 pm. On Sundays and holidays, leisure and food court from 11:30 am to 10 pm, and stores from 2 pm to 8 pm.
- www.morumbishopping.com.br

Shopping Pátio Higienópolis

Smaller and cosier, with natural sunlight coming through the beautiful circular dome, Higienópolis is extremely pleasant on a Sunday afternoon if lunch and a movie are on the program!

- Av. Higienópolis, 618, Higienópolis
- 3823-2300
- Every day, from 10 am to 10 pm. On Sundays and holidays, leisure and food court open at 11:30 am, and stores from 2 pm to 8 pm.
- www.shoppingpatiohigie nopolis.com.br

Shopping Paulista

- Rua Treze de Maio, 1947, Bela Vista
- 3191-1138
- Every day, from 10 am to 10 pm. On Sundays and holidays, stores are open from 2 pm to 8 pm.
- www.shoppingpaulista.com.br

Shopping Plaza Sul
- Praça Leonor Kaupa, 100, Jardim da Saúde
- 5077-7300
- Every day from 10 am to 10 pm. On Sundays and holidays, leisure and food court open at noon, and stores from 2 pm to 8 pm.
- www.shoppingplazasul.com.br

Shopping SP Market
- Av. das Nações Unidas, 22540, Interlagos
- 5682-3666
- Every day, from 10 am to 10 pm. On Sundays and holidays, stores are open from 2 pm to 8 pm.
- www.shoppingspmarket. com.br

Shopping Villa-Lobos
- Av. das Nações Unidas, 4777, Alto de Pinheiros
- 3024-4200
- Every day, from 10 am to 10 pm. On Sundays and holidays, stores are open from 2 pm to 8 pm.
- www.shoppingvilla-lobos.com.br

Shopping West Plaza
- Av. Francisco Matarazzo, Água Branca
- 3677-4000
- Every day, from 10 am to 10 pm. On Sundays and holidays, stores are open from 2 pm to 8 pm.
- www.westplaza.com.br

Top Center
Check out the food court downstairs.

- Av. Paulista, 854, Cerqueira César
- 3145-1819
- Mondays to Saturdays, from 10 am to 10 pm. Sundays and holidays, from 11:30 am to 10 pm, with stores open from 2 pm to 8 pm.
- www.topcenter.com.br

stationery shops

Casa do Artista
The name says it all – "the artist's house." The most complete store in its genre. All kinds of paint, crayons, brushes, papers, etc.
- Alameda Itu, 1012, Jardins
- 3088-4191
- For more locations: www.acasadoartista.com.br

Cristina Armentano
SEE PRINTING AT PAGE 179.

Kalunga
All stationery supplies, plus computers supplies.
- Av. Rebouças, 2360, Pinheiros
- 3347-7000
- For more locations: www.kalunga.com.br

Michelangelo
Office, artist & designer supplies.
- Av. Brig. Faria Lima, 2523, store 14, Jardim Paulista
- 3032-3110
- www.emporiomichelangelo.com.br

Scrapbooking

The scrapbooking craze has hit Brasil. You will find plenty of stores that cater to scrapbookers and lots of scrapbooking groups to join as well! Visit the websites

🌐 www.scrapsampa.com.br
🌐 www.paperchase.com.br
🌐 www.artepapier.com.br

and our best forum is

🌐 www.scrapworks.com.br

toys

SEE ALSO DISCOUNT STORES AT PAGE 180.

Best Baby

SEE CHILDREN'S CLOTHING AND SHOES AT PAGE 162.

Fábrica Idéias para Crianças

Great toy store with lots of educational toys – a nice place to browse with your children.

🏠 Rua Aspicuelta, 135,
   Vila Madalena
☎ 3034-3044

PB Kids

Mega toy store, offers a great variety of toys, including imported products. It also offers electronic appliances, CDs and DVDs for children.

🏠 Av. Rebouças, 2538,
   Pinheiros
☎ 3060-9808
🌐 For more locations:
   www.pbkids.com.br

L&T's best!

Pindorama

This inventive toy store offers alternatives to the bigger stores with the same brands, but the atmosphere is much more pleasant, and the staff very helpful. Educational toys, musical instruments and books can be found as well!

🏠 Rua Purpurina, 242,
   Vila Madalena
☎ 3032-7871
🌐 www.pindoramabrinquedos.
   com.br

Ri Happy

Good variety of national and imported toys.

🏠 Rua Teodoro Sampaio,
   2044, Pinheiros
☎ 3812-6876
🌐 For more locations:
   www.rihappy.com.br

Trenzinho

Educational and handmade toys.

🏠 Rua Fradique Coutinho,
   184, Pinheiros
☎ 3088-0936
🌐 For more locations:
   www.trenzinho.com.br

Vila Set

A fun place to take the kids, a micro "FAO Schwarz," carries mainly imported toys.

🏠 Rua Lourenço de Almeida,
   805, Vila Nova Conceição
☎ 3846-7161
🌐 For more locations:
   www.vilaset.com.br

Social

social clubs

Boating Clubs

FOR MORE INFORMATION ABOUT BOATING CLUBS AND EVENTS, SEE WWW.FEVESP.ORG.BR AND WWW.JETSKI.COM.BR.

São Paulo Yacht Club
⌂ Rua Francisco de Seixas, 225,
  Jardim Guarapiranga
☎ 5523-8366
🌐 www.spyc.com.br

Yacht Club de Santo Amaro
⌂ Rua Edson Régis, 481,
  Jardim Guarapiranga
☎ 5687-8847 / 5687-0836
🌐 www.ycsa.com.br

Yacht Club Itaupu
⌂ Estrada do Itaupu, 500,
  Riviera Paulista or
  Represa de Guarapiranga
☎ 5517-6229
🌐 www.itaupu.com.br

Equestrian Clubs

With riding schools. More information about equestrian clubs and events at
🌐 www.cbh-hipismo.com.br or
🌐 www.horseworldbrasil.com.br

Clube de Campo São Paulo

No temporary membership. However, should you wish to become a member, you can do so by paying the membership fees if you know someone who already belongs to the club.

⌂ Praça Rockford, 28,
  Vila Represa
☎ 5929-3111
🌐 www.ccsp.org.br

Clube Hípico de Santo Amaro

Horseriding school, also has a pool and other attractions.
⌂ Rua Visconde de Taunay, 508,
  Santo Amaro
☎ 5524-0600
🌐 www.chsa.com.br

L&T's best!

Jockey Club de São Paulo

Founded in 1875, it is the city's only racetrack and is an excellent place for a fun night out. There are races every Friday, Saturday, Sunday and Monday, but it's best to call beforehand to confirm the schedules. Betting is done directly at the track and opens three hours before the start of racing. The club, which houses over 2,000 horses, has two main tracks, one grass and one sand, both measuring around 2,000 meters. The Jockey Club also hosts other events such as fashion shows and concerts – it's a fabulous venue to celebrate marriages. Within the grounds, is a restaurant, catered by Charlô (tel. 3814-3547), whose terrace gives a panoramic view of the track. Charlô is open everyday, even when there are no races.

SEE UNDER RESTAURANTS AT PAGE 114.

📍 Av. Lineu de Paula
Machado, 1263, Gate 6,
Cidade Jardim
📞 2161-8300
🌐 www.hcj.com.br

Sociedade Hípica Paulista

Membership is not required for
riding classes. For inquiries into
temporary membership speak
with the administrative office.

📍 Rua Quintana, 206, Brooklin
📞 5504-6100
🌐 www.sociedadehipicapaulista.
com.br

Foreign Community

American Society

Anyone who has anything to
do with America would be happy
to join the society, as it does a great
job reminding Americans about
important dates in the U.S.A. (such
as deadlines for paying taxes,
voting day, etc.) Organizes events
to celebrate various American
holidays. Call them for help
finding a lawyer.

🌐 www.americansociety.com.br

Canadian International Women's Society

Founded in 1962 by the wife
of the Canadian Consul General
in **Sampa**, this non-profit
organization is yet another way
to meet Canadian women living
here, as well as women from
other countries. One of their
goals is to help local institutions
that care for poor children and
adults. Monthly meetings and
biannual charity events.
For more information go to
hike@originet.com.br

Gringoes

Information for the foreign
community in Brazil.

🌐 www.gringoes.com.br

Newcomers Club

International Newcomers
Club São Paulo.

🌐 www.newcomers-sp.com.br

SP Family

This English-language site
provides invaluable information.

🌐 www.spfamily.com.br

St. Andrew Society

Calendar of Scotish events.

🌐 www.standrews.com.br

The British Commonwealth Cultural Club

📍 Rua Ferreira de Araújo, 741,
first floor, Pinheiros
📞 3819-0135

Golf Courses

MORE INFORMATION ABOUT GOLF CLUBS AT:
WWW.GOLFEWEB.COM.BR.

FPG Kaiser Golf Center

Close to the city.
Golf Range.

📍 Rua Deputado João Bravo
Caldeira, 273, Jardim Ceci
📞 5587-5844
🌐 www.fpggolfcenter.com.br

PL Golf

Open to the public during the week. Games can be scheduled in advance, daily rates apply. On weekends, only by invitation from members. Restaurant and snack bar.

⌂ Av. PL do Brasil, km 6000, inside of the city of Arujá

☎ 11 4655-2622

🌐 www.plgc.com.br

São Francisco Golf Club

Games have to be scheduled in advance. No membership required.

⌂ Rua Martin Luther King, 1527, Osasco

☎ 3681-8752

🌐 www.golfsaofrancisco.com.br

Solar das Andorinhas Hotel Fazenda & Golf

A resort where you pay a daily fee, per person, and enjoy activities such as tennis, soccer, volleyball, basketball and swimming. Not a "professional" golf club in the proper sense of the term. Four holes.

⌂ Rodovia Campinas-Mogi-Mirim, km 121, Campinas

☎ 19 3757-2700

🌐 www.solarandorinhas.com.br

UniGolf

Hourly rate, has a restaurant, bar and massage facilities, managed by Luiza Sato Spa (SEE UNDER WELL-BEING CLINICS AT PAGE 152).
Entrance fee applies.

⌂ Rua Orobó, 125, corner with Marginal do Pinheiros, close to Shopping Villa-Lobos, Alto de Pinheiros

☎ 3023-5454

🌐 www.onneunigolf.com.br

Private Athletics Clubs

São Paulo has a number of private clubs that are more or less urban country clubs – without the golf! These clubs are great for the entire family as most have impressive athletic facilities, including tennis, swimming, soccer and a whole host of other activities. We've listed the clubs that extend temporary memberships to foreigners (this allows you to join without paying a very high entrance fee). If you are interested in one of the clubs that does not appear on our list you can always call them directly and ask them if they'll extend you the courtesy of a temporary membership.

Athletic clubs have many attractions during the year, including evening social events. A good place to make friends, practice sports or spend a weekend. Check for membership requirements and entrance fees.

Círculo Militar de São Paulo

⌂ Rua Abílio Soares, 1589, Ibirapuera

☎ 3884-4055

🌐 www.circulomilitar.com.br

Club Athletico Paulistano
⌂ Rua Honduras, 1400,
  Jardim América
☎ 3065-2000
⊕ www.paulistano.org.br

Clube Paineiras
⌂ Av. Dr. Alberto Penteado, 605,
  Morumbi
☎ 3779-2000
⊕ www.clubepaineiras.com.br

Esporte Clube Pinheiros
⌂ Rua Angelina Maffei Vita,
  493, Jardim Paulista
☎ 3217-5944
⊕ http://www.ecp.org.br/

São Paulo Athletic Club
⌂ Rua Visconde de Ouro Preto,
  119, Jardins
☎ 3217-5944
⊕ www.spac.org.br

your events

Children's Parties
Brazilians throw big, elaborate
shindigs for their children's
birthday parties. I have found
that when you throw a nice
"homemade" party for your child
at home, it is such a novelty that
everyone loves it! Typically
Paulistanos will hold a party in
a "buffet" – a large space with
toys, space to play, entertainers
(such as clowns or magicians) to
play with the kids, food & drinks
(including the birthday cake)
and party favors at an all-
inclusive price. You choose the

theme and the buffet does the rest
(FOR CUSTOM INVITATIONS, SEE STATIONARY
SHOPS AT PAGE 200). There are also
buffets for adult parties, weddings,
sweet sixteen parties, etc.

BUFFETS
Billy Willy
A full service children's buffet,
with lots of attractions such
as monorail, simulators and
climbing walls.
⌂ Av. Chibarás, 322, Moema
☎ 5052-7766
⊕ www.billywilly.com.br

Espaço Pindorama
An innovative indoor/outdoor
space, this children's buffet was
opened in early 2006. It offers
great arts & crafts workshops
for little ones and even tree
climbing for older kids.
⌂ Rua Comendador Miguel
  Calfat, 540, Vila Olímpia
☎ 3045-5190
⊕ www.espacopindorama.com.br

Happy Day
A great buffet for a small group
of little kids (under 4 years old).
⌂ Av. dos Tajurás, 49,
  Cidade Jardim
☎ 3814-6440
⊕ www.happyday.com.br

Mega Party
⌂ Rua Dr. Renato Paes de
  Barros, 154, Itaim
☎ 3079-6215
  For more locations:
⊕ www.megaparty.com.br

Planet Mundi

Big and roomy, with a nice area for grown-ups to eat.

⌂ Av. Chibarás, 285, Moema
☎ 5053-6700
🌐 www.planetmundi.com.br

OTHER OPTIONS FOR OLDER KIDS

L&T's best!

Helô Centro de Culinária

A cooking class! A great alternative to the buffet, Helô does parties for kids, starting at 7 years old.

⌂ Rua Lira, 75, Vila Madalena
☎ 3814-4854
🌐 www.helodoces.com.br

Kart In Jaguaré Racing Club

Try a go-cart party for kids. It's very noisy, but they love it!

⌂ Av. Jaguaré, 1133, Jaguaré
☎ 3719-0007
🌐 www.kartin.com.br

Kick Bola Urbana

Indoor soccer. Great place for an older child's birthday party.

⌂ Rua Bacaetava, 250, Brooklin
☎ 5093-2035
🌐 www.kickbolaurbana.com.br

Mega Play Morumbi Paintball

⌂ Rua Itapaiuna, 1809, Morumbi
☎ 3771-2969
🌐 www.megaplaymorumbi.com.br

Quadrifoglio Oficina de Arte

Paint your own ceramics. Another great idea for a children's birthday party, since it will entertain them, as well as help develop their creativity!

⌂ Rua Normandia, 25, Moema
☎ 5094-1864
🌐 www.quadrifoglioarte.com.br

Vidrada em Arte

Scrapbooking is a great party for older girls!

⌂ Alameda Jauaperi, 204, Moema
☎ 5051-8060
🌐 www.vidradaemarte.com.br

Should you decide to have the party at home (or in the *Salão de Festas* / Party Room in your apartment building) you can hire people to do just about anything – decorate the space, blow up balloons, bring moon bounces or giant slides to your locale, put on puppet / princess / magic / clown shows, bring mini zoos, etc. You can also call a "buffet" (catering) team to come to you – they will show up with cute little stands (*barracas*), each with a waiter, and they will serve mini hot dogs, mini pizzas, popcorn, cotton candy and much, much more! Important: don't forget the goodie bags (*lembrancinhas*) – they're very important to Brazilian kids!

DECORATION (BALLOONS)
Balloon Delivery
⟁ Rua Agostinho Gomes,
   1794, Ipiranga
☎ 6161-6725
⊕ www.balloondelivery.com.br

Dona Florinda
Balloon sculptures.
☎ 3209-2613
⊕ mofinholdt@uol.com.br

L&T's best!
Rica Festa
Entertainment (clowns, magicians), will come up with a theme for children's party, and provide the disposable party items and decoration, including balloons. Not limited to children's parties – also offers services for other occasions.
⟁ Rua Horácio Lafer, 61, Itaim
☎ 3078-1000
   For more locations:
⊕ www.ricafesta.com.br

Tio Maurício
⟁ Rua Dr. Teodoro Quartim
   Barbosa, 319,
   Vila São Francisco
☎ 3763-2662 / cel. 9931-5085

ENTERTAINMENT
Brincarte
They will organize the party at your place, take care of all the invitations and come up with entertainment for the children. Also, they provide food service and decoration and put on an art workshop.

☎ 3744-5508 / cel. 9187-2111
⊕ www.brincarte.com.br

Curumim Animações
☎ 5181-9399 / 5183-4569
⊕ www.grupocurumim.com.br

Paul & Jack
Magicians.
☎ 3772-6645
⊕ www.paulejack.com.br

Felipe Gonzáles
Magician.
☎ 4997-1019

Von Feffer Puppet Show
Classical fairy tales and famous characters come to life as puppets.
☎ 3845-5558 / cel. 9196-1510
⊕ www.vonfeffer.com.br

Cakes
Simple cakes are available at supermarkets and bakeries. (SEE SUPERMARKETS AT PAGE 185, AND PASTRY SHOPS AT PAGE 187). For something more elaborate try one of the following:

Bolos Glorita
⟁ Rua Pratápolis, 186, Butantã
☎ 3726-6767
⊕ www.glorita.com.br

Claudia Eid
Decorated cakes.
⟁ Rua Mourato Coelho, 1433,
   Vila Madalena
☎ 3031-5294
⊕ www.claudiaeidjordao.com.br

Isabela Suplicy Pâtissière

Makes unforgettable cakes for weddings.

☉ Rua Taques Alvim, 66, Cidade Jardim

☎ 3037-7080

Lílian Aiach

Homemade cookies.

☉ Rua Said Aiach, 48, Paraíso

☎ 3884-1568

Nininha Sigrist

☉ Rua Gracindo de Sá, 75, Jardim Paulistano

☎ 3064-2686

Equipment Rental for Parties

Cem por cento eventos

Upscale furniture and antiques.

☉ Rua Padre Domingos Tonini, 101, Vila dos Remédios, Osasco

☎ 3686-8039

🌐 www.cemporcentoeventos.com.br

Da Casa

China, cutlery, serving dishes (silver and porcelaine), crystal, etc.

☉ Rua Francisco Leitão, 347, Pinheiros

☎ 3085-10210

🌐 www.dacasaecia.com.br

La Table

They have all the glasses, cups, tables, chairs you need for a party.

☉ Rua Horácio Lafer, 517/523, Itaim

☎ 3078-8896

🌐 www.latable.com.br

L&T 's best!

Mesalinho

The "sister" shop of Da Casa will fulfil all of your linen needs. A good idea would be for you to take along the dishes you will be using, in order to coordinate colors, as choice is ample.

☉ Rua Francisco Leitão, 409, Pinheiros

☎ 3062-8519

🌐 www.mesalinho.com.br

Ritz Festa

☉ Rua Joaquim Antunes, 1019, Pinheiros

☎ 3037-7755

🌐 www.ritzfestas.com.br

Event Organizers

Alice Carta Promoções e Eventos

☉ Rua Bela Cintra, 2080, fifth floor, Jardins

☎ 3082-4855 / 3062-2745

🌐 www.alicecarta.com.br

Alicinha Cavalcanti

Promoter.

☎ 5051-8195 / cel. 9981-0877

Ça Va Eventos
Márcia Costa

Not only an event organizer, providing catering, decor, invitations and valet services,

Marcia's services extend to organizing conferences including interpretation, security, and all related services. In the business for the last ten years.

- 📍 Rua Caçapava, 49, room 51, Jardim América
- ☎ 3507-0757
- 🌐 www.marciacosta.com.br

Food

Banana Zoo

Stands with mini pizzas, cotton candy, etc.

- ☎ 6673-4510

João Onofre

- 📍 Rua Atílio Piffer, 672, Casa Verde
- ☎ 3966-2240
- 🌐 www.joaoonofre.com.br

Party Decoration

Embalagem Jardins

Disposable articles, plastic bags.

- 📍 Rua Augusta, 2080, Jardins
- ☎ 3085-6093

Festa Total

- 📍 Rua Augusta, 2063, Jardins
- ☎ 3082-1506 / 3082-9691
- 🌐 www.festatotal.com.br

Natalie

Seasonal and party articles, ornaments and decorations.

- 📍 Rua Estados Unidos,

2205/2219, Jardim Paulistano
- ☎ 3064-8364 / 3085-1066

> Definately take a trip down to 25 de Março; you'll find tons of party supply stores with great prices.

Star Pack

Plastic bags, disposable party articles, paper boxes, etc.

- 📍 Rua Tabapuã, 911, Itaim
- ☎ 3168-6287 / 3168-6448

Space Rental

Whatever the occasion, should you need to rent a space, São Paulo has many options to offer.

Some caterers have space available to rent, which can be included in the total package price. Also, most buildings have a "social area" which can be booked in advance for gatherings, functions or workshops. Some churches have halls which will accommodate wedding parties.

Another nice venue is the Jockey Club (SEE EQUESTRIAN CLUBS AT PAGE 204). A unique option is the culinary book store Mille Foglie. You can rent out the shop and give a dinner with the chef of your choise or you can be the chef! (SEE RESTAURANTS AT PAGE 114)

Hotels, in general, also have public rooms available for events (SEE HOTELS AT PAGE 65). Finally, a very nice option is to rent a space in some historical building (SEE HISTORICAL MONUMENTS AT PAGE 21) and museums (SEE MUSEUMS AT PAGE 94).

Glossary

In my view, this section is quite important as it gives one a "quick" insight into day-to-day translations and expressions, which are essential at the beginning. This is especially true if one likes to spend some time in the kitchen which, I might add, is quite therapeutic!

Although I had a full month of intensive Portuguese at Berlitz before moving to São Paulo, I was still incapable of going to the butcher and ordering my meat… This left me quite frustrated and the only way I was able to express myself was to point to certain parts of my body! I should also point out that Brazilian butchers cut their meats in a different way, therefore you might have to substitute certain meats for others.

Always remember that, in an odd way, every situation has some humor in it and if you keep this in mind somehow, believe it or not, your stress will be lessened.

BABY CARE / *Cuidados com o bebê*

Baby Food	Comida de bebê, sopa de bebê, papinha
Baby Wipes	Lenços umedecidos
Bottle	Mamadeira
Bib	Babador
Cotton Swabs	Hastes flexíveis Cotonetes®
Disposable Diaper	Fraldas descartáveis
Formula	Leite em pó
Ointment	Pomada
Teething Ring	Mordedor
Pacifier	Chupeta

CLOTHING / *Vestuário*

Bathrobe, robe	Roupão
Blouse	Blusa
Boots	Botas
Boxer shorts	Cuecas samba-canção
Bra	Sutiã
Cap, baseball cap	Boné
Coat	Casaco
Dress	Vestido
Dress shirt	Camisa social

Evening gown	Vestido de baile, vestido de gala
Gloves	Luvas
Hat	Chapéu
High heels	Sapato de salto alto
Jacket	Jaqueta, blazer
Jeans	Jeans
Jogging suit	Roupa de ginástica
Knee socks	Meias 3/4
Loafers	Mocassim
Long-sleeved shirt	Camisa de manga comprida
Long underwear	Ceroulas
Mittens	Luvas sem dedos
Nightgown	Camisola
Overcoat	Capa, sobretudo
Pajamas	Pijama
Pants, tights	Calças
Pantyhose	Meia-calça
Polo shirt	Camisa pólo
Pumps	Escarpim
Rain coat	Capa de chuva
Sandals	Sandálias

Scarf	Cachecol
Shoes	Sapatos
Short-sleeved shirt	Camisa de manga curta
Ski hat	Gorro
Skirt	Saia
Slippers	Chinelos
Sneakers	Tênis
Socks	Meias
Sport coat / blazer	Paletó
Sport shirt	Camisa esporte
Stockings	Meia-calça, meia fina
Suit	Terno
Sweatpants	Calça de moleton
Sweatshirt	Blusão de moleton
Tank top	Camiseta regata
Thongs	"Chinelo de dedo", Havaianas®
Tie	Gravata
Trenchcoat	Capa
T-shirt	Camiseta
Tuxedo	Smoking, traje a rigor
Underpants – male	Cuecas

Underwear – female Calcinha

Work boots   Botinas

DRINKS AND COCKTAILS

Cachaça or Pinga   Strong liquor made from sugar cane.

Caipirinha   It tastes like juice, but beware – it is far from it! Brazil's equivalent to Mexico's margueritas! It is made out of *cachaça*, lime juice and sugar (the traditional flavour) although you can substitute any fruit (passion fruit, strawberries, etc.) and use sweetener instead of sugar. Served with lots of ice, it is extremely refreshing.

Caipiroska   Instead of using *cachaça*, vodka is the liquor. You can also have it with sake, which makes it lighter.

Cerveja   Beer in bottle or cans, traditional or malted.

Chope claro   Draft beer, blond or dark.
or escuro

FOOD / *Alimentação*

CONDIMENTS, HERBS, SPICE / *Temperos, ervas, molhos*

Allspice   Pimenta-da-jamaica

Anise   Anis

Basil   Manjericão

Bay Leaf   Folha de louro

Bot Saffron   Açafrão

Caraway Seed	Alcaravia / Kummel
Cardamon	Cardamomo
Capers	Alcaparras
Cayenne Peper	Pimenta-malagueta
Celery Seed	Semente de aipo (salsão)
Chervil	Cerefólio
Chives	Cebolinha-Francesa
Cinnamon	Canela
Clove	Cravo
Coriander	Coentro
Cumin	Cominho
Curry Powder	Curry
Dill	Endro, aneto, dill
Fennel Seed	Erva-doce
Garlic	Alho
Ginger	Gengibre
Horseradish	Raiz-forte
Ketchup	Catchup
Leeks	Alho-poró
Marjoram	Manjerona
Mayonnaise	Maionese

Meat Stock	Caldo de carne
Meat Tenderizer	Amaciador de carne
Melissa	Erva-cidreira
Mint	Hortelã
Monosodium Glutamate	Glutamato monossódico, or Aji-no-moto®)
Mustard	Mostarda
Nutmeg	Noz-moscada
Oregano	Orégano
Paprika	Páprica
Parsley	Salsinha
Pepper	Pimenta-do-reino
Pepper Sauce	Molho de pimenta
Sage	Sálvia
Salad Dressing	Molho de salada
Salt	Sal
Soy Sauce	Molho de soja (shoyu)
Thyme	Tomilho
Tomato Paste	Massa de tomate
Vinegar	Vinagre
Worchestershire Sauce	Molho inglês

FRUITS / *Frutas*

Acerola	Acerola
Apple	Maçã
Apricot	Damasco or abricó
Avocado	Abacate

Banana   Banana
Different sizes and flavors: nanica, maçã, prata, ouro, da terra...

Blueberries   Frutos do vacínio or mirtilo
Mostly imported, hard to find.

Cherry   Cereja
Found fresh in December.

Coconut   Coco
Easily found in São Paulo, liquid inside referred to as "água de coco" and served as a beverage.

Dates	Tâmaras
Fig	Figo

Grapefruit   Grapefruit or toranja
Mostly imported, hard to find.

Grapes	Uvas
Persimmon	Caqui

Kiwi   Kiwi
Sweet, green fruit with brown skin, from Asia.

Lemon   Lima or lima da persia

Lime   Limão
There are many kinds: siciliano, cravo e taiti. The "limão galego" has a thin and smooth skin and it is the secret of a tradicional *caipirinha*.

Lychee	Lechia (pronounced "lichia")

Mango Manga
Tropical fruit; in many kinds: espada, rosa, coquinho, Bourbon, etc.

Mangosteen	Mangostão

Medlar Fruit	Nêspera or ameixa amarela

Melon	Melão

Orange Laranja
Many kinds: pêra, baía, seleta; the *laranja lima* has a very light, sweet taste, good for babies.

Papaya Mamão
Many kinds and sizes; the one known as Papaia is the smaller one, very sweet.

Peach	Pêssego

Pear	Pêra

Pineapple	Abacaxi

Plum	Ameixa

Pomegranate Romã
It is common in backyards, and in the countryside.

Prunes	Ameixa seca

Strawberry	Morango

Tamarind	Tamarindo

Tangerine Mexerica or tangerina
Many kinds: poncã, cravo, Morgot.

Watermelon	Melancia

BRAZILIAN FRUITS / *Frutas brasileiras*

Brazil is rich in native fruits, some only available fresh in their region of origin. Most are sold in São Paulo, fresh, processed or frozen, also in juices and in sweets.

See below the illustration of some fruits:

Assai   Açaí
Amazonia's native and dark red fruit, it is a good energy source. It is easily found frozen and processed, ideal for creams and juices.

Cashew Fruit   Caju
Northeast region's native fruit, usually found in São Paulo fresh, frozen and processed.

Ciruela Fruit   Umbu
Common fruit of the Northeast region, in São Paulo only found frozen and processed.

Star Fruit   Carambola
Indian fruit, it grows all over Brazil.
Yellow, sweet and sour fruit, its slices are star shaped – found all year.

Jaboticaba   Jabuticaba
Mata Atlântica's native small, rounded, tasty fruit with black skin. First you gently break the skin with your teeth. The filling must be white, and you may either swallow or spit the stone. If the filling is red, don't eat it, it's bad.

Genipap   Jenipapo
Indian and tropical American native fruit; it may be found in many Brazilian cities, good for liquor, comfit and medicine as well.

Guarana   Guaraná
Amazonian native energy berry, usually combined with other juices.

Guava Goiaba

Tropical America native fruit, it is popular and found all year long in every Brazilian region. Two kinds of pulp: white and red. Commonly used in jam and compote, or as a filling for cookies and cakes.

Hog Plum Cajá

Bahian yellow, juicy fruit, found in São Paulo only frozen and processed.

Jack-Fruit Jaca

Enormous fruit with a strong, sweet taste, very common in the countryside and the Northeast region.

Mulberry Amora

Dark red wild berry, its is not found for sale. It can be eaten from a tree or as jam or liquor.

Nectarine Nectarina

Fruit pink and yellow in colour; a kind of peach mixed with plum, produced in Brazil, Chile and Argentina.

Passion Fruit Maracujá

Brazil is the biggest producer of this native American tropical fruit, of two kinds: the sweet one, good to eat, and the sour one, ideal for juices and jams.

Pitanga Pitanga

Brazilian native fruit. A fleshy, dark red berry with a stone and a sour taste. Good for juices, liquor and sweets.

Sugar Apple Fruta-do-Conde or Pinha

Native Brazilian native fruit, it's very sweet and has a lots of stones.

Variet Myrtle Jambo

Asiatic origin, three kinds can be found here: red, pink and white. Good to eat, or in juices or jam.

HOW TO BUY? / *Como pedir?*

1/2 dozen	meia dúzia
dozen	dúzia
ripe fruit	fruta madura
unripe fruit	fruta verde

GENERAL FOOD / *Alimentos*

Almonds	Amêndoa
Artificial sweetener	Adoçante
Baking powder	Fermento em pó
Barley meal	Farinha de cevada
Beans	Feijão
Bologna	Mortadela
Bottled water	Água mineral sem gás
Brazil nut	Castanha-do-pará
Bread	Pão
Bread crumb	Farinha de rosca
Brown bread	Pão preto
Brown sugar	Açúcar mascavo
Butter	Manteiga
Cake	Bolo

Cake mix	Mistura para bolo
Candy	Balas
Carbonated water	Água mineral com gás
Cashew nut	Castanha-de-caju
Cassava	Farinha de mandioca
Cereal	Flocos de cereais or Sucrilhos®
Cheese	Queijo
Cheese spread	Requeijão
Chocolate	Chocolate
Cocoa	Chocolate em pó
Coffee	Café
Condensed milk	Leite condensado
Cookies	Biscoitos
Cooking oil	Óleo
Corn chips	Salgadinhos de milho
Corn oil	Óleo de milho
Cornmeal	Fubá, polenta de milho
Cornstarch	Amido de milho or Maizena®
Cottage cheese	Queijo Cottage
Crackers	Biscoito água e sal
Decaf coffee	Café descafeinado

Doughnuts	Donuts
Dried fruits	Frutas secas
Eggs	Ovos
Evaporated milk	Available at some grocery stores (imported)
Flour	Farinha de trigo
French bread	Pão francês
Fruit juice	Suco de frutas
Gelatin	Gelatinas
Green split peas	Ervilha seca
Heavy cream	Creme de leite
Herbal tea	Chá de ervas
Honey	Mel
Hot chocolate mix	Achocolatado
Ice cream	Sorvete
Jams	Geléias
Lard	Banha
Liquors	Bebidas alcoólicas
Low-fat milk	Leite desnatado
Macaroni (Pasta)	Macarrão
Margarine	Margarina
Milk	Leite

Mozzarella	Mozarela (pronounced "mussarela")
Nuts	Nozes
Oatmeal	Aveia
Olive oil	Azeite de oliva
Pancake mix	Mistura para panqueca
Parmesan cheese	Queijo parmesão
Peanut butter	Pasta or creme de amendoim
Peanuts	Amendoim
Pickles	Pepinos em conserva
Pie crust mix	Mistura or massa para torta
Pizza mix	Mistura para pizza
Popcorn	Pipoca
Potato chips	Batata chips
Powdered drink	Suco em pó
Powdered milk	Leite em pó
Powdered sugar	Açúcar de confeiteiro
Raisins	Passas, uva-passa
Red wine	Vinho tinto
Rice	Arroz
Rolls	Pãezinhos
Rye bread	Pão de centeio

Shortening	Gordura
Skimmed milk	Leite desnatado
Snacks (savory)	Salgadinhos
Soda	Refrigerante
Soft white cheese	Queijo-de-minas, queijo branco
Soup	Sopa
Soy oil	Óleo de soja
Spaguetti sauce	Molho para macarrão
Sugar	Açúcar
Sweet bread	Pão doce
Tea	Chá
Tomato sauce	Molho de tomate
Vegetables	Legumes / verduras
Walnuts	Nozes
Water	Água
White bread	Pão de forma
White sugar	Açúcar refinado
White wine	Vinho branco
Whole / wheat bread	Pão integral
Yeast	Fermento biológico
Yogurt	Iogurte

MEAT / *Carnes*

DELI MEAT AND COLD CUTS / *Carnes vermelhas*

Bacon	Bacon, toucinho
Corned beef	Bife em conserva
Eye of round	Patinho
Filet mignon	Filé-mignon
Goat	Cabrito
Ground beef	Carne moída
Ham	Presunto
Lamb chops	Costelinha de carneiro or bisteca
Lamb	Cordeiro or carneiro
Leg of lamb	Perna de cordeiro
Liver	Fígado
Liver patê	Patê de fígado
Meat soup	Carne para sopa (músculo)
Meat spreads	Pastas de carne, patê
Oxtail	Rabada
Pork chops	Bisteca de porco
Pork loin	Lombo de porco
Pork meat	Carne de porco
Pork tenderloin	Lombinho
Rabbit	Coelho

Roast beef	Rosbife
Sausages	Lingüiças, salsichas
Smoked pork chops	Kassler (defumado)
Spareribs	Costela
Steak	Filé
Stewing meat	Carne para ensopado
Sweetbreads	Miolo
Tongue	Língua
Veal	Vitela
Vienna sausage	Salsicha tipo Viena

TEXTURE, FLAVOR AND CUTS OF MEAT

Flank steak   Fraldinha
It's the only part of the bull that is well irrigated by blood circulation.

Hump of the Steer   Cupim
This is the flavorful fat-marbled meat of the Zebu (Brahma) steer.

Rib   Costela
This is the source of breast rib strips (*costela de tira*) and the breast rib point (*vazio da costela*).

Round steak   Lagarto
An excellent meat for steaks, roasts, and sauté beef dishes.

Round Steak Groin   Maminha de alcatra
From the lower part of the *alcatra*, this is a tender and flavorful cut.

Rump steak   Alcatra
Considered by many to be the sovereign cut of premium quality beef-round steak, groin cut (*maminha*). Served rare.

Sirloin   Contrafilé
This is a compact and flavorful cut of meat, cut from the frontal rib portion.

Special sirloin   Picanha
Comes from the center of the bull's rump (*alcatra*).

Tenderloin   Filé-mignon
This is an extremely tender cut of meat, as it has no point of contact with the animal's limbs.

POULTRY / *Aves*

Chicken	Frango
Chicken breast	Peito de frango
Chicken legs	Coxa e sobrecoxa de frango
Chicken wings	Asas de frango
Cornish hen	Frango de leite
Drumsticks, thighs	Coxas de frango
Duck	Pato
Hen	Galinha
Leg quarter	Sobrecoxa
Quail	Codorna
Turkey	Peru

SEAFOOD-SHELLFISH / *Frutos do mar*

Anchovy	Anchovas
Clams	Mariscos

Crab	Siri, caranguejo
Dried cod	Bacalhau seco
Flounder	Linguado
Haddock	Hadoque
Halibut	Tipo de bacalhau
Lobster	Lagosta
Mussels	Mexilhões
Octopus	Polvo
Oyster	Ostra
Salmon	Salmão
Sardine	Sardinha
Scallops	Vieiras
Shrimp	Camarão
Squid	Lula
Swordfish	Peixe-espada
Trout	Truta
Tuna	Atum
White fish	Pescada (mild file of sole)

SAVORY SNACKS / *Salgadinhos*

Coxinha de galinha Fried dough with chicken filling. Comes in two sizes and purchased at bakeries.

Esfiha   A version of the Lebanese pizza, comes either open or closed, consists of a pastry dough with a center filled with meat, onions and pinenuts. The Brazilians went a step further and "invented" a cheese version, a sausage version, and a vegetable version.

Kibe   A baked or fried meat cone with a filling of meat, onions, and peanuts.

Pastel   A fried pastry, comes with different fillings like meat and cheese. Popular at open markets.

Rissole   A fried Italian-style pasta with different fillings (cheese, shrimp, meats)

SAVORY FOOD / *Pratos salgados típicos brasileiros*

Acarajé   Deep fried bean bread filled with shrimps, *vatapá*, and lots of spicy condiments.

Churrasco   Barbecue

Cuscuz   A kind of a cake made from cornflour mixed with shrimp and sardine.

Farofa   A mix of manioc flour with different condiments, good with meat or beans.

Feijoada   Black beans with cooked with pork meat, served with rice, collared greens and oranges.

Moqueca   Stew with shrimp, tomatoes, peppers.

Pamonha   A type of pudding, which can either be sweet or savory, made from fresh corn.

Pirão   Made from manioc flour mixed in a fish broth, very good to eat with fish.

SWEET FOOD / *Doces brasileiros*

Beijinho	Candy made from condensed milk and coconut.
Brigadeiro	A very popular chocolate candy made with condensed milk and cocoa powder.
Cajuzinho	Candy made from condensed milk with crushed peanuts.
Cocada	Made from coconut, it's very tasty and popular.
Doce de leite	Sweet paste or bar made from milk.

Docinhos   Small home-made candies, can be purchased in bakeries or *docerias*. Made from different fruits, come in many shapes. A tradition at parties, especially children's.

Manjar	A flan made from coconut and milk, with a caramel sauce.
Olho-de-sogra	A dry, black prune filled with coconut candy.
Quindim	Puddim-like dessert made with egg yolks and coconut.
Romeu-e-julieta	White cheese (queijo-de-minas) served with guava jelly (*goiabada*).

VEGETABLES / *Legumes e verduras*

Acorn Squash	Abobrinha redonda
Artichoke	Alcachofra
Asparagus	Aspargo
Beetroot	Beterraba
Black beans	Feijão-preto

Broccoli	Brócolis
Brussel sprouts	Couve-de-bruxelas
Butternut squash	Abobrinha marrom
Cabbage	Repolho
Carrot	Cenoura
Cauliflower	Couve-flor
Celery	Salsão or aipo
Corn	Milho verde
Cucumber	Pepino
Chicory	Chicória
Eggplant	Berinjela
Garbanzo beans	Grão-de-bico
Green beans	Vagem
Green pepper	Pimentão verde
Heart of palm	Palmito
Kidney beans	Feijão roxo or "roxinho"
Lentils	Lentilhas
Lettuce	Alface
Manioc	Mandioca
Mushrooms	Cogumelos, champignons
Okra	Quiabo
Onion	Cebola

Parsnip	Nabo branco
Peas	Ervilhas
Pepper	Pimenta
Potato	Batata
Pumpkin / Squash	Abóbora
Radish	Rabanete
Red pepper	Pimentão vermelho
Sauerkraut	Chucrute
Savoy cabbage	Repolho
Spinach	Espinafre
Sweet potato	Batata-doce
Tomato	Tomate
Turnip	Nabo
Watercress	Agrião
Yam	Cará, inhame
Zucchini (squash)	Abobrinha

HEALTH / *Saúde*

HEALTH, SYMPTOMS AND COMMON DISEASES /
Doenças mais comuns, sintomas

Backache	Dor nas costas
Bleeding	Sangrar

Blood pressure	Pressão arterial, pressão sanguínea
Blood test	Exame de sangue
Break / broken	Quebrar
Bruise	Machucar
Burn	Queimar
Cavity	Cárie
Chest pain	Dor no peito
(The) chills	Calafrio, tremedeira
Cholera	Cólera
Cold	Resfriado
Congested	Congestionado
Cough	Tosse
Cramps	Cólica
Diarrhea	Diarréia
Dislocate	Deslocado
Dizzy	Sentir tontura
Ear ache	Dor de ouvido
Faint	Sentir-se fraco, desmaiar
Fever / temperature	Febre
Headache	Dor de cabeça
Hepatitis A and B	Hepatite tipo A e tipo B

Infection	Infecção
Itchy	Coceira
Laringitis	Laringite
Measles	Sarampo
Meningitis	Meningite
Nauseous	Náusea, enjôo
Nosebleed	Nariz sangrando
Polio	Pólio
Rabies	Raiva
Respiratory infection	Infecção respiratória
Runny nose	Coriza
Scrape	Esfolar
Scratch	Arranhar
Shortness of breath	Falta de ar
Sinusitis	Sinusite
Sneeze	Espirrar
Sore throat	Dor de garganta
Sprain	Contundir
Stiff neck	Torcicolo
Stomach ache	Dor de estômago
Strep throat	Amigdalite, dor de garganta

Sunburn	Queimadura de sol
Swollen	Inchado
Tetanus	Tétano
Toothache	Dor de dente
Tuberculosis	Tuberculose
Twist	Torcer
Typhoid fever	Febre tifóide
Virus	Gripe
Vomit / throw up	Vomitar
Wheeze	Chiar ao respirar, chiado
Yellow fever	Febre amarela

MEDICAL AND HOSPITAL

Anesthetic	Anestésico, anestesia
Bandages	Bandagens
Bandaid	Band-aid
Bed pan	Comadre
Bed rest	Descansar na cama, repouso
Bed table	Mesa-de-cabeceira
Cast	Gesso
Cotton	Algodão
Crutches	Muletas

Diet	Dieta
Gauze	Gaze
I.V.	Soro
Injection/shot	Injeção
Medical chart	Prontuário
Needles / syringes	Agulhas / seringas
Prescription	Receita
Sling	Tipóia
Stitches	Pontos
Tests	Exames
X ray	Raios X

HOME / *Casa*

CLEANING AND LAUNDRY
Artigos de Limpeza e Lavanderia

Alcohol	Álcool
Ammonia	Amoníaco
Bleach / clorox	Água sanitária or Cândida®
Brass cleaner	Polidor de latão e bronze
Broom	Vassoura
Brushes	Escovas
Bucket / pail	Balde

Camphor	Cânfora
Caustic soda	Soda cáustica
Cleaning fluid	Removedor or Varsol®
Clothes line	Varal
Clothes pins / pegs	Prendedor de roupas
Deodorizers	Desodorizador de ambiente
Detergent	Detergente
Disinfectant	Desinfetante
Drain cleaner	Desentupidor
Dryer	Secadora
Dust rags	Panos de pó
Dustpan	Pá de lixo
Fabric softener	Amaciante de roupa
Feather duster	Espanador
Floor wax	Cera de assoalho
Furniture polish	Lustra-móveis
Glass / window cleaner	Limpa-vidros
Hand vacuum	Aspirador pequeno
Insecticide	Inseticida
Iron	Ferro de passar roupas
Ironing board	Tábua de passar roupas

Laundry bags	Saco para roupas
Laundry basket	Cesto de roupa
Laundry detergent	Sabão em pó
Mop	Esfregão, pano de chão
Pine cleaner	Desinfetante à base de pinho
Recycling bin	Cesto para lixo reciclável
Rust remover for clothes	Removedor de ferrugem
Scouring powder	Saponáceo or "sapólio"
Scrub brush	Escova pequena
Shoe polish	Cera or graxa de sapatos
Silver cleaner	Polidor de pratas
Soap	Sabão
Sponge	Esponja
Sponge mop	Esfregão de esponja
Spot remover	Tira-manchas
Spray starch	Passe bem®
Starch	Goma
Static cling remover	Removedor de estática
Steel wool	Palha de aço
Trashcan/ garbage can	Lata de lixo

Utility sink	Tanque
Vacuum cleaner	Aspirador de pó
Vacuum cleaner bags	Saco de aspirador de pó
Washing machine / washer	Máquina de lavar roupas, lavadora
Broom	Vassourinha

HOUSEHOLD PRODUCTS / *Produtos domésticos*

Aluminum foil	Papel de alumínio
Can opener	Abridor de latas
Cat food	Ração para gatos
Clothes hanger	Cabide de roupas
Coffee pot	Cafeteira
Cotton	Algodão
Dog food	Ração para cachorros
Dryer	Secador
Firewood	Lenha
Fork	Garfo
Fruit cleaner	Esterilizante para frutas
Key	Chave
Kleenex	Lenços de papel
Knife	Faca

Lid	Tampa
Light bulb	Lâmpada
Light / switch	Tomada, interruptor
Lotion	Loção
Matches	Fósforos
Mirror	Espelho
Napkins	Guardanapos de papel
Oven	Forno
Paper towel	Papel-toalha
Plastic bags	Sacos plásticos
Plastic wrap	Filme plástico
Plate	Prato
Shampoo	Xampu
Shopping bag	Sacola
Shower	Chuveiro
Silverware	Talheres
Spoon	Colher
Step stool or ladder	Escada
Stove	Fogão
Straws	Canudos
Sugar bowl	Açucareiro

Toothpaste	Pasta de dentes
Tissues	Lenços de papel
Toilet paper	Papel higiênico
Toothbrush	Escova de dentes
Toothpicks	Palito de dentes
Towel	Toalha
Trash bag	Saco de lixo
Tray	Bandeja
Water filter	Filtro de água
Waxed paper	Papel-manteiga

INSECTS / *Insetos*

Ant	Formiga
Cockroach	Barata
Fleas	Pulgas
Larva	Bicho-geográfico
Lice	Piolho
Mosquito	Mosquito, pernilongo
Sand fleas	Borrachudos
Scorpions	Escorpiões
Spider	Aranha

PACKAGING AND CONTAINERS /
Embalagens e recipientes

Bag	Saco or sacola
Bar	Barra
Bottle	Garrafa
Box	Caixa
Bunch	Cacho, maço
Can	Lata
Carton	Caixa de papelão
Container	Embalagem
Dessert Spoon	Colher de sobremesa
Jar	Jarro, vaso
Liter	Litro
Loaf / loaves	Forma, formas
Pack	Pacote
Package	Embalagem or pacote
Roll	Rolo
Six-pack	Pacote com seis unidades
Stick	Cartucho, tablete
Tablespoon	Colher de sopa
Teaspoon	Colher de chá
Tub	Pote, tubo

QUANTITIES, PACKS AND UNITS OF MEASURE /
Quantidades e unidades

1 foot	30,48 cm
1 mile	1,60930 km
1 square mile	2,59 km²
1 square yard	0,83610 square meters (m²)
1 yard	91,4400 cm
1 inch	2,54 cm
1 ounce (oz)	31 gramas
Dozen	Dúzia
1 Gallon	3,8 litros
Half gallon	1,9 litro
1 Liter	1,000 ml
8 liquid ounces	Uma xícara
1 Pint	473 ml
1 Pound	1 libra (459,5 gramas)
1 Quart	946 ml

UNIT CONVERSION FORMULAS / fórmulas para conversão de unidades

Conversion from Celsius to Fahrenheit
degrees C x 1.8 + 32

Conversion from Fahrenheit to Celsius
(degrees F - 32.) / 1.8

O livro LIVING IN SÃO PAULO – THE L&T GUIDE, foi impresso
em São Paulo-SP, pela Quebecor World Ltda., para a
Larousse do Brasil, em maio de 2007.